Walking With Parkinson

Finding Faith, Purpose, and Peace

Corey D. King

Corey D. King

Copyright © 2017 Corey D. King

All Rights Reserved

ISBN-10: 1978204558

ISBN-13: 978-1978204553

Walking With Parkinson

To Amy, Andrew, and Rebecca

Corey D. King

Introduction to the Combined Edition

Almost six years ago, I created a blog called The Crooked Path to document my experiences with Parkinson's disease. At the time, I was the volunteer leader of a local support group organization in San Antonio, Texas, where I first discovered I was a person with Parkinson's (PWP).

My goal was to chronicle my journey with the symptoms of the disease, hoping that someone would find comfort in knowing they were not alone. I found I had more to say, though. With my wife Amy's encouragement, I wrote my first book, Walking The Crooked Path. I was surprised to find that it was not just about Parkinson's disease, but about finding a way to live with the challenges and surprises life had thrown my way.

Since then, I've retired, continued to volunteer, started and stopped several new hobbies, become battery-operated, and have fundamentally changed my view of the world and my place in it. And throughout, I have continued to write. I learned I enjoy writing, and sometimes the words strike a chord in someone.

A few months ago, I sat down to write my third book. I realized, however, that these three books are actually one continuous account that opens a window onto the enormous changes Parkinson's has brought into my life. It makes sense to me to put them all in one place.

The writing is what it is; I am not Hemingway. I did the best I could to be honest. Perhaps this is a chronicle of degeneration; if so, that's also honest, because Parkinson's is a degenerative disease. I think there's some good stuff here, though.

Other than a few "happy-to-glad" changes and correction of a few errors, the first two parts of the book you hold in your hands are as they were published in *Walking The Crooked Path* and *Stumbling Toward Victory*. Part III, *Seeking The Way Home*, is new.

I once read that the way to tell if you're writing what's in your heart is to revise until the writing makes you cry. I've cried more times over these books than in my previous fifty years. I hope that means something.

Corey D. King

Part I

Walking The Crooked Path

Learning to Live With Parkinson's

Corey D. King

Introduction to Part I

Many people have walked with me, supported me, encouraged me, chastised me, and made my journey richer and more rewarding. I wish I could thank them all, but then the acknowledgements would be longer than the book. However, some I must acknowledge individually.

To my friends in the PD advocacy community—thank you for being there for me, and allowing me to be there for you.

To Ronnie, my friend and colleague, and my last in a long string of great bosses—you are a great leader, manager, and engineer, and you're a wise and compassionate man completely dedicated to doing what's right. Thank you.

To Larry—thank you for asking your question, and for sticking with me while I answered it. Thanks for your constant, unflagging support, even when I didn't know it was there. And thanks for introducing me to the guys.

To Gene—of all the unexpected joys in my life, knowing you may be the greatest. You're my friend, my mentor, my confidante, and my shootin' buddy. More importantly, in you I see both a father and The Father. Thank you, my friend. I love you.

To Jeanette—even though I might have been a little rough around the edges as your first son-in-law, you accepted me, loved me, supported me during the most difficult parts of my journey, and treated me as a son. I'm grateful for your kindness and example, and I love you.

To Ken—I've walked the path with you my entire life, and although you're a phenomenal brother who's looked out for me and protected me, you're an even better friend and traveling companion. I hope the path before us is as long as we both want it to be. I love you, brother.

To my children—every father wants his children to be better than he was. Your path is still largely unwalked, but in different ways I see in both of you the things that I've always wanted to be. I'm so proud of you both, and I love you.

And to my beloved wife Amy—our path together has been

exceedingly crooked at times, but we've always walked together. Even when you've been angry enough with me to cheerfully strangle me, you've always been there. I regret the times I've taken it for granted, and the times I have lost sight of the important and been distracted by the urgent. The path ahead of me will be difficult, but with you beside me I can do anything. And when I can't, I know you can. *Tu es ma meilleure amie et ma joie de vivre, et je t'aime de tout mon coeur.*

Love builds up the broken wall, and straightens the crooked path…
- Maya Angelou

So live your life that the fear of death can never enter your heart…
- Chief Tecumseh

I believe; help my unbelief…
- Mark 9:24

Corey D. King

1
I've Got What?

I squirmed on the cold plastic chair in the doctor's examining room and thumbed through a limp copy of Texas Monthly Magazine, muttering to myself. I was already late for a meeting and I didn't have time for this nonsense. There was nothing wrong with me that I couldn't explain; sure, my hands and arms were stiff and sore, and occasionally didn't work quite the way I told them to, but I was sure the pain and stiffness were the result of creeping middle age and overexertion. I had taught a group of scuba students just a few days before, and I was always a little tired and sore after a class.

I hummed tunelessly along with a Muzak version of Elton John's "Rocket Man," and resisted the impulse to rummage through the drawers looking for rubber gloves to make balloon animals. I had just learned that the doctor was out, and my irritation level was climbing. I grumbled a string of complaints, "Waste of time... nothing really wrong with me... I need to get back to work... she always thinks she knows better than me... this song sucks... just overdid it in class last week... doctor's not even here today... wonder what she'll think of THAT... don't even have any good magazines..."

For more than ten years, the ache and stiffness in my left shoulder, elbow, and wrist had been a constant, unwelcome companion. My left hand and fingers were clumsy, I unconsciously carried my left arm curled against my chest, and I had developed a slight limp. Friends and colleagues asked, "What's with your arm? Why are you limping? You look stiff—what's wrong?"

I dismissed the questions with a variety of plausible explanations: weekend tree-trimming, old skiing injuries, ill-fitting shoes, overexertion in scuba classes. The symptoms had grown over more than a decade, so slowly that I didn't notice. Irritated and perplexed, I stiff-armed the well-intentioned concerns. After all, who knew better than me if something serious was wrong? I was always the smartest guy in the room: no one, especially doctors who had never met me before, could tell me something about myself that I didn't know first.

My wife Amy is blessed with many wonderful qualities, but patience and tact aren't always at the top of the list. Perhaps it's just the effect I have on her. She could also see physical changes in me, but she was as much a victim of the "boiling frog" phenomenon as I was—the changes were so gradual that she wasn't consciously aware of them either. She had an intuition that something serious was amiss, though, and it scared her. Fear usually manifests as anger with her, and that fear coupled with her self-described "Texas redneck" approach to problem solving resulted in colorful conversations.

"My arms don't move right. Look at this." I demonstrated moving my right arm and hand, making normal iron-pumping movements and clenching my fist rapidly.

"Yeah? So?"

"Well, look what happens with my left arm." I repeated the demonstration, and instead of rapid, smooth motion, my left hand and arm quivered spastically, jerked, and thrashed like a fish trying to throw a hook.

"You're doing that on purpose."

"I swear I'm not," I assured her.

"That's pretty messed up, hon. Why don't you go see a doctor?"

"Oh, I don't have time. Besides, they don't know anything."

"You always go in and tell them what's wrong, Ignatz. Why don't you try telling them what hurts then let them decide what's wrong?"

I choose to believe that "Ignatz" means "intelligent and noble love of my life" in a language that I don't speak.

I said, "Okay, but not next week. I'm going to DC next week, and then I've got a meeting with a client, and then…"

She rolled her eyes at me and walked away, and we tabled the subject until the next time I felt the need to demonstrate the right-left disparity.

Visiting the doctor was just below being water boarded on my list of favorite things, so several years passed before I made an appointment for a checkup. While I procrastinated, new physical difficulties emerged. The buttons on my shirt cuffs and collars inexplicably grew larger; pushing them through the buttonholes became a daily morning struggle. My neckties and shoelaces joined the rebellion, and resentfully resisted all my efforts to bend them into pleasing and useful shapes. Through years of repetition, I had honed my morning ritual to maximize sleep time: twenty-three minutes from alarm to key-in-ignition, backing out of the garage. As that time stretched from thirty minutes, to forty-five, to over an hour, I developed an uncomfortable suspicion that I was facing something more serious than simple laziness and middle-aged malaise.

I finally made an appointment for an annual physical. "Annual" was an exaggeration, since my last was over five years before. The doctor had some catching up to do. She proceeded with a detailed medical history, poked, prodded, took samples of various fluids, encouraged me to cough, and attached me to machines that plumbed my body's secrets.

As the exam came to an end, I mentioned, "Oh, I've been having problems with my left hand and arm. They hurt and feel stiff, and my hand shakes sometimes and it doesn't move right." I demonstrated.

The doctor agreed, although she didn't call me "Ignatz." We only know each other casually, and I'm clearly not the love of her life. "Well, yes, that probably shouldn't happen. Have you hurt your arm recently?"

We discussed several possibilities, including arthritis and joint problems from a variety of old football, baseball, skiing, and beer pong injuries. She talked about the wide-ranging effects of neck and shoulder damage, referred me to an orthopedic surgeon, and sent me on my way.

I saw orthopedic surgeons for my neck, shoulder, elbow, and hand, received multiple cortisone injections, had a series of MRIs and x-rays, and finally saw a neurologist for an electromyogram. This delightful procedure involves electricity and needles, and when the neurologist told me what he planned to do, I thought he was joking. He wasn't.

"So, you're really going to stick needles in my hand and arm, hook them up to a generator, and run current through them?" I asked.

"Well, it's slightly more technically sophisticated than that, but essentially, yes."

"And, by doing this, you hope to learn… what?"

"That's a little complex for the layman to understand, but rest assured, there's a purpose."

I imagine Jack the Ripper told his victims something similar, but I kept my mouth shut, hoping not to goad the doctor into higher voltage levels than strictly necessary. I thought I heard screams coming from his other examining rooms (no doubt in a nearby dungeon), but I'm sure my imagination was just in overdrive.

He inserted the needles and said, "Now, hold still." He cranked up the juice.

"I thought I told you to hold still; you're corrupting the data."

I was comforted to know he was actually collecting data and not engaging in some bizarre recreational activity, so I gritted my teeth, manfully didn't suggest that we switch places so he could be still and I could run the generator, and tried to stop my involuntary shaking. I couldn't, and both my anxiety level and his grumbling increased. After an eternity of jolts and tickles, he removed the needles and chased me out of his office, muttering about simple procedures and uncooperative patients.

The EMG indicated minor nerve problems in my elbow. I discussed the results with one of a series of orthopedic surgeons, and asked what I should do next. He told me he thought my symptoms would improve with elbow surgery to reduce nerve irritation and pressure. Feeling a little irritated myself, I asked, "Will surgery help with the shaking and stiffness, too?"

"Well, I really don't know what's causing that, but I think you should consider the surgery anyway," he said.

"So, you're not sure what's causing the symptoms, but surgery is the answer?"

Giving me a look that indicated that he, too, considered me to be an uncooperative patient, he said, "We could always try another cortisone injection." I suspected that his knife and needle were solutions in search of a problem I didn't have, so I thanked him and said I'd consider his advice. He was as glad to see me go as I was.

On a short vacation a few months later, as Amy and I walked together through Manhattan, I noticed she was avoiding walking on my right side.

"You keep whacking me with that darn college ring of yours when I'm on your right. You bruise me less when I'm on your left. You don't swing your left arm."

"Really? How long's that been going on?"

"Oh, I never really thought about it. Maybe ten or fifteen years—a long time," she replied. I hadn't noticed, but I realized she was right: my left arm didn't swing when I walked.

Over the next few months I noticed other anomalies. On a business trip to Washington DC in the winter of 2008, as a colleague and I walked back to our hotel after dinner, I had trouble keeping up with her. She said, "You've been dragging around all day, and you look stiff and you're limping. What's up?"

I was walking with a slow, uneven gait and dragging my left leg slightly. My left leg and hip, apparently taking lessons from my left arm and shoulder, were stiff and sore. My colleague was recovering from hip replacement surgery, but she had to wait for me to catch up with her a dozen times on the walk from dinner back to the hotel.

The collection of physical problems began to form a pattern, but I didn't see it. I enthusiastically explained away each anomaly—the shoulder pain was from a skiing injury, the neck stiffness was from a foolish, drunken encounter with the shallow bottom of Lake Austin that nearly left me paralyzed, the tingling and clumsiness in my left hand were due to nerve damage from either my neck or shoulder, the elbow pain was from carrying scuba tanks in diving classes, the leg pain was from muscle strain at the gym, or maybe from the new shoes that didn't quite fit. I always had an answer, and it was always wrong.

Amy finally ran completely out of patience and made an appointment with a specialist in internal medicine. "Just go," she told me. "Keep your mouth shut and answer his questions, and let him do his job."

I bit back a snarky comment about the difficulty of both answering his questions and keeping my mouth shut. I surrendered to the inevitable, but I thought, "I'll go, but he's not going to tell me anything I don't already know."

I knew something was wrong. Cancer, strokes, high blood pressure, and diabetes, which were all a part of my genetic background, explained some of the symptoms, but nothing I knew explained them all. My mother and father had both died only a few years before, and between their two medical histories I was potentially at risk for almost everything. I figured I had all the data I needed and that this was a puzzle I could solve. After all, why trust the doctors? They had repeatedly been wrong, and I was convinced I could do at least as well at diagnosis as they could.

The Muzak was now playing a watered-down, almost unrecognizable version of a Metallica song, and as I considered sneaking out the back door and coming back in a couple of years, the door opened and a nurse entered, bringing with her a whirlwind of activity. She was professional and competent, and I felt a little ashamed of myself. I still believed I was the smartest guy in the room, but only because I was the only guy in the room.

She began by taking a detailed medical history, and then introduced me to the neurological test I would later know as the "hokey-pokey exam." Finger taps, toe taps, fist clenching, heel stomping, put your left leg in, take your left leg out… it would have been difficult under the best of circumstances, and to my surprise, I performed poorly on many parts of the exam. I could tap my right index finger and thumb together at a rapid, regular pace, but my left hand lagged behind, and the same was true of any test that required coordinated movement between my left and right side.

"My wife claims I can't dance, either. Maybe I have an excuse," I joked. The nurse glanced at me and continued the exam.

"There are several tests we can't do here that I'd like to order for you," she said. She suggested multiple blood tests and a brain scan, commenting, "With your symptoms, a brain tumor is always a possibility and needs to be ruled out." Brain tumor? Brain tumor?? Elbow surgery looked good by comparison. Let's go back to that, I thought.

She finished the exam and left me alone again in the examination room while she made appointments for what seemed like several thousand additional tests, including a brain MRI. I finally left the office with a handful of orders and instructions to come back with the results.

In addition to donating several gallons of blood and urine to the testing gods, I spent an hour stuffed inside a cramped, noisy MRI machine, listening to a loud hammering sound and trying not to move. I was only partially successful; the MRI technician repeatedly called out to me by microphone from the control booth, "You're moving. If you don't stop, we'll have to repeat the test." I felt like a recalcitrant five-year-old being scolded for wiggling in church.

The torture finally ceased, and I collected my images and x-rays. The internist had arranged an appointment with a neurologist to discuss the imaging tests, and so in the summer of 2009, almost fifteen years after I first noticed a persistent ache in my left arm, I met with the neurologist.

It was the same neurologist who had performed my medieval torture test. I verified that electrified needles weren't on the schedule, and he looked at my brain images and pronounced them unremarkable.

I bristled. I liked my brain and it had served me well; I was offended that he didn't see evidence that it was a remarkable organ. In a tone that reminded me he hadn't forgotten my tendency to be uncooperative, he told me that to a doctor, "unremarkable" means, "I don't see anything here that's going to kill you," rather than, "what a boring, ordinary brain." He took a detailed medical history and then performed a much more comprehensive hokey-pokey exam. He finally completed his evaluation. We sat down, and he proceeded to change my life forever.

"I'm sorry, but your symptoms, tests, and medical history indicate Parkinsonism, most likely idiopathic Parkinson's disease. We'll need to do more tests, but I'm confident that's what you have."

I was shocked and almost incoherent. Through the fog of white noise in my mind, I tried to form reasonable thoughts and questions, but my first response was not the most complex thought I've ever had.

"Naaaah, can't be." I raised several objections, and the doctor patiently addressed each of them.

"But I'm too young for Parkinson's."

"Parkinson's affects people of all ages, although it's more common after age sixty. You probably have something called young-onset PD, but as I said, we'll need to do more testing to be sure," he replied.

"It's only on one side."

"That's not at all unusual. As a matter of fact, that's how it usually starts."

"I don't shake all that much. Isn't Parkinson's disease mostly about tremors?"

"The primary symptom of PD is often a rest tremor, but it doesn't have to be, especially in young-onset patients," he replied.

For the next fifteen minutes, I continued to search for the question that would undermine his diagnosis, and he continued to answer them all. He then told me he wanted to start me on a Parkinson's medication. If my symptoms improved, it would reinforce his diagnosis.

The long delay and uncertainty between my initial noticeable symptoms and an accurate diagnosis were frustrating but not unusual. PD can be difficult to diagnose, especially in younger people. The symptoms are subtle and gradual, and can have many causes. Doctors are taught to think of the most common causes first, and to leave the more exotic conclusions until the obvious and mundane has been ruled out. "When you hear hoof beats, think horses and not zebras," they say.

PD is a zebra, and is unusual enough in a younger person that it's often not considered until other diagnoses prove to be wrong. That's partially why my diagnosis was so difficult. My own insistence that I knew more than the entire medical establishment complicated the process, though, and injected additional delay and confusion.

My crooked path to the knowledge that I am a person with Parkinson's, or PWP, was only the first part of a longer journey. Along the way, I'm learning to cope not only with the physical and mental symptoms of an incurable, degenerative neurological disease, but also with radical changes in self-perception and outlook. PD changes everything; it has forced me to reexamine my identity, my most basic beliefs, and my purpose in living. It has changed my relationships with people I love, led me to reconsider my understanding of trust and control, and challenged everything I thought was true.

I'm also learning that even when my fellow travelers disappear and the path looks deserted, I'm still not alone. Parkinson's disease will eventually take everything, but in return it's giving me a surprising faith that I didn't expect and had actively resisted for my entire life. PD stripped away my pretensions and forced me to confront questions I thought I had answered long ago and wounds I thought were long healed.

There's an old Yiddish saying that I've always liked: "Man plans, and God laughs." Perhaps the idea is better stated in Proverbs 16:9, though: "In their hearts men plan their course, but the Lord establishes their steps." For most of my life, I've been convinced that I was in charge of my destination and that I chose the steps I took. I've come to realize that I've been wrong. God has apparently been gently amused at my presumption, and He has my attention now.

Corey D. King

2
Initiation

One of my first memories is of a bright light suspended above me. I learned later, as part of the set of stories I've come to call our "family mythology," that the light was a chandelier shaped like a wagon wheel hanging above the breakfast table in our house in south Dallas. It fascinated me, and I reached for the light from my high chair during meals with my parents, my big sister, and two older brothers gathered around the table. According to family mythology, the light was also the source of my first words. As I reached for the sparkling brightness with rapt attention, they repeated, "That's a light, Corey; light. Can you say 'light'?" They were overjoyed when I responded obediently, "ligh…," and they provided the proper correction.

"No, it's 'light'. Say 'light'."

I don't remember being irritated at the correction, but my second word was "…ighT," as if to say, "I GET it. Don't bother me."

I am the youngest in my family by six years, and family mythology also states that I was "the surprise." I took that to mean that I was unplanned, and I hoped that it was the, "Oh, look, we just won the lottery" type of surprise, rather than the "Oh, look, the dog found a dead muskrat and brought it home" type. The mythology remains silent on this subject.

I was a serious and thoughtful child, and my parents jokingly told me that I was the old man in the family. When my brothers and sister were joking, cutting up, or being loud and boisterous in the car, my parents rarely had to discipline them when I was there. Mimicking the words and tone I had heard, I scolded, "Behave, you kids," in a severe voice.

I earned the nickname "Eeyore," after the donkey in the Winnie the Pooh books that took a dismal view of every situation, expecting to be the butt of all jokes. I didn't see the humor; it was obvious that Eeyore had a clear view and common-sense approach. I wanted to be Christopher Robin, but Eeyore was my kind of guy.

My family told me that I was adopted (nothing wrong with being adopted—I'm not, but have wished occasionally since then that I had been), that I was overweight (my father's nickname for me for years was Tosca Fats—I was built like a greyhound, but that's what made it funny, get it?) and that I was Chinese (since every fourth child born in the world is Chinese, and I was the fourth child in our family). It was all done in good fun, of course, and perhaps with the underlying goal of shaking me out of my serious attitude. I think it worked. Now an adult, I think many things are funny that I suspect are actually not.

My sister Kathy doted on me, and was my second mother. She read to me from *Winnie the Pooh*, told me stories of Little Suzy the squirrel and the toy soldiers who protected her, and introduced me to the mysteries of *One Fish, Two Fish* and *Go, Dogs, Go*. She loved the Peanuts comic strip, especially Snoopy, and for some unfathomable reason she also liked folk music. I barely survived exposure to The Brothers Four and The Kingston Trio, but I loved reading with her.

The younger of my two brothers, Ken, looked after me and made me laugh. He was my hero. He could do everything I wanted to do, everyone liked him, and he wasn't embarrassed to have me tag along. Over the years, Ken taught me to throw a baseball, climb a tree, tell a joke, talk to girls, and a few other things I might have been better off not learning. I idolized Ken; although Kathy was my second mother, Ken was and will always be my big brother.

My oldest brother, Marc, was a mystery to me. He was quiet and reserved, and his room smelled like English Leather aftershave. He was an Eagle Scout and he liked building airplanes; the balsa wood and tissue paper creations that adorned his room were fascinating, and looked hopelessly complex. I always hoped he would teach me how to cut and glue the tiny wooden parts to make a wing or fuselage, or show me how to fly, but he didn't have much patience for a little brother with too many questions and clumsy fingers. To complicate matters, the fluid that he used to tighten and stiffen the tissue paper on his planes was called "dope." I had heard repeatedly about the dangers of doing dope, so I figured I would be better off avoiding Marc's airplanes, at least until I was older.

I was six. I loved school, had friends, had a crush on the little girl three houses away, and looked forward to the Griff's hamburger my mother bought for me almost every day after half-day kindergarten. My grandfather, whom I called Pappy, took me for haircuts, which were always followed by toys at the Ben Franklin five-and-dime store and ice cream. My favorite was the peppermint stick ice cream at the Polar Bear ice cream shop down the street, and I had the shortest hair of any kid in school; if I could have gotten a haircut every day, I would have been happy. I felt safe and slept soundly at night, and my occasional nightmares faded unremembered with the light of day.

When I was seven, we moved suddenly from Dallas to Washington, DC. I didn't know why we moved, I only knew that everything familiar and comforting in my life had disappeared. My memories of the six months surrounding the move are mostly of whispered conversations that I wasn't supposed to hear. I remember that we moved in the fall after I started first grade. I don't remember much about the previous summer, other than the morning that I learned Marc was in the hospital.

Marc was ten years older, we were not close, and I was slightly afraid of him. He was still my brother, though, and I was upset that he was in the hospital. I was equally upset that no one would tell me why. My father was a policeman, and I knew from other whispered conversations that nothing good comes from sudden visits to the hospital in the middle of the night.

Marc remained in the hospital for several weeks and I was not allowed to visit. In Texas during the 1960s, young children were not welcome during hospital visiting hours, so I moped in the lobby with a succession of relatives—my sister, my mother, my grandmother. I knew something terrible had happened, and my imagination filled in the gaps.

I decided that a monster had attacked Marc. No one wanted me to know, I reasoned, because if the monster knew you were thinking about him, he would come for you, too. I resolved to try very hard not to think about the monster, and thus keep myself safe.

Don't think about a penguin. It's impossible—making a conscious effort to avoid a particular thought practically guarantees failure. Day and night during Marc's hospital stay, I imagined what he looked like, what the monster had done to him, and where the monster was right now. I sweated and shivered in fear, convinced the monster knew I was thinking about him, and I lay awake at night, listening. I knew the monster had taken Marc at night, because he was there when I went to bed and was gone before breakfast. So, I waited. I was dreadfully sure I would be next.

Marc finally came home and confirmed my suspicions. He had been badly injured and walked with silver crutches that wrapped around his forearms and made a disturbing clicking sound. He seemed injured in other ways, too. He seemed not only quiet and reserved, but also angry and withdrawn, and he rarely spoke to me. I grew more afraid, not just of him but of what I imagined had happened to him. I wanted to ask, but even then I recognized the scent of danger in the air. It was a familiar odor in our house. Some subjects were off limits.

Eventually, the monster faded from my conscious thoughts and was replaced with the excitement and anticipation of my first days in "big school." I settled into a first-grade routine of "Tip and Mitten," timed multiplication tests, and civil defense drills. I'm part of the last generation to learn to duck and cover in school, and I vividly remember the teacher blowing her whistle and commanding us to climb under our desks with our backs to the window. I had no idea why we were huddled on the floor, although I knew it had something to do with "the Soviet Onion." I had no idea what the Soviet Onion was, but I didn't worry excessively. I did wonder why I was safer from it under my desk, though.

I forgot about the monster until the day I came home from school to learn that we were moving. No explanations—I was only a child and wasn't entitled to them. My fears rushed back. The monster had found us again and we were moving to get away, I thought.

It seemed that one moment I was in my familiar bed in Dallas, and the next I was in a new house, in a new school, with teachers I didn't know, surrounded by people I didn't recognize. Kathy was away at college, and amidst the turmoil of the move and my unfamiliar surroundings, my dreadful sense of the monster's presence returned. This time, however, I was confused. Had the monster attacked Marc, or was Marc actually the monster? Through my childish eyes, he even looked like the monster I feared.

Our new house in suburban Maryland was much larger, with empty rooms and hardwood floors. It creaked and echoed. As I lay awake at night, listening to the echoes, I imagined that I could hear the monster moving from room to room.

"Click click, thump, click click, thump, click click, thump..." I knew what I heard was Marc walking upstairs on his crutches, but I imagined the monster was searching the house for me. Maybe those clicking claws and stubby monster feet, thumping down the hall, were coming for me right now.

I huddled in bed as fear and dread trampled through my chest on stubby feet, and in reaction to the stress and anxiety that was common for me over the next ten years, I vomited. The pattern repeated night after night for months. I learned to do my own laundry by washing sheets in the middle of the night so my parents wouldn't know.

They knew, of course. I remember listening through the bedroom wall as my father muttered to my mother, "He does this every night. Can't you keep him quiet?" They both knew. I sometimes wonder if they might even have been proud of me for trying to hide the truth, as if I had learned the family way: "Keep it to yourself; tough it out; no one needs to know our business."

I never knew, and still don't know, the details of Marc's accident. The incident is a taboo subject in the family, not even addressed by the family mythology. Marc won't talk about it even now, at least to me; our relationship is almost non-existent. Over the years, I've pieced together some of the details, attempting to understand—not out of curiosity, but to help fill a hole in my own history and explain a family sickness that still goes uncured. Amidst the rumors, guesses, and speculations now almost fifty years old, the only facts I have found were in a very short article from the Dallas Morning News, dated Tuesday, May 6, 1969, buried in Section D, under Local News:

"OFFICER'S SON SHOT IN BACK – The 16-year-old son of a high-ranking Dallas police officer remained in satisfactory condition at Baylor Hospital after he was shot in the back early Sunday morning in a neighbor's home. Police said he was shot once in the lower left back as he tried to flee the home of Bob C. Tinsley, 2233 Tosca Lane, about 2 a.m. Sunday. Tinsley told officers he was awakened by the screams of his wife who told him there was a prowler in their bedroom. Tinsley said the prowler jumped up and ran from the bedroom and into the kitchen. Tinsley chased him, stopping at a closet to get a .22 caliber pistol. He ordered the boy to freeze at the back door, and then fired one shot which hit the youth and a second which struck the door. Police took affidavits from Tinsley and his wife and talked with the boy, a Kimball High School student. Charges were pending a full investigation, police said."

There was no follow-up story, no mention of charges, and no reference to my father anywhere. He was then an assistant chief in the Dallas Police Department, a front-runner to be selected as chief, and Mr. Tinsley, our next-door neighbor, called him first that night. It was my father who found Marc unconscious on the driveway.

I don't know what happened next, but another assistant chief was selected to be chief, my father resigned from the department, and we moved less than six months later. The Dallas Police Department denies having records of the shooting, and it's not clear that there was ever any further investigation. The incident simply evaporated, leaving behind my brother's physical and emotional scars and an unhealed family trauma that continues to fracture us.

My brother was not the monster in the house, nor is his story mine to tell. He was as much of a victim of the real monster as I was. The real monster was secrecy. As I washed sheets in the middle of the night and finally learned to sleep on the bathroom floor when I knew I was going to have a bad night, I learned: when bad things happen, keep quiet.

I had ample opportunity to practice this simple lesson for the next twenty years. I didn't challenge the monster until my own son was born and I could no longer keep a secret I had hidden for almost my entire life. The first person I told was Amy, and she reacted in a way I found familiar—she threw up.

My father, by all appearances a good father, husband, and public servant, molested me repeatedly as a child and young adolescent. I never understood what motivated him, and when I confronted him several years before he died, he couldn't give me any insights. His only interest was in keeping the secret, even after it was out in the open between us. His reaction was to tell me that he didn't think it was necessary for my mother to know about it. For her protection, you see. What use would there be in hurting her?

With Amy's encouragement, I paid him a visit in late 1998 in the retirement community where he lived with my mother in Dallas. I invited him to go for a drive and told him I didn't mind driving. I took his car keys and drove with him for hours through Dallas streets and highways. With him as a literally captive audience, I began asking questions. He handled them all as skillfully as a lifetime in law enforcement, public administration, and executive management could allow. Interrogation was nothing new to him—he had had years of experience before I was even born, and he had nothing to fear from me.

We drove for over four hours. I wanted to see him break. I bludgeoned him with my memories of the things he had done, with his corruption of a relationship that should be sacrosanct. I told him I thought his entire life was a lie, and that nothing he had ever done would matter unless he made this right. I said I didn't trust him around my children, and that was why Amy and I didn't leave them alone with him. I described how it felt to grow up thinking he might kill me someday to keep the secret; if he could do those things to his own son, where were the boundaries? Were there any boundaries at all? I thought I needed him to feel the fear, revulsion, shame, guilt, and confusion he had created in me.

He took it all in stride. He was calm, unperturbed, and as smooth as silk. He might have been screaming on the inside, but he never let it show, and he never expressed regret or asked for forgiveness. I am sure I will never see such a display of misguided, misapplied strength of will again in my life. He died never having raised the subject with me again.

His abuse had two major impacts on my development and outlook. First, I became unable to trust, especially authority figures who claimed to be righteous and virtuous. Father figures, whether in the form of coaches, mentors, military commanders, bosses, or God—the ultimate father figure—were not reliable. I unconsciously and repeatedly searched for a replacement father to trust, and was repeatedly disappointed.

I was also firmly convinced that the abuse was my fault, and that if I had only been stronger, braver, more observant, or more in control, I could have avoided it or stopped it. My father had practiced the application of force and intimidation for his entire adult life, and he was a master at management of people and events, but I still thought I should have stopped him. I became convinced that I was weak and powerless, and my father exploited those feelings as part of the pattern of abuse. Many of my life choices and attitudes can be traced back to my response to my father's abuse.

We all have dark spots on our histories and challenges to

overcome. Worse things happen to children at the hands of trusted relatives every day, and my experiences are no excuse for curling up and dying. It's only one of the threads in the tapestry of my life. Like having PD, I would have never wished for it, and I would be heartily grateful if it had never happened, but it eventually helped me to develop the ability to live with adversity, and it led me to believe that I can endure anything.

Even as I write this, though, a voice whispers at the back of my mind, "What are you doing? No one needs to know—you're just embarrassing yourself and everyone else. This is family business—keep your mouth shut."

Throughout my life, this voice has been an overbearing taskmaster, telling me to ignore the truth, hide weakness and failure, and keep family business to myself. Couched in noble terms such as "strong and silent" and "keeping my own counsel," the voice kept me from exposing a family sickness that could have harmed my own children, acknowledging a physical limitation that nearly cost me my life, and coming to terms with Parkinson's disease earlier. The voice once sounded like my father's, but now it's mine. It still whispers, but I've learned not to listen.

3
Information And Belief

I left the neurologist's office clutching my bag of medication samples, thinking, "Well. Parkinson's disease. Maybe that's not so bad. Michael J. Fox has Parkinson's, and he's about as cool as they come. And if I only have to take one of these pills a day, I can do that. Yeah—Parkinson's; at least it's not a brain tumor." For a moment, I was relieved to have a label for my collection of physical problems.

Amy was traveling in Africa, so I had time to research and develop a plan to manage the challenge. One little white pill per day and some minor lifestyle changes; no problem, I figured. I'd accomplished harder tasks.

My sense of relief lasted until I sat down in front of my computer. I mentally flipped a coin and settled on Wikipedia, typed in "Parkinson's disease," and started reading.

I read for hours, scarcely believing what I learned. I finally pushed back after ten hours with a myriad of new terms and concepts buzzing in my head and a growing sense of unreality. How could this be? What had I done wrong? I was sure there was a mistake. Parkinson's disease was serious, and except for minor illnesses and middle age, I was healthy. This couldn't be true.

The neurologist instructed me to take the medication he had given me for six weeks. He'd then evaluate the results. Simple and easy, I thought, and definitely will prove I don't have PD.

I swallowed the first pill with a mix of trepidation and anticipation. I half-expected my left hand to suddenly leap into life, and for the whole day after that first dose, I wandered around the house, periodically sitting at the computer and typing a few lines as a test to see if anything had changed. No changes; no effect.

The doctor warned me about possible side effects, and told me to call him if they were too bad. I took the first dose on a Saturday morning, thinking that if there were going to be problems, I'd see them Saturday or Sunday, and would be on top of it by the workday on Monday. Reasonable, logical, and wrong.

I felt fine all day Saturday, but there were no changes my symptoms. Sunday, I repeated the process—still no changes in my hand and arm. I went to bed feeling just a little out of sorts on Sunday night.

On Monday morning, the alarm rang at the normal time. I rolled out of bed and promptly fell down as the room turned on its side. I had read that dizziness and disorientation were possible side effects, but this wasn't dizziness. This was a carnival Tilt-a-Whirl ride missing a few important bolts. I decided to relax on the bedroom floor for a few minutes and consider my options.

I discovered I could control the disorientation if I kept my head still and moved very slowly. So, looking like the Tin Man on a rainy day, I made my way to the couch to recover from the process of getting out of bed. After a few minutes, the dizziness faded enough that I could eat. I made several telephone calls—one to my office to let them know I would be working from home, and then to the neurologist to ask, "So, what is THIS nonsense all about?"

He called back later that day, and it was a short conversation:
Me: "I'm very dizzy."
Doc: "Yes. That's one of the potential side effects."
Me: "I'm sorry, I wasn't clear. I'm VERY dizzy."
Doc: "Yes, we discussed this. You may experience some unpleasant side effects at first. They will likely fade over time. It's important that we determine how well you respond to medication."
Me: "Dizzy. Very dizzy."
Doc: "Is there anything else? No? Feel free to call anytime."
I had started down the path that all people with Parkinson's, or

PWPs, walk: the balancing act between the benefits of various treatments and the unavoidable side effects that can be worse than the disease. And this was just the first few days of a simple drug challenge to validate the diagnosis.

The dizziness eventually eased, but the benefits did not appear. After six weeks, I visited the neurologist again and reported the news. And over the next three months, the pattern repeated with a succession of drugs. Most caused violent nausea and vomiting with every dose. I had side effects by the truckload, but I was still not seeing any noticeable benefits. I had the same stiffness, slowness, unsteadiness, and lack of fine motor control.

After a very unpleasant trial with a new drug, I called the doctor's office again. I needed information. The drugs don't appear to be working; what does this mean? Is the diagnosis a mistake? Do I have a brain tumor after all, or do I just need a better diet? The doctor called back quickly, and as I stood on the outside patio of a local restaurant, he gave me his rundown.

I clearly had the symptoms of Parkinson's disease, but the cause was unknown. It didn't appear that I was responding to medication—that was called drug-unresponsive Parkinsonism. There were several possible culprits. "Space-occupying defects" in my brain had been ruled out, as had several other unusual possibilities. There was something called "atypical Parkinsonism" that could be responsible. Only time would tell. We would have to wait.

Unfamiliar technical-sounding terms are irresistible to me, so I hit the web again. This time I wanted more detail, so I went to the Mayo Clinic website. I found new information about atypical Parkinsonism: the common characteristic is a rapid degeneration of physical and mental function ending in death.

I was stunned again. Only months ago I was happily unaware, enjoying time with Amy and my kids, teaching scuba diving on weekends, learning a new job, and living a normal life. Today, I "would have to wait" to find out if I had a disease that would quickly steal my health, my body, my mind, and, finally, my life. In desperation, I sought another medical opinion.

I searched throughout the country for the best neurologists for a second opinion. There were multiple options, including road trips to the Mayo Clinic(s), Washington, Cleveland, Houston, Dallas, and many other places. There were excellent options in San Antonio, though, and I had learned enough to know I wanted to see a movement disorder specialist, so I made an appointment.

During my first appointment, the doctor listened patiently as I gave him a quick synopsis, and he asked a number of pointed and probing questions about my medications, my symptoms, and my history. He asked questions that I found a little strange, such as, "does your arm or hand ever do things on its own, or feel like it doesn't belong to you?" and then administered another hokey-pokey exam, this one more comprehensive than any other. I walked up and down, tapped, dragged, clenched, touched, and twisted as directed, wishing for a little music to make my timing better. He also snuck up behind me and pulled on my shoulders suddenly. I didn't realize at the time that it was part of the exam, and just thought he had a unique way of interacting with his patients.

We then sat down for a discussion. He was clear, straightforward, and direct.

"Well. It's apparent to me that you have Parkinsonian symptoms, and they're markedly asymmetric, which raises questions. There are some possibilities we have to rule out, so here's what we're going to do…"

I left his office with an order for another test to make sure all the useful parts of my brain were getting enough blood, an order for a test with an interesting specimen collection process (I'll never again trust a bottle of apple juice in the refrigerator), an additional blood test to eliminate several metabolic possibilities, and a particularly detailed day-by-day plan for conducting a drug challenge with the right Parkinson's drug. He was clear that, given my history, I would probably have nausea and vomiting problems from the medication, but that I should just bear it as well as I could.

He was absolutely right on all counts. The brain scan showed no blood flow abnormalities in my brain, and the other tests showed nothing more significant than a Vitamin D deficiency. All that remained was to judge my response to medication.

For some PWPs, response to the medicine is like flipping a switch; the effects are quick and obvious. They were assuredly quick and obvious for me: horrible nausea and vomiting after every dose. The doctor made some changes to my daily regimen that made a radical difference, and I embarked on a long, slow, nausea-free increase in dosage. After two months of pills and uncertainty, I went back to my new neurologist for another hokey-pokey exam.

He concluded that I showed significant improvement in motor function. He guessed that my previous violent reaction didn't leave enough medication in my system to have an impact, and that the right combination of drugs made all the difference.

After almost twenty years of slowly growing symptoms and fifteen years of physical disability, I finally had an answer: young-onset idiopathic drug-responsive Parkinson's disease. Even this was only a provisional diagnosis, the result of a winnowing process that had ruled out other conclusions. I learned from my frantic research that even the most careful PD diagnosis was only about 75% accurate, so I had to ask, "Is it possible that this isn't really even Parkinson's?" His response brought the stark reality of my new situation clearly into focus.

"You need to understand that if you don't have Parkinson's disease, the only other possibilities are much worse."

I had been a normal, healthy middle-aged man with some unexplained soreness and stiffness only weeks before. Now, the best I could hope for was life with an incurable, degenerative neurological disease. I was devastated, and had a completely new set of unanswered questions. How could I fight back? What could I do to control this new reality? What should I do next?

Corey D. King

4

Preparation

By the time I was fifteen, I had almost convinced myself that the abuse hadn't really happened. It had stopped several years before, and it was such an unbelievable and horrible anomaly that I coped by ignoring it. I tried once to tell my brother Ken, but he was only a teenager himself and simply didn't know what to do with the information. I let it drop, and didn't bring it up again until many years later.

From the outside, my junior high and high school years appeared normal; I was prone to nightmares and anxieties, but I had friends, played sports, and made good if not outstanding grades. The secret I carried, and my belief that I was not only at fault but also faulty in general, sank below the surface; not to heal and disappear, but to fester and wait for the future.

I was tagged as a gifted and talented student in elementary school, and although I was happy with the perceived achievement, I was uncomfortable with being singled out. As I grew older, I developed a love-hate relationship with my academic ability. I was smart, but I hated for adults to comment on it in front of other kids. It made me feel peculiar, and I needed no additional reason to feel different.

I enjoyed the feeling of power that being the "smart kid" gave me, though. I craved the sense of control that knowing the answers gave me, and it came naturally. I was curious about everything, and one of my favorite pastimes was to choose one volume of our World Book Encyclopedia, starting with "A" and continuing through "X-Y-Z," and read it cover to cover. I must have read the entire encyclopedia a dozen times between the ages of eight and fourteen, one letter at a time. The World Book helped me develop an appreciation for the value and power of knowledge, even if many of the facts I learned from its pages were wrong, as I've discovered over the years.

Although I needed the power that academic achievement gave me, it was at odds with another powerful drive: my need to hide. I felt defective and wrong in a way I couldn't define, and I felt much safer and more secure when no one noticed me. These two forces were in constant opposition inside me. I craved the spotlight and the sense of accomplishment and approval it brought, but I also wanted to stay in the shadows.

As an outgrowth of the love of reading and books I received from my sister Kathy, I became a science fiction fan. I immersed myself in tales of spaceships, space exploration, and the steely-eyed, square-jawed heroes who could both out-think and out-shoot bug-eyed monsters and space pirates. As I lost myself in those created worlds, I developed a future vision of myself that combined my intellect with an air of power, fearlessness, and bravery. I wanted to be Virgil Samms, First Lensman of The Galactic Patrol, but I decided that I could settle for being an astronaut. I resolved to become the person I imagined I could be—smart, but strong; a thinker and a doer; equally comfortable at the blackboard or in the cockpit. I wanted to be Alan Shepard, Neil Armstrong, and a less wimpy Luke Skywalker combined.

I developed The Plan. First, I would obtain an appointment to the Air Force Academy and earn a degree in engineering. I would become an Air Force fighter pilot and test pilot. I would eventually earn a Ph.D. in either engineering or physics, and then be assigned to NASA as an astronaut. I resolved to be the first man on Mars.

I gleefully ignored the fact that I became violently carsick on our occasional drives through the mountains in the Shenandoah National Park, and that I had never met a roller coaster that didn't make me vomit. I was on a mission, and naysayers be damned.

I had played baseball, football and basketball when I was younger, but I chose track as my sport in high school. I was a sprinter and quarter-miler, and I was fast enough to compete well and win regularly. My SAT scores were excellent, my grades were good, I didn't have any juvenile felonies on my record, and I cleaned up reasonably well, so an appointment to the Air Force Academy seemed possible.

I completed the Academy application and received nominations from my senators and congressmen. My Academy liaison officer informed me I was a shoo-in, so I decided to have confidence and didn't apply at any other academies or universities. And so, of course, the appointment went to a football player from my high school who also applied, a nice guy who left the Academy under duress during his sophomore year as a result of a youthful indiscretion that involved a young lady and some unusual behavior at a local dance hall. Or so I heard.

Shocked, discouraged, and without much time, I conducted a quick survey of possibilities. I had been offered a track scholarship to Brown University in Rhode Island, but I still wanted to pursue a degree in aerospace engineering and follow The Plan; Brown, although an excellent choice, wasn't much of an engineering school. I was months past the application deadline for most other top-tier engineering schools, so I looked at state schools in Texas and Maryland, the two states where I could claim residency. After rejecting Texas A&M University (mostly because my father recommended it), I enrolled at The University of Texas at Austin and joined Air Force ROTC. I obtained an AFROTC scholarship after my first semester, and after four years as a Longhorn, I earned a degree in aerospace engineering, a promise of a place in Air Force Undergraduate Pilot Training after graduation, and commission as an Air Force Second Lieutenant. I also met my future wife at UT, which, in retrospect, is the best thing I did during my college years.

My entry onto active duty was delayed several months after graduation. I spent the delay working at General Dynamics in Forth Worth on the F-16 fighter and exercising my new American Express card for dinners with my future wife. Finally, I departed for Undergraduate Pilot Training in Columbus, Mississippi. After a minor ripple in The Plan, I was on my way, I thought.

Boy, was I wrong.

5

Where Are All The Good Alternatives?

I was confused and frustrated during my long journey to a Parkinson's disease diagnosis, but I was satisfied to finally have an answer. After years of wondering, I now had a label and could develop a plan of attack. I was relieved until reality set in.

Dr. Elisabeth Kubler-Ross described grieving as a five-stage process: denial, anger, bargaining, depression, and acceptance. I've been in all five of those places, sometimes on the same day. It's not a steady progression, and I'm not finished yet. Although Parkinson's disease shortens expected lifespan, it's not a directly fatal disease. Many people with Parkinson's live long lives after diagnosis, with slow progression and years of good function. Unfortunately, although the speed of progression and the details are different for everyone, the direction and result is always the same.

Parkinson's is both complex and very simple—it's all about "on" and "off." For a PWP who's on, the various medications and treatments are working as well as they ever do, the symptoms are at a minimum (although never gone), and life is manageable. During off time, though, the full weight of the disease comes crashing down and nothing works. Our arms and legs don't move or move too much, our hands shake or are immobile, our bodies scream with the pain of rigid muscles that won't relax, we shuffle, freeze, and fall, we struggle to eat, to speak, to sleep, to stay awake… in short, on is good, off is bad. Daily life for a PWP is a constant battle to maximize on time, minimize off time, and predict the transitions from one to the other. It's a full-time job, and it can be exhausting, frightening, and discouraging. Parkinson's steals not only the ability to move and communicate effectively, but it also damages self-esteem, destroys relationships, halts promising careers in mid-stride, and sentences both PWPs and their loved ones to a seemingly eternal cycle of medication, daily struggles with the basic activities of living, and a slow decline in spite of heroic efforts. A friend and fellow PWP once told me that Parkinson's is "like being stuck on the railroad tracks in front of a slow-moving train—you know it's coming, but even though it takes years to arrive, you can't get out of the way and you can't make it stop."

After my diagnosis, I adjusted the medications and fought my way through debilitating side effects just as every other PWP does. I lost friends I had known for years who stopped responding to attempts at communication, and I made many new friends in many places. My family and I also tried to manage the fear, uncertainty, and anxiety that accompany a progressive, incurable illness. How long would I be able to continue functioning? What would happen when I couldn't work anymore? How fast would the disease progress? How would our family change? Would we be okay?

It quickly became clear that I was unusually affected by side effects from PD medications. Nausea, dizziness, disorientation, fatigue, insomnia, sleep attacks, hallucinations, compulsive behavior, dyskinesia—they were all a part of my PD experience. Since PD is not well understood, the drugs used to relieve the symptoms often cause as many problems as they solve.

Sleep disruptions and hallucinations were particular problems for me. I had had occasional bouts of insomnia prior to being diagnosed, but when I began taking a particular PD medication, I learned what insomnia really is. I would regularly be unable to sleep at night for two or three nights in a row, and even when I did sleep, it was not for more than an hour or two at a time. I tried a variety of sleep medications, but although they helped me sleep slightly longer, I would awaken unrefreshed, disoriented, and sluggish.

It wasn't as if I couldn't catch occasional catnaps, though. I had sleep attacks—sudden, uncontrollable sleepiness during the day. I fell asleep in meetings, during meals, and during one-on-one conversations. In the past, I had occasionally fallen asleep during lectures or business presentations, but it was a new experience to fall asleep during a presentation where I was the one speaking. I imagine it was novel experience for the audience also.

I also fell asleep behind the wheel. I had enough warning to pull into a parking lot or to the side of the road before the uncontrollable sleepiness overtook me, but it was dangerous and disconcerting. I fell asleep several times at stoplights, and only woke up when the irritated drivers behind me blew their horns. Once, I woke up from one of these short naps to a concerned woman knocking on my car window. I rolled down the window.

"Are you okay? Do you need an ambulance?"

"No, thanks," I responded. "I'm just a little sleepy."

"Well, maybe you shouldn't be driving, then, hmm? Why don't you get off the road before you kill yourself or someone else?"

I debated telling her about Parkinson's disease, dopamine agonists, and sleep attacks, but decided that this really wouldn't be the right time for an awareness and education session. Besides, I wasn't sure I could make it through the discussion without falling asleep again.

I also hallucinated. I had never had this particular experience before, so the first time that I saw a squirrel run across the living room floor, I was startled and shocked. We had a backyard full of squirrels, and I enjoyed watching them steal seed from the bird feeder in the mornings and fight with the birds. I thought, "Oh, great. I left the door open—how am I going to get that tree-rat out of here?" I spent thirty minutes trying to find the damned thing in the house, with the cat sitting on the couch watching me with patient contempt. Our cat, a huge Siamese that tolerated no nonsense from anyone or anything, was a serial killer of birds and squirrels, and ruled the house from the couch like a furry dictator.

I saw the squirrel again from the corner of my eye, and glanced over at the cat. He gazed back at me as if to say, "Yes? Is there something you can do for me?" I was astounded that this killer didn't see the squirrel and make it pay for its impudence. When I saw several more small furry animals running just out of clear eyesight across the floor and the cat didn't react, I began to suspect that maybe they weren't really there.

Over the next two years, the sleep problems and hallucinations became slowly worse. One memorable evening, I was sitting sleepless at about 3:00 AM, writing an email to a friend, when I had an eerie sense that someone was standing behind me and looking over my shoulder. I looked quickly and was grateful I didn't see anyone, but the feeling didn't go away. From that time on, I have had the pervasive feeling that there is someone standing behind me, just out of view. I habitually check over my shoulder. Although I know that it is a hallucination, it is upsetting and disconcerting.

I also heard whispering just out of earshot; the sound of people talking quietly in the next room. The long nights of insomnia were lonely, but now I felt like I was living through my own personal version of "The Shining," complete with ghosts moving in the shadows, small furry creatures scurrying across the floor, and barely perceptible whispering from the next room. I have never reached the point of delusion where I believe that these manifestations are real, but it is a wholly unwelcome experience anyway.

I had reached the point where my high medication dosage caused unacceptable side effects, and attempting to decrease the dosage resulted in unacceptable symptom control. My neurologist recommended that I consider a surgical treatment: deep brain stimulation (DBS) surgery.

When he suggested the idea for the first time, I had only been diagnosed for about two years. I said, "You've got to be kidding—that's for late-stage Parkinson's, after everything else stops working, isn't it?" I apparently have a limitless capacity for being wrong, and I was this time, too. DBS actually works best for people who are still benefiting from medication, but with unacceptable side effects. It also works best for people who are relatively early in the disease, who don't have other complications or significant cognitive impacts, and who are not falling often. In other words, me.

So, after weighing the risk factors and evaluating the data, I decided to have DBS surgery in June 2011. The surgery required preparation—a full-anesthesia MRI for brain mapping, a neuropsychological test to make sure I wasn't demented enough to be a bad surgical risk, and a "putting my affairs in order" process. We're talking brain surgery here, after all. Even though the likely outcome was positive, there were major risks, and my family and I had to prepare for all possibilities. My typical approach of hoping for the best and preparing for the worst gained a new intensity.

Hope is good—it provides the courage to press forward even in the face of fear and uncertainty. I was afraid of the procedure, but I was encouraged by my neurologist who always tells me the truth even when it stings, and by many fellow PWPs who had braved their own fear and apprehension with good results. Amy and the kids supported me also; they were willing to do whatever it took to give me a chance at a better quality of life even if none of us knew what that meant. With that going for me, a little brain surgery seemed like a good risk.

Corey D. King

6

Aviation

I'd arrived at Columbus Air Force Base, Mississippi in the fall of 1984, full of determination and ready to be an Air Force pilot. I had been slightly diverted on Step One of The Plan, but I had found an outstanding alternative; who but a Texas Aggie wouldn't want to be a Texas Longhorn? I had also met the love of my life. The future looked bright.

Pilot training commenced with physical training and academics, and I quickly found that my bachelor's degree in aerospace engineering wasn't an asset. Rather than discussing the lift equation that governs an airplane in flight, I learned that airplanes flew because of the "lifties" on the wings. When you turned, the lifties rolled off the wings, and that's why you had to add power and pull on the stick to stay level. So much for Bernoulli, Navier, and Stokes—all pinheads without silver wings. I decided I could live with that—I was certain flight test school would be different.

Finally the long-awaited day arrived—my first flight in an Air Force jet trainer. In 1984, Air Force student pilots flew in the T-37B and the T-38, and my "dollar ride" was in the left seat of a T-37B Dragonfly. That's not what the aircraft was really called, of course.

The T-37 was a "Tweet," or, if you were wordy, a "6000-pound dog whistle."

I had passed the Air Force Reserve Officer Training Corps Flight Instruction Program in college, which was designed to give cadets headed for the cockpit enough small-aircraft flight hours before Air Force pilot training to limit the likelihood of sheer incompetence or unresolvable lack of coordination. I did well in FIP in a small plane, but here was the real thing—a twin-engine jet aircraft. My dream was coming true. With my flight suit, parachute, helmet, and oxygen mask, I thought I had died and gone to heaven. Later (1.3 hours later, according to my logbook), I was sure I had died, but I was no longer sure I was in heaven.

The official purpose of the dollar ride, named for the silver dollar each student was expected to pay the instructor for his or her first flight, was to introduce a new pilot-training student to the aerospace environment. Unofficially, the instructors competed to see if they could make their students airsick. Never one to disappoint, I puked enthusiastically. We all laughed, and the dozen or so of us who left the flight line that day carrying white plastic bags caught a little good-natured teasing, but no one held it against us.

We usually flew three training missions a day, interspersed with simulator time and academics, and the days were long. Report time in the flight room was 2:30 AM during early week, and 4:30 AM during late week. A duty day was twelve hours long—a perfect environment for someone living out their calling and preparing for what they were born to do. Unfortunately, I learned over the next six months that, in addition to whatever else I was destined to do, I had been born to heave.

My problem was complicated by the weather in Columbus and my predisposition to ear and sinus infections. Whenever I gained ground on the airsickness, I would come down with an ear infection and be placed by the flight surgeon on non-flying status. I would typically be grounded for a week or so, which was just long enough to lose my progress in controlling the airsickness. I developed a pattern and a reputation, but I was determined to fight through it.

Airsickness in pilot training fell into two broad categories—it was either an unavoidable physical characteristic of a particular student's inner ear and brain, or it was something they euphemistically called "manifestation of apprehension," or MOA. The distinction was important—they were willing to work with physical problems, but with MOA, the Air Force was uninterested in even allowing the student to remain on active duty. They determined the difference with dexscope.

Dexscope is a combination of the drugs Dexedrine and scopolamine. Scopolamine numbs the inner ear and makes motion sickness effectively impossible, at the cost of severe drowsiness. It's also called the "zombie drug," and in larger doses can cause agitation, delusions, psychosis, and hallucinations. Dexedrine is, well…speed. It keeps you very awake and crispy, makes your skin crawl and your eyeballs itch, and gives you an overwhelming desire to talk fast on the radio. Truly a combination made for the high-speed aerospace environment.

Someone taking dexscope could be strapped in a roller coaster upside down eating raw buzzard all afternoon and feel fine, but if fear and anxiety caused the sickness, dexscope didn't help at all. The flight surgeon decided to try dexscope.

I flew three missions on dexscope, and they were the most sublimely wonderful aviation experiences of my life. I felt free and limitless; the aircraft went where I told it to, and I felt like I was wearing it rather than sitting inside it. Loops, spins, cloverleafs, barrel rolls, Immelmanns, chandelles, split-s's—for so long I had wanted them to be beautiful and effortless, and now they were. The sky was blue, the clouds were puffy, and I could even understand the radio. I was finally in heaven. I was heavily medicated and I was sure I could feel my hair growing, but I wasn't airsick.

The experiment satisfied the flight surgeon and squadron commander. I wasn't one of those MOA types, so they were willing to give me the benefit of the doubt. They were clear, though—one more episode of post-solo airsickness, and I was done. I think I might have been fine if not for yet another ear infection.

When I recovered a week later, I flew one dual mission with my instructor to make sure I hadn't forgotten everything, and then I went up solo on a mission to practice aerobatics. Unfortunately, I actually tried to practice aerobatics, and that was my downfall.

I took off uneventfully and proceeded to my assigned practice area, a pie-shaped wedge of sky defined by distance and heading from the navigation beacon at the base. I arrived without incident and flew a couple of experimental Immelmanns and loops—a few twinges of nausea, but not too bad. I decided to push a little and I set up for a cloverleaf—four loops with a ninety-degree turn near the top of each loop. I remembered how much fun it was when I was heavily drugged, and I wanted to see if could do it without benefit of pharmaceuticals.

I was at the top of the third leaf when I felt a familiar sensation—it was time to hurl. I was disappointed, but I had been through this before and I was a pro, I thought. I was drifting lazily over the top of the loop as I twisted slightly in the ejection seat to reach the supply of white plastic bags in my flight suit leg pocket. I was below stall speed, but I was almost weightless and the airplane didn't notice, even though my inner ear protested violently.

As I twisted to reach the bag and slapped the mask off my face to do what came unnaturally, my leg slipped and I kicked the right rudder. Hard. Below stall speed, upside down, nearly weightless. I should have had better sense (aerospace engineer and all that), but I was young and stupid. The aircraft lurched, and in reflex and inexperience I jerked back on the stick and stalled. The aircraft stopped flying and started falling. Before I could even think, "oh, s**t, that was dumb," I was involved in my first, last, and only inadvertent inverted spin.

Emergency procedures are a critical part of Air Force pilot training, and some emergency procedures are important enough that they print them in large block letters in your checklist and make you memorize them. They're called "boldface procedures" and spin recovery was a boldface procedure. I still remember the steps:

1. THROTTLES – IDLE
2. RUDDER AND AILERONS – NEUTRAL
3. STICK – ABRUPTLY FULL AFT AND HOLD
4. RUDDER – ABRUPTLY APPLY FULL RUDDER OPPOSITE SPIN DIRECTION (OPPOSITE TURN NEEDLE) AND HOLD
5. STICK – ABRUPTLY FULL FORWARD ONE TURN AFTER APPLYING RUDDER
6. CONTROLS – NEUTRAL AND RECOVER FROM DIVE

I had completely forgotten about my need to vomit, and was instead focused on my need not to plummet to the ground and end my life in fiery embarrassment. I had forgotten everything else, and couldn't have even told you my own name, but I remembered that boldface. It must have worked, because I found myself in level flight again, muttering the same obscenity over and over. I now had time to puke; this time, it might have been a manifestation of apprehension.

All this excitement occurred in the first twenty minutes of a planned, 1.3-hour mission, but my zeal for aerobatics had cooled. I extended the speed brake and flew back and forth in the training area, burning fuel and thinking about my future. My thoughts ranged between extremes, from, " I can play this off—maybe no one saw me," to, " I should probably just eject now, walk back to Texas, and get a job at a gas station." When I had burned enough fuel to give me options, I headed back to the base for the last landing of my military aviation career.

The supervisor of flying and the squadron commander were waiting for me. They summoned me as soon as I had put my helmet and parachute away. The SOF spoke first.

"Lieutenant King, how was your mission?" he said.

"Not bad, sir," I said. No blood, I thought.

"Question for you, Lieutenant. Is a spin an authorized solo maneuver?"

"No, sir, it's not."

"Then what the hell did you think you were doing out there solo, spinning my jet?"

Before I answered, I thought about my dream of being an astronaut, my reluctance to show weakness, my desire not to quit or look foolish, and my practical need to have a job so I could marry the girl I had fallen in love with (and, much less importantly, to pay for the new sports car I had bought). I compared those things to being dead, and answered, "Sir, it was an accident. I was airsick, and…" The unvarnished truth came out. I was never a good liar, and they knew what had happened anyway. The crew chief had seen my little white bag.

The squadron commander finally spoke. He said, "Son, go see the flight surgeon," and with those words, my Air Force flight career and my aspirations for glory in space were over. They were over long before that, actually; I just refused to see the truth.

Corey D. King

7
It Looks Like An Ink Blot

My decision in the spring of 2011 to have DBS surgery was difficult, but there's nothing easy about any of the elements of this disease. There are always tough decisions, trade-offs, and hard choices between unpleasant options.

Two facts complicated the decision: the fact that I was very young (forty-eight is young, isn't it?), and the fact that I had only been diagnosed for two years. Those two facts recurred in conversations about my decision to have the surgery. "REALLY? You're having brain surgery? On purpose? You look fine to me—why would you want to do that?"

Most PWPs must repeatedly address the last comment, even with family members and close friends. On some days we do look and feel better than on others, and we're grateful for those days. It was difficult for me to know how to respond to those well-meaning comments. It didn't seem right to say, "Thanks very much for saying that; however, let's not forget that I'm not better, I'm not going to get better, and tomorrow I'm going to look terrible again." There's a fine line between reminding people that PD is variable, capricious, and incurable, and just accepting a nice compliment and the good wishes and concerns that lie behind it at face value. It reminded me of the Saturday Night Live skits that feature Debbie Downer—she never had anything good to say. It tends to stifle conversation when you feel the need to say, "Yes, it is an absolutely beautiful day, and I've never seen the sky so blue and the sun so bright. I have Parkinson's disease, you know."

Those two facts, coupled with the fact that I sometimes appeared to be unaffected by the disease, troubled me as I weighed the pros and cons, sifted through the mountains of available information, and talked to dozens of patients, doctors, experts, family members, and friends. I was young for DBS surgery. Although DBS is now being used more often for younger patients, one of my neurosurgeon's nursing staff mentioned that I was the youngest person she had seen to have the surgery. In addition, I had only been diagnosed for a short time; many people who have this disease manage their symptoms and treatments well for years, and have no interest in or need for DBS.

Sleep disturbances were the main problems that drove me toward DBS. I hoped that DBS would eventually help me taper the amount of medication I was taking, reduce side effects, and help me sleep, and not just in the car driving to work in the morning.

The first step was easy: a two-hour full-anesthesia MRI. I only remember the smiling faces in the MRI room, the IV in my arm, and a chemically-induced black curtain that came down momentarily and then came up again in the recovery room. The nurse said, "Well, welcome back. How are you feeling?"

Blearily, I responded, "I think I was abducted by aliens for a moment."

I experienced no ill effects and no post-anesthesia complications. The detailed map of my brain the neurosurgeon obtained allowed him to plan a precise implantation path for the DBS electrodes, avoid some of my favorite parts of my brain, and finish in exactly the right spot in my subthalamic nucleus. I didn't even know I had a subthalamic nucleus until then.

According to my neurosurgeon, DBS is not a difficult procedure to perform. The key to success is to perform the procedure exactly the same way every time, with the same equipment and the same processes, in the same order, with the same team, carefully and without fanfare. He told me he wasn't interested in being famous, writing journal articles on new processes, or trying all the latest equipment. He just wanted to perform every procedure with predictably excellent results. Coupled with his experience level (well over 1000 successful implantations at this point), his approach made my choice of surgeons easy.

The next step was a neuropsychological exam. Some people are better candidates for DBS surgery than others, and one of the major contraindications for DBS is dementia. The neuropsych exam looks for signs of dementia, and also sets a baseline for cognitive function, memory, coordination, and spatial orientation. With this information, we could compare my pre-surgery state with post-surgery, and see both improvement and decline.

The surgery was scheduled for June 9, 2011, and would last for three to four hours. I would actually be awake for about half of the procedure. I had heard that the brain itself has no pain receptors; I thought that was a fascinating concept. I was more concerned about the process of getting to the brain, though. Past experience with wildly pitched baseballs, tree branches, cave ceilings, and open kitchen cabinets made me quite confident that my scalp and skull enjoyed no such freedom from pain. I hoped the surgeon had thought of that.

I had researched the procedure and talked to other patients, so I thought I knew what to expect. I would arrive at the hospital early on the ninth and receive a new look—I would have my head shaved, a new experience for me. I couldn't recall having seen my own scalp before, except for brief periods in the Air Force when I was overenthusiastic at the barbershop. After the shaving, the surgical team would then install a stereotactic frame—a metal ring that would be screwed into the bone of my skull to keep my head completely still during the procedure. A brain scan to validate my alien-abduction MRI would follow, as a double check that I hadn't done something to change my brain and to verify that the surgical plan was still correct.

I would then proceed to the operating room, where I hoped they kept the serious painkillers. The surgical team would open up my scalp, drill into my skull, and implant two electrical leads in my brain, following the predetermined path. I would be awake, perhaps so I could provide color commentary and tell jokes. After they determined that all was well and everything was where it should be, they would finally let me sleep. I was looking forward to that part of the procedure.

They would anchor the electrodes to plastic plugs in my skull connected to long electrical leads. Those leads would be placed under the skin of my scalp, neck, and upper chest, and terminate in a new battery pack and stimulation computer implanted under the skin of my upper chest below my collarbone. After I healed, the only visible signs would be a slight bulge in my upper chest and two small bulges on the top of my head. I would spend two weeks recovering from the procedure, and then after six to eight weeks, my neurologist would program the device. After tuning and adjustment, I would be a new, electrified man.

My work colleagues thought my surgery might be a unique opportunity to push the boundaries of science and experiment with the man-machine interface. In the lab I helped to manage, we developed ways to make complex technical systems do things their designers didn't intend (we didn't use the term "hacker"—it's rude and inaccurate). We took our work seriously, and I had the sense some of my team took it too seriously. I learned to smile and nod at the comments about the "Six Million Dollar Man," questions like "so, will you be Borg after this? Will we be assimilated?" and even my new nickname, "One of One," a play on "Seven of Nine," a half-robot/half-human character from one of the Star Trek TV shows. However, I drew the line at questions like, "What did you say the control system signal looked like? Do you know anything about the effective range of control? What kind of processor is in the stimulation system? Do you mind dropping by the lab for a few minutes when the system is installed? We'd like to test a theory." Engineers are just hilarious, in an incomprehensible kind of way.

In May 2011, I completed a major milestone on the way to the surgery date. I didn't know what to expect from the neuropsychological exam, but like many parts of the process, it was fascinating. The exam lasted about three hours, and started with a Minnesota Multiphasic Personality Inventory (MMPI), a delightful collection of 576 questions that, if you were not already disturbed, could easily make you that way. I had an easy time with questions like, "I often hear voices that tell me to do things I shouldn't do," and, "Demons often inhabit my body." I knew the right answers, regardless of what the truth might actually be. I had a little more trouble with questions like, "I believe I would like the work of a forest ranger," and, "I believe I would enjoy being a woman." I may have overthought some of the questions; surely, it depends on which forest ranger and which woman, doesn't it?

There were many other tests in the neuropsych exam. Most of them activated my sense of competitiveness, and I worked hard. It was clear to me, however, that on some segments I didn't do well, and I wondered whether it was just a normal effect of growing older or whether it was Parkinson's disease. One of the tests involved saying as many words that started with a particular letter as I could in one minute. Piece of cake, I thought. I completed F and N without any problems, and then came the letter A. I started off strong; "apple, aardvark, archive, argument," and then stalled. I couldn't think of a single word that started with "A." I had an intense dialogue with myself trying to break through the A-word logjam, but that entire section of the dictionary had disappeared.

"Oh, come on, there're all kinds of words that start with A. How about... no, I used that one. Now, there's... no, not that one—too vulgar. Well, there's... no, that's a proper noun, and he said I couldn't use those. I wonder if he'd notice if I just got up and left the room? How long IS one minute, anyway? This is just getting ridiculous now. A, A, come on—you're a smart guy—please, just one more..."

"Time's up," the psychologist said.

"Oh, thank God," I said. "What just happened?"

In typical psychologist form, he said, "What do YOU think just happened?" I fought an internal battle with myself, and avoided ruining the whole test by strangling him. It's the small victories that are the most satisfying.

One of the final tests involved dozens of cards printed with different numbers of colored shapes. My task was to match the cards and figure out what the rules were for matching. My inquisitor laid four cards face-up on the table and gave me the rest of the deck.

"You place the cards where you think they go, one at a time, and after each one I'll tell you whether it's correct or incorrect." Great, I thought. I'm good at this kind of thing.

I started slapping cards down confidently. It went well, briefly.

"Let's see—three green squares. Does that go with the two green triangles, the one blue square, or the three red circles? Let's try... the circles," I thought.

"Correct."

"Ah. Numbers. Now, one yellow triangle ought to go with one red square…"

"Correct," he said again.

"Way too easy," I thought. Confidently, I continued to slap the cards down, receiving each "correct" as my due reward for being so darned smart. I placed three yellow circles on three red triangles, and was already reaching for the next card when I heard him say, "That's incorrect."

"Huh? No, it's not."

"I'm sorry, but it is incorrect," he said. "Okay," I thought. "I just have to revise the algorithm a little bit. New data; no big deal. Numbers go with numbers, unless there's a match of colors and shapes. So, three yellow circles go with any number of yellow circles first, then any card with three of anything. Got it…"

"Correct, correct, correct, incorrect." WHAT???

"Okay, another revision… shapes plus colors, then numbers, then colors alone, but only if… no, wait. Shapes, then colors, but only if there isn't a shape-color match, or if there are more than six cards in my hand, or if it's Tuesday and not a leap year… no, wait." My mind was awash with nested if-then loops, conditional rules, cases, and other logical constructs that my software development colleagues lived and breathed, but that I only vaguely remembered from my one software engineering class in graduate school. My tendency to overthink didn't occur to me then. There was a mystery here, and I was going to figure it out.

"Correct, correct, correct, incorrect, incorrect, incorrect, incorrect, incorrect, incorrect, incorrect, incorrect, incorrect, correct…"

"Can we go back to the "A" words now, please?"

Whenever I thought I finally understood the rule set, he said, "that's incorrect." I suspected that this wasn't about placing cards, but instead about judging my tolerance for frustration. I resolved to be imperturbable.

"Correct, incorrect, incorrect, incorrect, incorrect, incorrect, incorrect, incorrect, incorrect, incorrect…"

"Oh, come on. Now you're just messing with me."

In his best Sigmund Freud voice, he said, "Hmmmm. Do you often think that people are messing with you? What do they do to mess with you? Does everyone mess with you?" Again the internal struggle, again a small victory. He lived, and I stayed out of jail.

After roughly ten years in hell, I finally came to the end of the card deck. I pushed back slightly from the table, looked my new friend in the eye, and said, "Okay. What's the story? How does this work?"

"Well, I'm really not supposed to tell you…"

I debated telling him about my internal struggle, and how we might both lose if he didn't cough up the answer, but I decided that might work against me. In my calmest, most non-psychotic, non-frustrated voice I said, "I think it would be really good for us both if you told me what I wanted to know."

"It's actually pretty simple," he said. "For the first few minutes, you're supposed to match the numbers. Then you're supposed to match the colors, and then you're supposed to match the shapes. You seemed to be having a hard time with that."

I stopped breathing momentarily, and even stopped shaking, which is a significant event for someone with Parkinson's disease.

"You were CHANGING THE RULES? Let's discuss for a moment what a rule actually is, shall we? Let's talk about horses in midstream; let's talk about consistency; let's talk about what you don't do in the middle of a test. Okay? Okay?"

"So, consistency is important to you? Do you expect the world to be consistent? How does it make you feel when people are not consistent? Was your mother consistent?"

Apparently, I passed the test. They didn't cancel my surgery.

Corey D. King

8
Coercion

The Air Force and I agreed that I could keep my commission if I never again tried to pilot a military jet aircraft. I spent several months in the spring of 1985 working in the Columbus base commander's office as an errand boy while the Powers That Be decided my future. While there, I met a major who had been a flight commander in the student squadron, responsible for a dozen or so instructor pilots and perhaps forty students. He had fallen from grace with the Air Force for some reason, and had been stripped of both his command and his wings. He and I were in a kind of limbo, waiting to learn what our futures held.

I saw him regularly in the cafeteria, so out of politeness I struck up a conversation with him one afternoon.

"Hi, Major. How are things going?"

"Hello, Lieutenant. Have you accepted Christ as your personal Lord and Savior?"

I was taken aback. I stammered, "Well, I'm not sure. I used to got to church, but I haven't had time recently, I was a student here but I washed out for air sickness, my dog ate my homework, I think I hear my mother calling me, I've got to go find anything else to do, sir, goodbye and enjoy your lunch," as I backed toward the door. I probably could have handled the situation more tactfully, but I had never been asked that directly before, and I didn't know what to say. I knew my answer was, "No, and I don't want to hear about it from you, either," but I also sensed that would be the wrong thing to say. I hid in the base historian's office for the rest of the day and hoped I wouldn't see the major again before I left for my new assignment.

Of course, I saw him every day for the next two weeks. I finally tired of ducking into doorways and diving into the shrubbery every time he appeared, so when he approached me in the base library, where I was using my engineering degree to update a section of the base history document, I resigned myself to a conversation I really didn't want to have.

"Hello again, Lieutenant. Do you know Jesus?"

I admitted that I didn't, but that I had gone to church when I was younger. I just didn't see the point any longer.

He began a long, rambling monologue filled with Bible verses, commentary about the nature of sin, personal anecdotes about his conversations with God, and the evil nature of the modern Air Force. He then said, "Are you willing to get down on your knees with me right here and accept Jesus?"

I felt trapped and embarrassed, but I was surprised that I also felt a touch of fear. I remembered that this was how I felt when my father abused me. Trapped, ashamed, frightened of what this crazy person here with me might do, shocked by my belated recognition that he wasn't what I thought he was, wanting to be anywhere else but frozen in place by my perception of his authority over me. An unexpected anger pounded in my temples.

"No, Major, I am not. I'm not interested in your God or anything you have to say. Do you really think you're doing the right thing? You don't know me, sir, and you don't have any right to pressure me like this. If you talk to me again, I'll tell the wing commander and base commander. Leave me alone." I wished I could have kept the quaver out of my voice, but I was both enraged and apprehensive. I didn't know why then, but I also felt a slight sense of liberation that I attributed to telling a senior officer to bug off.

"Lieutenant, my duty is to God, and my mission is to save souls. That's why they want me to leave. You won't be telling them anything they don't already know."

I was dumbfounded, but I was on a roll. "Major, you're making me really uncomfortable. Even if I were interested, and I'm not, bullying me on duty is wrong." In memory, I imagine myself looking like Dirty Harry Callahan, but Barney Fife is probably closer to the truth.

He shook his head. "I'm just trying to save your soul from Hell. That's where you're headed." He walked away.

The only other time I saw him was my last duty day at Columbus, as I was out-processing. I had gone to the base gym to get a signature verifying that I didn't have any of their basketballs in my possession, and I saw him sitting at a desk in the hallway between the men and women's locker rooms. It was his desk, complete with a pencil holder, a telephone, and his nameplate, and he was filling out forms. The leadership at the base was shaming him, because no one wanted him in their organization while they drummed him out of the military. I never learned whether his infraction had only been his inability to reconcile his religious zeal with the responsibility he had accepted with his commission, or whether there was more to it. My indignation had cooled somewhat, but I still thought he deserved everything he was getting; he had turned his back on duty, honor, and country, and used his rank and position to achieve personal goals that didn't have anything to do with his obligation as an officer. I pitied him, but he still disgusted me, and I was sure that he must be seriously mentally deranged.

In retrospect, I overreacted. I was in the grip of forces and motivations I didn't understand but that had bubbled close to the surface for many years. I associated religion with coercion, and coercion with abuse, shame, and guilt. I wanted no part of it, and I began to consciously reject God and religion in any form.

Corey D. King

9
Denying The Brutal Truth

The neuropsychological exam forced me to confront a scary subject I had been avoiding—the cognitive side of Parkinson's disease. I had been focused on the physical symptoms of Parkinson's: the movement symptoms, the autonomic nervous system problems, the degeneration of my body and physical competence. I had been ignoring the other part of this insidious disease: the potential decline of executive function, memory, complex decision-making, multitasking, and other higher-level cognitive abilities. This characteristic of PD was the most disturbing and frightening to me. I relied on my ability to think and to solve problems as part of my profession and of my basic personality; the possibility of losing my mental competence and not "being me" was deeply troubling. The neuropsych exam emphasized that possibility for me. How would I know what was happening if my instrument of observation was compromised? Would I feel it slipping away, like HAL 9000, the computer in the movie *2001: A Space Odyssey*? "My mind is going. I can feel it, Dave. I can feel it. I'm...

afraid."

A Parkinson's diagnosis is devastating for the PWP, but in some ways it's actually easier on a PWP than it is on his or her family. Every day, I'm free to choose how I respond to PD, but Amy, my children, and my extended family don't have the same freedom. None of us asked for PD, but I have more control than the people who surround me. I dance to the tune PD calls, but I am free to choose how I dance. They not only have to dance with me, they also have to be patient as I lead the dance, and try not to complain when I step on their feet.

My diagnosis was difficult for my whole family, and we all responded differently. After the initial shock, I tried to become a Parkinson's expert. I wanted to know everything about the disease: symptoms, causes, treatments, prognosis, ongoing research, and alternative therapies. I read constantly, and haunted online support groups and chat rooms. It was my normal approach to a threat—using knowledge and information as a weapon. It usually wasn't effective, but it gave me something to do and let me maintain my illusion of control.

I eventually had to step away from my intense focus on learning everything about Parkinson's. It was obsessive, and I focused too much on the horror stories. I threw myself into advocacy instead. I joined a local support group that became a surrogate family for me. I found people who knew what I was going through because they were also going through it. With the support group, I discovered a sense of community and belonging that I craved, and an opportunity for leadership that was particularly satisfying. Leaning on my leadership and management experience from almost thirty years in business and the military, I became the president and board chairman of the local chapter of a national Parkinson's organization. I spoke at support groups, was interviewed on the radio, and even was the subject of a feature story in the local newspaper. Instead of being someone who happened to have the disease, I started to become the disease—it became my identity. I even began wearing a silver representation of a dopamine molecule on a chain around my neck. I can only imagine how irritating I must have been.

Amy, on the other hand, was facing the possibility for the first time in our lives together of having to be the primary breadwinner, and it panicked her. She threw herself into her career and tried to establish a twenty-year foundation over the course of twelve months. She was upset and frightened by the gradual changes she saw in me, and unconsciously began to draw away. We were unable to talk about the details of my disease, make plans for the future, or bond together as a team to meet the challenge. I missed her companionship, but I was in a tailspin myself. I felt guilty and ashamed that my illness and I were the cause of so much upheaval and turmoil in our lives, and knowing how frightened she was, I didn't push.

I needed someone to talk to, and I began to rely on a female friend more than a married man should. I didn't have any evil intent, but I placed myself in a position that could potentially have gotten out of hand, and I didn't even realize I had done it.

Amy and I have been married for almost thirty years now, and we have stood together against challenges large and small. She was there for our children when I was in the Air Force, traveling constantly and never at home even when I was in town. We had lived through periods when we weren't sure where our next meal was coming from, and periods where the activities and priorities of an affluent lifestyle threatened to overcome our better natures. Through it all, we always stood together. Briefly, Parkinson's disease stole that from us.

"For better or worse, in sickness and health, forsaking all others…" These are important words, but they're vastly more than words—they're the core of the strength that has held us together for over a quarter century. They don't just apply to romantic entanglements that can threaten a marriage, but to any relationship that takes on too much importance, regardless of the cause. Parkinson's and all the stresses and baggage it brings tried to steal our strength. Thankfully, Amy and I both recognized it and we fought back. We both received a loud, ringing wake-up call, and just in time. Although there was damage to repair, there was no large-scale destruction, and today we once again stand shoulder-to-shoulder to face the real enemy. The disease will eventually win the war, but it's going to lose this battle.

Not everyone is as blessed as I am. PD is like a wolf tirelessly circling the house, looking for a way in. It not only destroys health, vitality, and life, it also tears families apart, destroys relationships, and can steal the joy from life. The divorce rate for the general population in the US is around fifty percent for first marriages, and somewhat higher for subsequent marriages. For marriages where one spouse is newly diagnosed with PD, however, the divorce rate by some estimates is higher than eighty-five percent. Parkinson's, like other degenerative, chronic diseases, places stress on every element of a relationship, and finds weaknesses that might have gone unnoticed under more normal circumstances. It's a daily battle, and both the enemy and the battlefield change constantly, but we cannot just give up and let it win. Where do you find the strength, however, when just getting out of bed takes all the energy you have?

10

Service

In late May of 1985, I finally received a new duty assignment and orders for a permanent change of station. I was rebranded as a space operations officer and shipped off to Denver, Colorado for training.

Several months before the nearly spectacular end to my flying career, my girlfriend had become my fiancée, and we settled on June 8, 1985 as the date we would be married. As further evidence that God protects drunks, fools, and unsuccessful pilot candidates, I was ordered to report to Lowry Air Force Base in Denver on June 9, 1985, no later than 1:00 PM. We had time to be married and have a slice of cake with our guests, but just barely. We left Bergstrom Air Force Base in Austin, Texas, where we had decided to hold the wedding, at 5:00 PM on the eighth. We headed to Denver in my sports car, packed to the brim with the accessories of our new life together.

The trip was largely uneventful, except for an incident that I didn't actually see. Being manly, protective, and mindful that our wedding guests were watching, I was driving when we left Austin. At about 1:00 AM on the back roads of west Texas, I could no longer keep my eyes open and Amy volunteered to drive. We swapped places in the car, and I was asleep within seconds.

Some time later (it might have been minutes or weeks; I was like a corpse in the passenger seat), I awoke to a sudden lurch, a loud thump, and Amy's screams. I was covered in black wetness from the coffee she was drinking while she drove.

"What happened? Are we dead?" I slurred, trying to focus my eyes through a film of sleep and coffee.

"We hit something," she said.

"No... kidding," I responded, remembering at the last moment that we had only been married a matter of hours, and perhaps my new wife wouldn't appreciate my sarcastic, dry wit right at that moment. "Are you okay? Is the car okay? What do you think it was?" At least I got the order of the questions correct.

"I think it might have been an armadillo," she said.

"Felt more like a water buffalo," I cracked, unable to contain myself. I was right—she didn't appreciate my wit.

We stopped at the next town, Dalhart, Texas, and rented a room in a small motel until the sun rose. The owner was not pleased at all to be dragged from his bed at 3:00 AM by two bedraggled newlyweds, wild-eyed and smelling of coffee and fear-sweat, and I think the room he gave us was actually a storage shed. We didn't notice—we collapsed and slept in our clothes for three hours, then continued on our journey with the rising sun.

We arrived in Denver the next day without further incident, and our lives together and my Air Force career (v2.0) began in earnest. After several months in Denver, we again crossed the country to my first duty assignment in Air Force space operations. I had been assigned to be a crew commander at the East Coast PAVE PAWS ballistic missile warning radar site on Cape Cod. I learned that PAWS stands for "Phased Array Warning System." I have no idea what PAVE stands for ("Pretty Awesome and Very Expensive," perhaps).

My job was to wait patiently for World War III, to calmly report that everything was working correctly (if indeed it was) in the event that my radar actually detected the beginning of World War III, and then to be destroyed along with most everyone else in a radioactive hailstorm of submarine-launched ballistic missiles. You'd think that there wasn't much training required for a job like this, especially parts one and three. Part one came easily for me. I'm naturally patient, and I had a wide streak of fatalism that fit with my role as a professional apocalypse-watcher. Part three came easily enough also—it doesn't take great skill to be vaporized, although I did have extensive training in vaporization avoidance. If the bombs began falling, I had a secret plan: I would climb under my desk as I was taught in first grade, and wait the Russians out from there.

Part two actually did require extensive training, however. Even if it is a natural reaction, "Oh God, oh God, we're all going to die," was not an acceptable crew commander response to detection of rising sea-launched ballistic missiles. It was just as likely that detection of a massive Soviet missile attack was an exercise or a system malfunction, and shrieking like a child about it only invited ridicule at the officers' club.

So, we trained. Not only did my crew and I participate in the simulated destruction of the world many hundreds of times, we also handled hundreds of fake fires, floods, hurricanes, tornadoes, power failures, system malfunctions, terrorist attacks, heart attacks, printer paper outages, and swarms of locusts. Pharaoh should have trained with the 6th Missile Warning Squadron; then he wouldn't have been so upset by all those plagues, and he would have kept a flawless, detailed, time-stamped log while they were happening.

Occasionally, the real world intruded on our parade of training catastrophes. I was the crew commander on duty on January 28, 1986, a day when we expected the radar to detect a ballistic missile launch for a scheduled event from Cape Canaveral, Florida. It was my sad duty to repeatedly report "no detection" for the launch of the Space Shuttle Challenger, which exploded seventy-three seconds after liftoff, killing all onboard. Challenger never rose high enough to be detected by our radar.

Military operational environments are often dangerous, with hazards both known and unknown. In the Air Force, the danger inherent in flight and strategic weapon system operations and other combat-related activities is expected. Pilots, missile crews, forward air controllers, Air Force Special Operations teams, and other front line operators accept the danger every day and still do their jobs, usually without fanfare or thanks. Every other member of the military does as well, but some jobs are more dangerous than others, and the danger and duty to execute in spite of it are not always obvious. That may be why I was surprised the night my missile-warning console tried to kill me.

During the third of four midnight-to-8:00AM shifts in my crew's duty rotation, about three months before the end of my duty tour on Cape Cod, my crew was working quietly, following one of our innumerable training exercises. The two junior crew members were busy tracking high-interest satellites, and my crew chief and I were chatting about our performance on the exercise and listening to jazz music. He had an encyclopedic knowledge of jazz, and was telling me a story about how he had met a musician with the improbable name of Mongo Santamaria in New Orleans as a teenager. I was arguing that no such person existed, and if he did, his mother should be ashamed, when I heard a loud BANG, and the operations center began to fill with acrid white smoke.

The PAVE PAWS radar, although one of the most modern in the Air Force at the time, was composed mostly of 1960s-era technology, and the radar display consoles were huge, 500-pound monstrosities with circular green cathode-ray tube screens, packed with analog electronic components. Chief among these components were cylinder-shaped devices called capacitors. They ranged from thimble-sized to the size of oilcans, and were filled with oil that was rich in polychlorinated biphenyl, a toxic chemical. One of the oil can-sized capacitors in my console had exploded and caught fire, and had sprayed my left arm, torso, and legs with hot PCB-laden capacitor oil.

Under other circumstances, the crew and I would have beaten a hasty exit from the ops center. The air was laced with smoke and I was greasy and stank like a Radio Shack set ablaze. But the fire didn't appear to be getting worse, so we used the fire extinguisher on the console and then did what any operations crew does under similar conditions—we ran the checklist.

In military ops, there's a checklist for everything, so we flipped to the right one and began checking off steps. The crew chief and I conferred briefly, and I decided that satellites could go untracked for a while and sent the junior crew members out of the ops center. The fire was out, no one was immediately in danger, the fire response team was on the way, and everyone who needed to be notified had been. We had a dilemma, though—it was four in the morning on a Sunday, and we were the only two people on the entire site qualified to respond to a missile warning alert. We fully expected the Powers

That Be to declare our radar non-operational and let us leave the ops center, but they hadn't done it yet. We sat and waited. We were Cold Warriors, and the Russians were sitting in their giant subs just offshore, waiting for us to leave so they could destroy our country, the American way of life, and freedom in general. We weren't going to let that happen. I may have had an overblown perception of our role in the process.

We had both donned Scot Paks (personal breathing devices) and we looked and sounded like Darth Vader. We sat and waited for the phone to ring. After about two minutes, my crew chief sighed and said, "You know, I really wanted to be a jazz musician..."

It finally occurred to me that I didn't necessarily have to wait for a call, so picked up the phone. I was surprised to note that only six minutes had passed since the loud BANG.

"Missile Warning Center."

"This is Otis. We are OPSCAP RED for a fire in the operations center as of 1022 Zulu." I waited, expecting them to anticipate the punch line.

"Yes? You reported that status at 1024 Zulu." Tough crowd; they didn't take the bait.

"My crew chief and I are sitting in the SOC wearing Scot Paks and watching the gauges drop to zero. Request Missile Warning Center permission to abandon the SOC until the fire teams arrive and declare the site safe."

"Stand by, Otis." Stand by? After thirty seconds that seemed like three hours, he returned.

"Permission granted, Otis. Report status and estimated time to return to operation when able." Cold, man, cold. No Christmas card for YOU next year.

By that time, the squadron commander and operations officer had arrived, the fire team was working, and the physician's assistant was checking my crew and me for burns, smoke inhalation, and signs of toxic chemical exposure. We all had headaches, and I felt sick to my stomach. After the commander and operations officer asked questions about the event and our response, they sent us home.

I was off duty for about a week. During that week, I developed a minor skin rash and had occasional periods of nausea and vomiting. For some reason, the PA was concerned about my liver (perhaps he had heard about some of my off-duty recreational activities), so I had a series of liver function tests as well. I don't recall hearing anything about the tests, so I suppose they were normal. I recovered and went back to work, seemingly unaffected by the incident.

A short time later, I was reassigned from Cape Cod to Shemya Air Force Base, Alaska to command a crew at the COBRA DANE radar station. I had volunteered for the assignment almost nine months before, with the understanding that the Air Force would give me a follow-on assignment to Johnson Space Center in Houston on the military side of the Space Shuttle program. The Challenger disaster effectively ended that program, so there was no follow-on assignment to Houston. Just to demonstrate that they could keep at least half the bargain, the Air Force sent me to Alaska anyway on an unaccompanied remote tour for a year. I left behind any concerns about my toxic exposure as well as a very pregnant, very morning-sick wife who went home to live with her parents while I was away.

My year at Shemya ("It's Not The End Of The World, But You Can See It From Here," say the tee-shirts) was simple. I was either working, sleeping, or at the gym. After six months, I received a phone call: Amy was in labor with our son, and it was time to come home. I arrived in Dallas only three days later, traveling constantly by military aircraft. I expected to have missed the main event, but Amy and unborn son had considerately waited for me, and I was able to be present at the birth of our first child. Three weeks later, I was back on the Rock, this time leaving behind not a pregnant wife, but a growing family that I would not see again for another six months.

I never knew what either COBRA or DANE stood for; we passed the time making up colorful suggestions when we weren't working, sleeping, or at the gym. Shemya was a fascinating place then, with multiple tourist attractions: Fifty-Caliber Beach, where the foolish and brave could collect live World War II-vintage ammunition; Shipwreck Beach, where amongst the debris of an old Japanese freighter you could find Coke and 7-Up bottles from the 1940s; numerous fishing holes containing a frighteningly mutated variety of the Dolly Varden trout, which we were warned not only not to eat, but not to even touch, and hundreds of blue foxes from an old, abandoned Russian breeding operation, all with the same genetic defect: a shriveled and useless hind leg. It seemed not to bother them. They hopped on three legs faster than I could run on two.

I also discovered toward the end of my year-long assignment that the drinking water there had been contaminated with diesel fuel. I didn't consider the ramifications until years later.

The remainder of my Air Force career—in Ohio, Colorado, New Mexico, and many unnamed garden spots around the world—was by turns exciting, stressful, rewarding, frustrating, and uniquely satisfying. Amy and I learned to live together, overlook each other's faults, and adjust to the changes and stresses we encountered. We had a beautiful daughter to go with our handsome son, and were blessed by their ability to survive our mistakes and good intentions. I did fascinating and meaningful work with colleagues I trusted, and I had the opportunity to see and do things that I'll never be able to talk about openly, but which served to solidify the worldview I had held since childhood: the world was hostile and uncaring, and full of malicious intent that could only be challenged and defeated through preparation, analysis, and constant vigilance. During the remainder of my military career, I also continued to serve in operational, research and development, and technology testing assignments that exposed me to a wide variety of environmental hazards and toxic materials. I didn't dwell on it, though. I was doing my job. I was and still am proud to have contributed and honored to have served.

It was a hard way to live, and I didn't have much use for what I called "magical thinking." Magical thinking, by my definition, included wishing, prayer, belief, and hope. One of my father's bits of wisdom that had stuck with me through the years was, "if you wish in one hand and piss in the other, you know which hand is going to fill up first." As vehemently as I tried not to be like my father in any way, that attitude had taken root in me, and it left me a little humorless and intolerant. I was also not much fun at parties.

My ten years in the Air Force were marked by restlessness. I was searching for something that I couldn't find; I didn't even know what I was looking for. I changed jobs more often than normal, and the constant upheaval caused hardships for Amy and my children, even beyond the usual hardships of a military lifestyle. We lived like nomads, moving eight times in those ten years.

I mourned the loss of the fantasy life I imagined would rid me of the feeling of powerlessness and weakness I carried with me. Because of airsickness, sinus infections, and other factors I couldn't control, I would never be a fighter pilot, a test pilot, an astronaut, or the first man on Mars. I knew consciously that it was foolish and childish, but unconsciously I believed those achievements would wash away my shame and self-loathing. I was a military officer, a husband, and the father of two children, but I was also still the preadolescent boy that, paralyzed with fear and dread, had prayed for deliverance and had not received it. I still blamed the God I claimed not to believe in for leaving me alone in the dark as a child, and for denying me the chance to reinvent myself as a strong, fearless, and capable adult.

I wore the trappings of religion like camouflage. Since adolescence, I had had no inward sense of the presence of God or other supernatural phenomena, but I knew better than to be openly scornful. It was unbecoming of an officer and gentleman, or the father of young children and the husband of a good-hearted, loving wife with a strong, sustaining faith. So, I pretended. I taught Sunday school because it looked good on my performance reports, and I helped teach my children the tenets of faith because that's just what one did. I went to church and kept my scorn and criticism to myself (or so I thought; Amy knows me better than anyone, and she was hurt and saddened by my obvious lack of sincere faith). I felt superior; I told myself that a scientist, engineer, and self-proclaimed "rational thinker" knew better than to waste mental energy on medieval superstition, but that if I needed to go along to get along, I would. I was ethical, concerned about doing right and avoiding wrong, and I believed in truth, justice, and the American Way, but I was convinced that there was no otherworldly basis to these beliefs—they were just social convention and the result of evolution acting on social groups. I had it all figured out, and had slapped a coat of paint on my worldview—nothing could penetrate it. God, if He existed, had abandoned and ignored me; I was returning the favor.

Boy, was I dumb.

11
Can You Feel Anything When I Do This?

June 9, 2011 finally arrived—the day of my deep brain stimulation system implantation. The neurosurgeon had asked us to be at the hospital no later than 5:00 AM. Making a 5:00 AM appointment was not a problem, because I was often still awake then. The night before the implantation had been another sleepless night, but not with apprehension or anxiety, which usually was not the cause anyway. It was just another long night of Parkinson's insomnia, with a touch of added anticipation. Although the likelihood of severe complications from the procedure was very low, I had to assume the worst; so, I had said the things that needed to be said, done everything I could think of to do, and was somewhat at peace.

And then I fell asleep. Parkinson's is like that. Just when you think you have it figured out, it surprises you with something new. So, after eighteen months of incessant insomnia, I was running late for my DBS surgery because I overslept. Amy woke me, and I took a shower with a wonderful disinfectant product called Hibiclens. This was the second of my Hibiclens showers in twelve hours, and was designed to make me less of a threat to myself from infection than I usually am. The primary complication for DBS implantation surgery is post-surgical infection, and my neurosurgeon was taking great pains to avoid that. In general, he had thought through every possible screw-up, unforeseen circumstance, and snafu. I think he might have done this before.

After my leisurely five-minute napalm shower, I threw on some clothes and jumped in the car. We arrived uneventfully at the hospital right at the stroke of 5:00 AM for an abbreviated trip through the admissions office. We had been pre-admitted several days earlier; doing paperwork at three-thirty in the afternoon is much easier than at five in the morning. In rapid sequence we worked our way through surgical admission and then to a holding room for some final medical history and drug interaction discussions.

It became very clear to me that you should never just give yourself over to the system. After a nurse had relieved me of yet another vial of blood, I spoke with another nurse about drug allergies and drug interactions. Those with Parkinson's disease have to be very careful of drug interactions. Some can be fatal, such as the interaction between Demerol and Azilect. I had a very difficult time helping the nurse understand that I wasn't just allergic to Demerol, but that if they gave it to me it would probably kill me. Not that they intended to give me Demerol, of course; however, the longer I talked with her, the more certain I became that as soon as my back was turned they would stab me with a needle full of the stuff. We finally came to an understanding. She told me, "we won't give you Demerol because Azilect has Demerol in it, and you're taking Azilect."

"Not true, but good enough," I said to myself. "I'll just let this one go and take the risk." Amy calls me pedantic, but I think I'm just prudent.

We made our way into the surgical prep area about 5:45 AM, where they started my IV with promises of wondrous treats to come with names I didn't recognize. The surgical nurse told me, "just think of it as a couple of margaritas." That, I could understand. They moved me then to a sheltered corner of the surgical prep area where the first big event of the day would take place—The Shaving. I wasn't overly apprehensive about losing my hair for a short time, but it was still a landmark event for someone who had enjoyed a full head of hair for his entire life. I had no idea what they would uncover. A former college roommate and one of my best friends told Amy, "If you see the number 666 emerging from the hair, try to pretend that it says 999." A Biblical scholar and comedian in one package.

I discovered an interesting phenomenon; when someone has his or her head shaved in the hospital, everyone shows up. Amy, my daughter, the neurosurgeon's entire surgical team, the medical device representative, the nursing staff, the orderlies, and some guy named Walter who wandered in from the hall were all standing around watching as my head was shaved. I wondered who would actually do The Shaving, and was surprised to find that the neurosurgeon himself ran the clippers. Apparently it's all just part of the service.

The Shaving was uneventful, with lots of laughing and joking and comments about the emerging smoothness of my skull, and there were no numerical messages about my role in Biblical prophesy in evidence. The only comment that really stands out came from the neurosurgeon, who apparently moonlights as a standup comedian.

"I've never seen anybody with hair this thick," he said. "You've got hair like a chinchilla."

I didn't have much time to enjoy my new smoothness. Soon after The Shaving was done, Amy and my daughter were escorted to the waiting room and the serious work began. The next major step was installation of the stereotactic frame, which involved local anesthetic, large chunks of machined metal, and some of the biggest screws that I've ever had screwed into my skull. The margarita drugs had started to flow, and my reaction was something like, "OWW!! That hurt.... wha? Hmmm. Look—there's a kitty."

With the contraption now firmly anchored to my skull, they wheeled me down the corridor to the operating theater. I vaguely remember as we were rolling that the anesthesiologist kept telling me, "You don't have to hold your head up off the gurney. Just relax." Yeah, right. Relax.

After a stop for a final CAT scan that I apparently slept through, we arrived at the operating theater. I was awake for the first half of the procedure. From the local anesthetic in my scalp, to the installation of the rest of the stereotactic system, to the distinctive sound of the surgical drill boring nickel-sized holes in the top of my skull, I remember it all. The neurosurgeon told me, "Sorry, this is mashing your nose a little." I think I remember saying, "No biggie; I'm not using it for anything right now anyway."

I remember knowing that they had started to implant the electrodes in my brain, and being satisfied that they were right—it didn't hurt at all. With the benefit of modern pharmaceuticals, I was supremely unconcerned and completely comfortable.

I was also reportedly "pretty chatty" during the first part of the procedure, telling jokes and stories and providing a running commentary on my impressions of the procedure. Perhaps in part to shut me up, they put me to sleep to tunnel the electrical leads under my skin and implant the battery and pulse generator in my chest. The overall procedure was shorter than usual because, according to the neurosurgeon, the electrode placement and the data that they gathered was "just fantastic," and they didn't need to go through the usual neurological testing process to verify placement of the electrodes. That's one of my strongest memories of the whole procedure—the neurosurgeon muttering to himself, "fantastic, just outstanding, this is wonderful, superb…"

I woke up in the recovery room after what seemed like only minutes, with the recovery nurse leaning over me. She smiled and said, "Well, I see you're back." A short time later, Amy came in to visit, and we sat together briefly before they asked her to leave. I spent a long time in recovery, being repeatedly reminded to breathe. The anesthetic they had used depresses respiration, so the nurse kept telling me, "Corey, breathe deeper. Corey, you're not breathing. You need to breathe, Corey." I thought, "Can't you leave me alone? I'm trying to sleep here."

After I left recovery, I headed to the neurological progressive care unit, where I stayed for about thirty-six hours. My family and friends dropped in to wish me well or to make fun of my new look (sometimes both), or to go on walks with me around the corridors. I left the hospital on Friday, just a day and a half after major brain surgery. I could make comments about advances in modern medicine, but I think it's more likely that my insurance company preferred to have me in a lower-cost environment, like my own living room. I had no complaints; I was ready to go home.

I immediately noticed both positive and negative effects from the procedure. Electrode implantation causes some minor damage to the area around the subthalamic nucleus that can result in improvement in Parkinson's symptoms. This effect, called the lesioning effect or the honeymoon period, fades over time, but for two weeks, I could do the neurological testing "finger taps" with my left hand better than any time in the previous five years.

On the negative side, I saw some cognitive changes. There are those who say that I'm always confused; however, I felt that way for several weeks. I thought more slowly, it was difficult to start and finish simple tasks, and I fell asleep unpredictably.

DBS surgery is not a cure, and it's not disease modifying. DBS, like the available drugs, masks the symptoms of PD, but the underlying disease still progresses at the same rate. Having the surgery gave me the gift of time, though. It made time for the biomedical research community to find a cure that can help me and others like me. If there is no cure, it still gave me time to live a fuller, more productive life with the people I love, and vastly improved my quality of life. I was grateful for that time, and I resolved not to waste it.

Corey D. King

12

Transition

In 1994, after nearly ten years on active duty, six permanent change of station (PCS) assignments, a Master's degree courtesy of the US Government, years spent in windowless rooms filled with arcane machinery and documents with colorful cover sheets, and over one million frequent flyer miles on various airlines, Amy and I decided to take advantage of an early-out program offered by the Air Force.

The Department of Defense seems to oscillate between two states: "too much" and "not enough." During the mid-1990s, officers in my career field and year group fell into the "too much" category, and the Air Force was offering money if I would resign and go away. At the time, I was a captain stationed in New Mexico, and I had just been considered and not selected for promotion to major two years early. Amy was weary of the constant moving and searching, my children were old enough that the uprooted lifestyle of the Air Force brat was beginning to take a toll, and I wanted to see how the other ninety-nine percent lived. So we decided to take the offer and separate from the

Air Force.

While on active duty, I was involved in a variety of operational, scientific, and engineering activities, almost all of which I still can't discuss. I was exposed to some harsh environments, stresses, and toxins, as many of my colleagues and fellow service members also were, but when I separated, I was as healthy as I had ever been. I was offered the opportunity to be evaluated for service-related disabilities, but I couldn't identify any, with the possible exception of a minor hearing loss. I decided it wasn't worth the effort, and I took my separation paperwork and bid military service farewell almost exactly ten years after entering active duty.

I didn't go far, though. My first civilian job was with a defense contractor that served some of the same organizations I had been aware of while on active duty. It was a familiar environment, and a gentle transition. My leadership and management skills and my technical background were valuable in my new life, and I found I had the ability to project a sense of confidence that I actually didn't feel, but which opened new doors for me. I also found that civilian life, in addition to paying much better than military life, also promoted more quickly, and sometimes for superficial reasons. I rose in the management structure of my new company, and after several years, found myself in the lead of the company's regional office in south Texas, with about 200 employees and a multi-million dollar profit and loss responsibility. I made mistakes, learned from some of them, tried not to repeat them too often, and worked to fill in the huge gaps in my business sense and leadership approach. I constantly felt unqualified for my position, but I was advised by several trusted friends and colleagues to "fake it 'til you make it." Not exactly a winning corporate mission statement, but it got me through the worst times. I learned, faked, and lost sleep, and was successful after a fashion. I was not a naturally talented businessman, but I learned one of the primary secrets to executive success: surround yourself with talented people, give them what they need, and stay out of the way. I was still "looking for it," though, and wanted a new challenge.

A software prototyping project I had supported turned out to have commercial potential, and after a short period of analysis and "walking in the woods" to decide what to do, I became a senior executive in the start-up company formed to commercialize and market the new technology.

I was massively unprepared to be a senior start-up executive, but I had the confidence of youth and inexperience, and I was excited to be a part of a dynamic group of very smart people who had great ideas and wanted to use them to change the world and become rich. This was the late 1990s, at the start of the dotcom boom, and the new conventional wisdom was that you didn't have to show a profit to run a successful business with a lucrative exit strategy. I figured I could make the opportunity work—great ideas, lots of energy, but no actual "P" in the P & L.

Of course, business fundamentals still applied even to dotcoms, and lack of sales eventually whittled away at the company. It was the hardest and most humbling work I've ever done, and I was more talented at some parts of the job than others. Once again, I found I wasn't a naturally talented businessman, but I did have a talent for putting difficult concepts into simple language, and for helping people understand those concepts. I enjoyed teaching and explaining more than deal-making, and I found I was happiest at the front of a room filled with other executives, at a white board or with a set of PowerPoint charts, making the complex simple and the crooked straight.

I began to have periods of severe depression toward the end of my two years in the high-tech start-up world. I blamed unresolved issues from the past and the intense pressure I was under to play a role that didn't fit. The depression became gradually worse and began to noticeably impact my work performance. The downward spiral might have continued to its inevitable conclusion, but circumstance saved me—a large software company showed interested in acquiring the business. They didn't want our customer base (it was laughably small), or our staff (they could have just hired them—we were probably six months from closing the doors anyway). They were interested in our technology. It was truly cutting edge, and one of the reasons we were having trouble selling it was that, in a sixty-minute sales call, we would spend fifty-five minutes explaining the basic concepts and five minutes selling. Potential customers appreciated the education, but wrote no checks.

My depression eased somewhat, but never went away. After the deal was done and all the investors and creditors were paid, there was very little money left for the team (with my cut, I think I bought carpet for the house and a six-pack of good beer), but I had learned a new phrase: founder's stock options. I became an employee of the new company and worked there for the next six years as the value of my options grew, the stock split four times, and a theoretical windfall became real.

I continued to have periods of depression and other odd, seemingly unrelated nuisances and irritations. I noticed that I sometimes would type only with my right hand because my left was aching and stiff. During my many business dinners, I ordered wine less and less often. I didn't enjoy it anymore because I couldn't taste or smell it. On long plane flights, I was restless and uncomfortable and often had to get up and take laps around the plane. And when I was very tired or stressed, my left thumb would twitch. I was working eighty-hour weeks and traveling constantly, so I attributed it to job stress and kept reaching for the gold ring.

I was running out of energy and ideas, though. I became less effective, had more trouble handling company politics and the inevitable infighting and jockeying for position, and I was constantly exhausted. Finally, in the midst of a major merger with another company, I quietly melted down.

Amy could see it coming, although she had no better idea than I did the reason it was really happening. Several months before, she had persuaded me to put our large, expensive executive home on the market. So during the same week that my son, our firstborn, left home to enter college, we also signed a contract to sell our home and I resigned from the company. All we needed was a divorce, a death in the family, and a jail term to round out the list of the topmost stressful events a family can experience, and in typical overachieving style, we did them all simultaneously.

With the temporary reduction in stress that my deconstruction of our entire life brought, I felt free and optimistic again. We moved into an apartment to keep our options open, and I began planning a new type of life for us, free from stress, doing the things that made me happy and fulfilled. My depression and most of my strange afflictions evaporated or lessened, and I told myself, "See? Job stress. Everything will be fine now."

Boy, was I wrong.

13
Riding The Lightning

After my DBS surgery in June of 2011, my incisions healed, my hair grew in true chinchilla style, and I became accustomed to the new lumps, bumps, and ridges on my head and chest. The lesioning effect finally disappeared, but it gave me a preview of how the stimulator might help me and I was eager to turn it on. I had already reduced some drugs and eliminated others, and the device wasn't even working yet. I was sleeping better and the hallucinations had almost disappeared, but in the normal give-and-take of Parkinson's treatment, I was having more tremors and dyskinesia (involuntary wiggling and writhing movements). I didn't miss the squirrels, cats, and phantom people moving around just out of direct sight, though. Life was good, but I was eager for turn-on day.

Exercise is a potent weapon in the battle against PD, and after the surgery I saw again how important it was. When the lesioning effect was at its peak, I decided to stop using the cane I had grown to rely on, and I began to walk for what seemed like several hundred miles every day in an unusual location—the hospital where my DBS surgery was performed. I tried walking in my neighborhood; potentially heatstroke-inducing behavior in south Texas if the walk starts after the sun rises. I tried walking in the mall, too. No. Just no. If I have to explain why, you've never been in a mall.

The hospital was huge, had more corridors than I could walk in a month, and had even more stairs. As an added benefit, no one gave a second glance to the bald guy with the staples in his head walking up and down the stairs and halls with a beautiful and intense woman behind him screaming, "swing your arm, lift your knees, doggone it!" I loved it. I swear.

I had plenty of time while walking to think and talk with Amy about solutions to all the world's problems, and one of our topics of conversation was my cane. I was eager to give it up but I found that it was harder than I expected, and I spent some time examining why. There were the obvious reasons—stability during balance disruptions, help getting in and out of my car (difficult for anyone—I hadn't given up my sports car yet), and added confidence getting up and down stairs. All were completely reasonable physical needs, but not the only reasons the cane was hard to give up, as it turned out.

The physical symptoms of PD can change and worsen over the course of just a few hours, and can ease and improve just as quickly. Some days are better than others, and when I'm doing well, I appreciate comments about how good I look. I know that ninety-nine percent of those comments are honest, sincere, and rooted in kindness and truth. However, I have an unreasonable discomfort with the remaining one percent when I think I can sense an undertone of something else; perhaps an unstated question about how serious this whole thing is anyway, or a level of skepticism about why I'm making such a big deal out of this disease, or a bit of irritation about why I have handicapped license plates on my sports car.

I remember a day when everything seemed to be on a peak The drugs were working, I had slept well, and I was moving with relative ease. I stopped at a local sporting goods and outdoor outfitters store. Out of habit, I had parked in a handicapped parking spot, knowing that the trip back out could be different than the trip in, and that I could go off at any minute. I left my cane in the car.

When I came out of the store an hour later, I found a penciled note on my windshield.

"You shouldn't park in a handicapped parking spot when you don't need it, asshole," it said. "Just because you have the tags and it's legal doesn't mean it's right."

I felt a sick sense of indignation. I wanted to find the person who left the note and explain that I wasn't that guy, that I sometimes looked okay but that I really wasn't. I also felt ashamed, as I remembered that there were other people who used handicapped parking spaces who needed them all the time, and were in much worse shape that I was. I resolved then to be more careful about when I used the privilege, but to use it without regret when I needed to.

I discovered, to my surprise, that I carried and used my cane as a kind of explanation, and even an excuse. Why does he limp? Oh, he has a cane; there must be a reason. Why does he fumble with his wallet in the checkout line, drop his change, and take so long? Oh, he has a cane; he's probably sick or injured, and not drunk or clumsy. Why is that young guy parked in the handicapped space? He looks fine; oh, wait, he has a cane. Never mind.

For me, the cane had been not only a physical aid to movement, but also a method for answering questions before they were asked, and a way of opening up conversations about PD on my terms. It was a defense mechanism in the most classic sense, and it showed to me that I wasn't as far along on Dr. Kubler-Ross's five-stage process as I had thought.

I resolved to try to let go of the cane and to trust that the DBS system would do what it was intended to do: reduce the severity of some of my motor symptoms. I also resolved to let go of the one percent and be grateful when I heard, "You really are looking great. I'm glad you're improving."

Turn-on day for my DBS system finally arrived, and was a combination of "rather remarkable" and "no big deal." The neurologist had carefully set my expectations, and I wasn't expecting immediate major changes. As with other elements of my treatment, the neurologist was slow and careful in turning on the stimulator, "titrating up" in electricity just like for new drugs. I was a little disappointed that there was no "oh-my-gosh-I-can-run-jump-and-play-look-at-my-hands-move" moment, but I was happy the thing was working.

The actual programming session didn't take long at all, although I had to stay at the neurologist's office for about two hours after it was done, presumably to see if I would suddenly start picking up radio stations or opening garage doors with my head. The neurologist began by explaining that he would first test the electrical integrity of the leads, and then he would adjust the system to determine how I responded. He was clear that I would leave this first session with the device set at a low level and probably without noticeable effects, and that I would come back in two weeks to have the system tweaked again.

With my expectations properly set (and steam rising from the campfire), he began. I couldn't see the screen of his handheld programming device, so I didn't know what was going to HOLY CRAP, WHAT WAS THAT? I felt a buzzing twitch run down my right arm, and the fingers of my right hand momentarily went into business for themselves. It shut off as abruptly as it started, and I said, "That was strange."

"Yes. That means that the electrode on the left side of your brain is working." For reasons that escape me, the left side of the brain controls motor activity on the right side of the body and vice versa. I started to comment on that fact when my left hand and arm began to twitch and tingle, and my hand became more rigid and immobile than usual. It also was returned to my conscious control quickly, and I had a fleeting thought about the Control Voice at the beginning of the old "Outer Limits" TV show from the early 60s. "There is nothing wrong with your brain. Do not attempt to control your own body. We will control the horizontal, we will control the vertical. We can make you twitch and shake, and if you upset us we will make you sorry."

Things were quiet for a few moments, as the neurologist and the medical device expert discussed next steps in low tones. I was anxiously waiting for the next lightning bolt in some part of my body, but I only felt a few minor tickles and buzzes here and there. I began to relax (always a mistake), and as I tried to settle into the chair and get comfortable, I found that I couldn't. There was no pain or real discomfort, but I couldn't sit still.

"Well, THIS is weird," I said.

Amy, recording the session, said, "What's happening?"

"I can't sit still," I said.

"Are you just trying to get comfortable?"

"No," I replied. "I think I'm trying to dig a hole in the chair."

The neurologist had set the stimulator voltage level, and it caused an immediate and uncontrollable bout of dyskinesia; not painful, just strange. When he reduced the voltage, the dyskinesia evaporated like rain on a Texas street.

Hope is a funny thing. Sometimes you have it without knowing it, and just a little extra information changes the picture. I remembered the neurosurgeon's comments about how the "signals were great." That indicated two things: the stimulator was working, and there was no question that I had Parkinson's disease.

You'd think that would be no surprise to me, but I found that I had been holding out some hope that I fell into the fifteen- to twenty-five percent of Parkinson's patients who are misdiagnosed. Diagnosis by neurological exam, medical history, and ruling things out still leaves room for uncertainty, and in a small number of cases, a person treated for Parkinson's for years never actually had the disease. I was still hoping that I would one day wake up without symptoms and find that this had all just been a colossal misunderstanding, even after experiencing classic PD symptoms for years, being diagnosed by five of the best medical professionals in the US, and showing improvement in symptoms after taking levodopa.

I still had hope: for an eventual cure, for a good, productive, happy, and long remainder to my life with people I love, for a manageable progression to this disease, and for long-term effectiveness of DBS. However, I finally had to put away the unreasonable hope that I didn't really have Parkinson's disease.

Corey D. King

14

Recreation

In the summer of 2006, after I resigned from the company that had made us financially secure, sold our dream house, sent our first born off to college, and tossed the rest of my family into upheaval and uncertainty, I looked around for something else to do. I settled on scuba diving.

My true intent was to take some time off from the stresses and aggravations of the high-tech business world, find out what I really wanted to do, and do a complete reset and reboot of my professional life. Amy and I, after discussing the goals, approach, and available resources, decided I had about a year to decompress and figure it all out. We also discussed the pros and cons of renting either an apartment or a house for that year. We wanted flexibility in case The Plan (version 3.0 now) took us to another city, so we didn't want to buy another house.

We decided to rent an apartment so that our fifteen-year old daughter, who had been ripped up by her roots from her comfortable home, could have the novel experience of apartment living. There are other novel experiences, in retrospect, that would have been better choices: a root canal for her birthday, a sleep-away torture camp, or a new burlap and barbed-wire wardrobe, for instance. We all survived, but we still call our year in the apartment and the year that followed, "The Lost Years."

I was hard at work, though. I tried on multiple hats and looked at investment opportunities, alternate careers, and new ways of living. For the first time in my life, I carried a tool kit to work, installing computer and video equipment as an independent consultant with an old friend and former colleague. I hung out a shingle of my own, and did IT security consulting. I considered becoming a real estate agent, a general contractor for home renovations, a franchise restaurant owner, and a safety and training diver in the NASA underwater weightlessness training facility in Houston. The only thing I didn't consider was being an astronaut. That had already been checked off the list.

Between consulting engagements and investment opportunity webinars, I dived. I was a scuba divemaster and assistant instructor for several of the national scuba certification agencies, so I taught classes at a local dive shop, worked with students who were having difficulty with specific skills, filled and carried scuba tanks, handed out equipment, and lived the life of a dive bum. To give all this activity a veneer of respectability, I developed a business plan for opening a dive shop in an exotic location. Dive shop conventional wisdom says that to make a million dollars in the dive business, you should start with two million dollars. Not so, according to my business plan. It clearly demonstrated how to turn $3.26 million into $1.0 million in just three years. With this bit of due diligence out of the way, I focused in earnest on diving.

I dived almost every day, even if it was just to teach a buoyancy class in the pool or show a problem student how to do a water rescue. My wetsuit never dried out, my skin smelled like chlorine, and my hair was as blonde and brittle as my son's when he was a high school swimmer. I was invited to be the divemaster on a dive trip to Saba, a small island in the Netherlands Antilles, and it was wonderful. I just couldn't figure out how to make being a dive bum support a family of four.

I also began to see some of the old, familiar physical issues return.

I had trouble turning the valves on scuba tanks with my left hand when I was filling them, and my left arm and shoulder ached and throbbed constantly. When I was standing in the shallow end of the pool, demonstrating a skill to a group of students or showing them how a piece of equipment worked, I often shivered and shook, even if the water was warm. One of the most obvious issues was apparent on a day I was teaching a group of advanced students underwater navigation skills. As part of the class, each student had to measure the time it took to swim 100 feet underwater in a straight line. As I demonstrated, I was dismayed and embarrassed to discover that I couldn't do it. No matter how carefully I kicked, I curved to the left and ended up twenty-five feet or more from the target at the end of the 100-foot course. The students all got a laugh out of it, but it concerned me. It was obvious that my left leg was much slower and stiffer than my right, and that was something new. I attributed the problems to strain and overuse, and even wondered if with all the diving I had been doing the cause might have been decompression sickness, or "the bends." It didn't get noticeably worse, so I lived with it.

I was no closer to finding the new life I had been seeking and time was passing. I felt like I had jumped from an airplane wearing a parachute harness that either contained a parachute or my dirty laundry, and the only way to find out which was to pull the ripcord, which I had agreed to do within a year. Amy was growing concerned.

"You know, you're probably not going to be able to make a living at diving. Maybe you should start looking for a job."

"I have been looking for a job. I check Monster.com every morning, and I sent a resume out just today," I snapped.

She gave me a familiar look. "I know you wanted something else, but it's been nine months, and now you're just playing. And I also know that you don't really believe you can find the right job by sending out resumes and checking websites."

I fumed, but eventually admitted that she was right. I began looking for a position in my former career field, and hoped that the year-long break would give me a fresh sense of perspective.

I called old colleagues and friends, looking for a way back into the world that I had so unceremoniously abandoned. I found that, regardless of assurances to the contrary, reentry was much more difficult than departure. The economy was starting to falter, positions were filled, people had moved on or retired, and a few held grudges and concerns about my reliability because of my hasty departure from corporate America less than a year before. I found a few entry-level positions, a couple of openings for one hundred percent commission sales jobs, and a few interesting opportunities in San Francisco, Cupertino, or San Jose, the home of the $2 million, 1000-square foot bungalow. I didn't find anything that would work for all of us, though.

Although I was concerned about the return of the pain and stiffness in my arms and legs, I still dived regularly, and volunteered to be the rescue diver for the swimming portion of a local triathlon. It was a simple job—in my wetsuit and with full scuba gear at the ready, I sat in a small fishing boat in the midst of about 100 swimmers and watched and waited. The boat driver was in radio contact with other watchers positioned around the lake, and if any of the racers began to have problems or disappeared below the surface, I would strap in, roll off the boat and be a hero (in theory, anyway).

Fortunately, no one tried to drown, so the boat driver and I struck up a conversation while we scanned the water. He asked me what I did for a living when I wasn't sitting in a boat. I gave him a capsule synopsis, without some of the more colorful elements: Longhorn with a BS in aerospace engineering and an MS in space operations, former Air Force officer, experience with radar, satellite operations and communication, software development and sales, computer security, consulting services, laboratory management experience, business experience in public, private, and start-up companies, currently a dive bum but ready to get back to work. I asked him what he did when he wasn't driving a boat.

"Well, I run a research and development laboratory organization here in town. We do contract-based applied research on communications and electronic systems, and we have a big business in spacecraft subsystem software design. We're trying to build an information security business with commercial and government clients, but we don't have anyone who has the business experience and the interest. I also need some proposal development help, and some general management expertise."

We both sat quietly for a moment, continuing to scan the water. He spoke first.

"Umm, do you think you might like to come in for an interview?"

"I think that would be great," I said. "Since almost every experience I've had in my life up to this point has prepared me for this conversation, it would be ungrateful not to."

I talked with him and his team several times over the next two months, and they agreed to let me work with them. I wasn't a perfect fit; these people were as good or better than every scary-smart scientist or engineer I had ever met, and I had let my hardcore engineering skills atrophy in favor of developing business skills. They recognized they weren't hiring me for my 1980s and 1990s-vintage engineering expertise, but for a combination of engineering outlook and business experience. They were kind enough never to use the phrase, "a mile wide and an inch deep" in my presence.

I started work there, and as expected, the learning curve was steep. As the leader and manager of people smarter and more technically current than myself, I was expected to keep up, and to also find paying work of my own I could do (no one likes a freeloader). I had learned a few tricks along the way, though.

In meetings during the first few months, I struggled to come up to speed quickly. I took copious notes, and when anyone asked my opinion or wanted direction, I cultivated the thoughtful look and the chin-stroke, and said, "Well, what are your recommendations? Surely you must know what you'd like to see happen here?" I usually escaped unscathed, and I could then spend all evening on the Internet answering the same question over and over again in different technical areas: "What in the world does THIS mean?"

I loved the work, I respected and admired the people I worked with, and I found that the man I had met unexpectedly in a boat on a lake was the best boss I had ever had—he was not only a gifted engineer, but he was a good businessman and a genuinely good person, and he became a friend as well as a colleague. My job stresses were normal and manageable, especially after having had experience in the Roman arena of commercial high-tech, and I felt that, at long last, I had finally found home. I intended to finish my professional career there. As it turned out, I did.

One by one, the physical symptoms and collection of strange difficulties that had plagued me for almost two decades returned. This time, I couldn't ignore them or blame job stress. I had no choice but to find out why this was happening.

Corey D. King

15

I'll Have Twenty-Two Helicopters and A Fudgsicle

My neurologist activated my DBS system in July of 2011. I had a programming session about every two weeks for several months, and the benefits of DBS soon became clear. I had more consistent symptom control, and my medication side effects were much more manageable. I also had an electronic device embedded in my body, which I thought was pretty cool.

Although my neurologist instructed me in strong terms not to play with the device, I felt it was only prudent to understand how it worked, and to know how to turn it on and off if I needed to. Perhaps I should have I should have read the FULL manual before I began claiming that my stimulator battery was malfunctioning, and begin hauling medical device representatives, neurosurgeons and neurologists, and people off the street into a room to discuss what was wrong with the darned thing. When, oh when will I ever learn to listen to my wife?

Amy said, "It's probably just the batteries in the patient programmer, don't you think?"

I didn't think—that was my first problem. My second problem was that I didn't listen to Amy.

"Naaaah, can't be. I remember clearly that someone at some point said something about a percentage level, related to something that I don't remember but that I'm convinced has to do with the stimulator battery. That makes sense, doesn't it?"

It didn't. The neurologist placed me under strict orders to think about topics other than my stimulator, and to give the "Electro Boy" fascination a rest. How unfair, I thought. What's the fun of having a new electronic device that's actually inside my brain if I couldn't have a little fun with it now and then? In retrospect, perhaps I had the wrong attitude about the whole situation. My credibility suffered, and I pouted that I was being unfairly blamed for a natural response, especially for someone who had a passion for electronics. I consoled myself by playing with my fleet of helicopters.

Which brings me to a slightly more serious subject, although at the time it didn't seem all that serious. Over a period of about eighteen months, I developed an interest in model helicopters. They were fascinating—they're complex little devices, you can break them and put them back together endlessly, and with practice you can fly them around the room and chase the cat with them. For someone with both aeronautical and electronic interests, they are an almost perfect diversion.

You'd think that one or two would be enough to satisfy nearly anyone. Not so, particularly someone with compulsive behavior side effects from Parkinson's medications. It was slow and insidious, like many things associated with Parkinson's disease, but over a year and a half I developed quite a fleet of model helicopters. At one point I had twenty-two of them. In the clear light of retrospection, even I can see how bizarre that was. It's not unusual behavior for someone with PD taking a dopamine agonist drugs, however. As matter of fact it's benign given the possible spectrum of behaviors.

Compulsive behavior caused by dopamine agonists can include compulsive gambling, hypersexual behavior, compulsive shopping (for helicopters, for instance, or home electronics, or home automation equipment, or Fudgsicles, just to name a few random possibilities), or an obsessive focus on almost any activity or object. The behavior is a medication side effect, but the consequences are real and can cause upheaval, relationship damage, and financial ruin for the unwary. Like the physical symptoms that I was able to explain away, I was able to justify my focus on model helicopters as a healthy way to replace other interests that I had lost: scuba diving, sports, running, skiing, and most other physical activities. After all, everyone needs a hobby, right?

My compulsive behavior was relatively easy to control, and the impacts were minor (although I did have a few pounds to lose from all those Fudgsicles). The realization that I was behaving compulsively, however, opened up a new set of possibilities to consider. They were hard to contemplate, but they are a part of Parkinson's disease and can't be ignored.

In addition to the motor and autonomic nervous system symptoms associated with PD, there is a spectrum of potential cognitive impacts. They range from minor short-term memory disruption to severe dementia almost as profound as Alzheimer's disease. According to the medical literature, nearly every Parkinson's patient experiences some cognitive issues, even if they are mild and not significantly more noticeable than the usual effects of aging.

My family and friends had noticed initial indications of something called "executive dysfunction" in me. Although it sounds like a bad quote from a Dilbert cartoon, it's related to the ability to multitask, to think abstractly, to remember and apply facts, and to interpret motivations and read situations effectively.

I had trouble remembering new facts, and regularly missed appointments even though I kept a calendar on my phone. My job required me to juggle the details of dozens of complex technical projects; if I had enough time I could retrieve the information I needed from my failing brain, but there was never enough time. I became more and more ineffective at business development and customer relationships; my occasional stammering, difficulty remembering details, and slowness in switching subjects left me a half-step behind, and I avoided activities that were critical to my job performance.

My DBS system made my motor symptoms more manageable, and exercise and physical therapy improved my movement problems. My autonomic nervous system irregularities could be improved by a combination of lifestyle changes, medications, and simple tolerance. However, the combination of physical and newly emerging cognitive problems caused significant disability.

So finally, in August 2011, after twenty-seven years of a satisfying and varied professional life as a military officer, an executive in public, private and start-up companies, and a leader and manager in the nonprofit research and development world, Amy and I decided that it was time for me to retire. I began disability leave from work, and given the nature of this disease, I don't anticipate returning to my professional career. It was the hardest decision of many hard decisions we've made since I was diagnosed, but it was the right one.

I made the choice in the initial stages of the disease to be aggressive in addressing the symptoms. Some doctors and PWPs will counsel "saving some for later." For instance, young-onset patients like me often are counseled to avoid a drug called carbidopa-levodopa for as long as possible, because long-term exposure usually has the side effect of significant disability from dyskinesia. However, without it, I was always "off" (the term a PWP uses to describe a period when the symptoms are at their peak, and when they're not getting much or any relief from the treatments). I decided to take the risk of debilitation from dyskinesia later for the reward of better function and enhanced quality of life now, and I began taking carbidopa-levodopa almost immediately. The same rationale applied to my decision to have DBS surgery, and to an extent, to my decision to retire from professional life. I decided to do everything I could to maximize quality of life now, and to leave the future to medical research and good fortune.

When I retired, the changes in me were sometimes less apparent during the day. In particular, some of the changes Amy saw only she was able to recognize, because no one knows me as well as she does. She was there when I got out of bed in the morning, and saw what I was like before my morning handful of pills. She saw me stumble and trip at night when I had had an exhausting day, and meds and DBS together couldn't mask my symptoms. She saw me struggle to find words, hesitate, and lose track of a conversation. And she saw the radical increase in all my symptoms from simple, everyday work stress. She knew better than anyone that it was time to let go, and she helped me to see it, too.

Everyone approaching middle age begins to have physical and

cognitive problems, some worse than others. Taken in isolation, each of the challenges I was managing was inconsequential. But, when coupled with other inconsequential problems that were fundamentally out of character for me, a pattern began to develop. I could tell there was something changing. It was slow and hard to notice—one day was not significantly different than the next. But one week was slightly different from the next, one month was noticeably different the next, and last year was significantly different from this year. I could deny it or I could acknowledge it, fight it, and live with it where I couldn't fight it. I'd had enough denial.

Corey D. King

16

Do Not Go Gentle…

In the first several months after I retired, I had trouble wrapping my head around the concept that the change was real and permanent, barring an act of God or a miraculous cure. Although I could find plenty to occupy my time, I felt like I was playing hooky from school, and I couldn't shake the feeling that my e-mail box at work needed attention. There must be some sort of natural law related to conservation of e-mail, however, because my personal email stepped into the gap.

I discovered that while I had been focusing on work in the last few years, I had seriously neglected my handy-man responsibilities around the house. I was surprised and dismayed to find out that my sprinkler system didn't work very well and that Amy had known it for years. So, without considering the limitations imposed by chronic illness and recent surgery, I pitched into the project of repairing the sprinkler system. I didn't think too deeply about the fact that there was a terrible drought in progress in south Texas, with lawn watering restricted to no more than once per week. Regardless of how well the sprinkler system worked, the yard was going to be dead anyway, but that seemed beside the point.

That summer was among the hottest in Texas history, also—a perfect time to spend hours in the sun doing manual labor that I had been completely unaccustomed to doing in recent years. The good thing about working on a sprinkler system is that you can pretend to be examining the function of the sprinkler heads and adjusting the spray pattern with a little screwdriver, when you're actually letting the sprinkler spray you in the face and praying for a cloud to come by so that you don't die from heat stroke.

Although I tried not to dwell on it, I was still finding new ways that Parkinson's disease intruded on activities I used to take for granted. Most people probably know that a sprinkler system is underground. I didn't realize that "underground" is a significant journey for someone with PD. It takes quite a while to get there, and it takes even longer to get back after you've spent some time there. Digging up sprinkler heads and valves is challenge for anyone when the Texas sun is roughly thirty feet away and the temperature in the shade is like a summer day on Venus; PD only adds additional fun.

It's also advisable to sit on the ground while working; bending over becomes painful, and you end up with a sunburn that's hard to explain. For someone with Parkinson's, blood pressure variations from changing posture (postural hypotension) can turn the act of standing up into a quick trip back to the ground and a brief nap. A little prior planning was in order.

I hadn't done much of this kind of work in the recent past, and I had to make a few accommodations. Gravity is helpful on the way down, as long as you don't make the trip so quickly that the impact causes discomfort. However, climbing out of the gravity well again was an entirely different experience than I remembered from just a few years ago. I understood how a box turtle must feel, lying on his back, waving his claws in the air and slowly roasting on a Texas highway.

There's a way to solve any problem, though, even mobility problems caused by Parkinson's disease. I started carrying a small chair with me so the up-and-down journey was not quite as disconcerting. To combat the heat, I soaked my Harley-Davidson do-rag with water from the hose, draped it over my nearly bald head, and covered it with a baseball cap to protect my freshly healed DBS scars. I thought I was clever, and maybe even a little bit cool because I was wearing Harley logoware, until I saw my neighbor laughing and shaking his head. Maybe it's just that I was wearing the wrong color do-rag. I had no idea the neighborhood was Crip instead of Blood.

Everything takes longer with PD, so I had plenty of time to think as I spent thirty minutes screwing six screws into a sprinkler system valve cover, and that was with an electric screwdriver. Why was it important to me to do these things? Since having DBS surgery, I had risked heatstroke, rattlesnakes, Gila monsters, and fatal sunburn while working on the sprinklers, as well as Amy's displeasure for falling through the bedroom ceiling while working in the attic pulling Ethernet cable. Why?

The fact of my recent retirement provided a partial answer. Under different circumstances, I might have had another fifteen to twenty years of useful work left to me, doing important and valuable work that would have continued to give me a sense of fulfillment, mission, and purpose. I grieved for that lost potential, and I took on projects as a way to continue to have a sense of value and purpose, even if my capacity was not what it used to be. I enjoyed my ability to make things work, to fix broken machinery, and to solve problems. Occasionally those problems were of my own making, but if you're going to dig yourself into a hole, it's helpful to be able to dig out again. Although it took ten times longer than in my pre-PD days, fixing the sprinkler system reminded me that I still had the capacity to solve problems and to accomplish difficult tasks, even if the definition of "difficult" had changed.

Another equally important answer to the question, "why do I do these things?" was that it was a way to fight back. Life with PD is a daily battle: against exhaustion, drug side effects, nausea, stiffness, slowness, tremor, pain, and all of the other baggage this unwelcome visitor brings. I tend to think in military metaphors, and I once described Parkinson's disease as a long battle against overwhelming odds from a succession of fallback positions. There are many ways to feel like a loser in this situation, but there are just as many ways to feel like a winner. One of those ways is by simply not giving in. I was not successful every day, but every day brought another opportunity. I fixed the sprinkler system, pulled Ethernet cable, expanded the home automation system, and even flew those helicopters as a way to say to Parkinson's, "Today, I win. Tomorrow may be different, but just for today, the battle goes to me." That was worth aching muscles, minor sunburn, blisters, losing ten screws for every one I got into the right place, and even the occasional need to patch a hole in the ceiling. PD may be an overwhelming, unstoppable adversary, but I resolved to make sure it knew it was in a fight.

17

Rationalization

I remember the smell—cigarette smoke, Old Spice aftershave, sweat, and a peculiar sour odor I would later recognize as fear. I was six years old, and when I sat in my father's police cruiser, I always got dizzy and sick to my stomach because of the smell.

My father was already a captain in the police department when I was born. I knew very little about his role as police officer as I was growing up; he left in the morning before I got out of bed, and I didn't see him again until shortly before bedtime, when he would come home smelling like his police cruiser, place his service weapon in the cabinet above the refrigerator, and sit down to dinner.

I lived in awe and fear of my father. Our family used to say that my dad could "shout with his eyes." He rarely had to raise his voice to get our attention. When he was happy, he was magnanimous and jovial, witty and funny, everyone's friend. But when he was not, you could tell by the storm clouds in his eyes.

As a police officer, my father used fear and intimidation as behavior management tools. He told stories at the dinner table about keeping criminals and prisoners in line by intimidating them with the threat of violence without actually needing to use violence. He prided himself on never having had to draw his service weapon, except the one time that he drew his 1911 pistol to repeatedly apply it to an unruly prisoner's head in the elevator on the way to the booking room. The pistol broke, he said, and I presume the prisoner's skull did as well. That was unusual for Dad, though. He could apply the concept of deterrence just as effectively as the US government did to control Soviet aggression during the Cold War.

My father was not typically physically violent, but he understood the application of force and the use of mental and emotional intimidation to control other people. He was proud of his ability to use the power of his personality to get what he needed and wanted from others, including his wife and children. My dad scared me, but like any six-year-old boy, I longed to be like him. After all, he obviously wasn't afraid of anything; he made other people afraid, and that gave him a power that I craved. When I was older, I overheard him tell my brother, "Make sure they never know just how far you're willing to go. Keep them wondering how bad you might hurt them, and they'll comply." I believed him completely; I had seen it.

A mythology grew around my father as I grew older. He was larger than life. His wife and children willingly assumed the burden of recounting the family history, and he was usually the central figure in that history. The victors write history, and my father always made sure he was the victor.

"Remember the time that Dad ran out of gas, and all the rest of us were too afraid to say anything? Corey was too young to know better, and he kept asking, 'Dad, why are we stopping? Why are we stopping, Dad? Are we there? This doesn't look like the campground. Are we camping here?' We had to pin him down in the back seat and hold our hands over his mouth to keep him from making Dad mad. Wasn't that funny?"

"Remember when Kathy snapped Dad on the butt with the dish towel, and he told her not to do it again or she would be sorry? She did it again, and he took the dishtowel away from her and began whipping her with it. She ran out the front door, and he chased her down the block for nearly half a mile whipping her while she screamed. Wasn't that funny?"

"Remember when Mom told us about the time when they were newlyweds and Dad said she should never hit him, because she wouldn't like what would happen in return? Mom didn't think he was serious, and so she playfully slapped him once, and he slapped her back nearly hard enough to knock her out. Dad sure is a man of his word, isn't he?"

"Remember when Dad told Ken that he was the laziest tennis player he had ever seen, and if he wasn't going to try harder to live up to his potential, Dad wouldn't waste his time coming to see him play? Dad was tough, but he just wanted us to do our best."

We told these stories proudly, adding our family interpretation of each event just as we had been taught. Only when we began to tell these stories together after my parents died in late 2000, or when I told them to people outside the family, did a different interpretation begin to emerge.

Some of the proudest stories in our family mythology concern my father's role in a national crisis during the early 1960s. Although he was not actually present at the Kennedy assassination, he played an integral role in press relations in the following days, and he testified before the Warren Commission concerning his and the police department's activities during the subsequent investigation. Although I was too young to remember the actual event, I do remember the stories.

"When Kennedy was assassinated in Dallas, Dad was the police chief's right-hand man with the press. He worked for three days straight, doing almost all the press conferences because the chief disliked talking to the press. He didn't come home for almost a week. He really worked hard for the things he believed in."

"After Oswald killed Officer Tippit, Dad helped manage the fund of donations for his family. When the fund became bigger than anyone expected, and the Chief wanted to put some of the money in the Police Widows and Orphans Fund, Dad argued with him and finally told him, 'That money belongs to Mrs. Tippit. If you do this, my first stop will be at the personnel office where I will resign. My second stop will be the Dallas Morning News editorial office, where I will tell them everything.' Dad was really able to put it all on the line for the things he believed, wasn't he?"

I had the rare opportunity of seeing a YouTube video of one of my father's press conferences during the crisis, and I was amazed at what

I saw. He was calm, competent, and in charge, and it made me unwillingly proud to see him. He was at the focus of the derision and criticism of the entire world for a time, and he was masterful.

Certainly, press relations between police departments and the press have changed in the last fifty years, and are now much more open. But, I also recognized what I saw in my father's eyes. I saw the storm clouds there, and I knew how angry he was.

He was angry that the reporters would dare to second-guess the department's actions during the crisis, and was personally offended by their insinuations that the department was incompetent. He was angry at having to justify the actions of men who he considered to be heroes, and I remember more than once in later years that he said, "The whole world thought that we were Keystone cops. They just didn't get it." And, I also think he was angry that the power of his personality and his ability to intimidate and coerce were not effective. He couldn't control perceptions as much as he wanted, and it enraged him.

He could control his own emotions, though. He was calm, cool, and professional, and didn't overtly display the rage I had learned to recognize in his eyes. Fifty years after the event and ten years after his death, I felt a chill as I watched that video. I thought, "Don't they know how mad they're making him? Don't they know what could happen?" And I realized, no, they didn't. You had to be family to know.

The Kennedy assassination became a subject that we never discussed at home. Dad would not answer questions about it from us, and he scoffed at conspiracy theories and accusations of involvement of the department, the FBI, and the Secret Service in the assassination. He had about as much use for alternative theories of the assassination as he did for the Beatles or for long hair.

Although I believe that doing the right thing was important to my father, it was clear that appearing to do the right thing was at least as important. "Avoiding even the appearance of impropriety" was a phrase that I heard repeatedly as I grew up with my father. His message clearly was that, regardless of what might actually have happened, appearing to be without reproach was ultimately the most important thing in any situation.

My father was a mix of good and bad, and I suspect he knew it. He was respected and loved by many of his colleagues, who spoke glowingly of the positive influence he had had on their lives, and how much of a role model he had been. I couldn't count the number of people who came to me at his memorial service to tell me stories about how honorable, noble, and selfless he was. I smiled and nodded, thinking, "You just didn't know him." It didn't occur to me until later that perhaps they knew things about him that I didn't know or couldn't see.

Dad craved that kind of adulation, but he also had his own demons. I had seen him struggle with anxiety and panic attacks since I was old enough to observe and understand. There was always an alternate explanation: throat spasms that caused him to choke and wheeze, stomach problems, job stress, heart disease. Any explanation was better than the truth, because the truth wasn't a part of the carefully crafted public persona he had built. I think the truth was that he was haunted by many of the things he had done, and he couldn't admit it even to himself.

"Mother is the name for God in the lips and eyes of little children," according to the novelist William Thackeray. If that's true, I think it's equally true that Father is the voice and face of God. For most children, the first view they have of God is their own father. I was afraid of mine, and later revolted by him, and then ashamed and deeply disappointed in him. In the end, the fiction he created and maintained at all costs was more important to him than I was, and I rejected everything he taught and claimed, regardless of its truth or value. And in that mix, I rejected the possibility that God might exist, and then built rational reasons for holding that view. My own truth, though, is that the rejection came first and the reasons came later.

My reasons for rejecting even the concept of God were specific and well developed. A treasured family friend once asked me, "What has having PD done to your theology?" His innocent, well-intentioned question was the beginning of several years of email correspondence and personal visits, during which I laid out the carefully reasoned basis for my lack of belief. I argued, pointed out inconsistencies of fact in the Bible, used analogy and metaphor, applied inductive and deductive logic, and expounded learnedly about biology, physics, mathematics, and philosophy. I endlessly defined and redefined terms, talked about the scientific method, waxed poetically about the value of uncertainty and the quest for truth and knowledge, and quoted everyone from Bertrand Russell to

Carl Sagan. I was earnest and sincere, and I convinced myself many times over. However, I never admitted or recognized that all this reasoning didn't come first—the rejection did. Regardless of the validity of the arguments, they were built on sand. I didn't reject God because reason led me there. I rejected God for emotional, non-rational reasons, and then used reason to help me stay there. It was time to start over, and build up from the foundation again.

18
The Electric Jitterbug

About six months after the DBS system was implanted, I began experiencing a recurrence of the "on-off" phenomenon—fluctuations in my physical symptoms due to changes in medication levels. One of the reasons for using DBS was to help smooth out those variations, but I had started to crash again after a medication dose wore off. Two or three times a day, I suddenly and unpredictably became stiff, slow and shaky, and I stayed that way until the next dose of medication took effect. I discussed the problem with my neurologist, and he suggested that increasing the DBS voltage level should help. By then this was familiar territory, so I was unfazed by the normal tickles, buzzes, and jolts I felt as he tested the system. He settled on a new stimulation level, and since I seemed to tolerate it well, he suggested I have lunch and come back in an hour or so.

As I left the office and headed toward my car, I started to feel... well, I don't know how to describe it. "Twitchy" might be the right word, but it really doesn't do the feeling justice. I began having trouble walking when I was about 100 feet from the car, and by the time I unlocked the door I was having trouble standing. My entire body was completely uncontrollable, with jerky, thrashing movements that were worsening by the minute.

I had a completely inappropriate response to the situation—I began to laugh. I've been a Monty Python fan for years, and I imagined suddenly having become a charter member of "The Ministry of Silly Walks." I got in the car, telling myself, "Well, this is kind of funny, but I need to calm down. I'm hungry, and I can't drive like this." I decided that through sheer force of will, I could stop thrashing so I could have lunch.

My force of will had no effect. The dyskinesia steadily worsened, and I grew concerned. The uncontrolled movement had become violent, and the first time I punched myself in the face I decided I had had enough. I tried to cross my arms and hold my hands still, but that wasn't working either. My legs were kicking and thrashing, and my arms were beating against the steering wheel, the gearshift, the rear view mirror, and my own face and body. It took me ten minutes to get back into the doctor's office.

I looked like a rag doll in a high wind, and I caused quite a stir in the waiting room. The doctor's assistant knew immediately what had happened, and he hustled me back to an examination room. It didn't take long to readjust the stimulation level and stop the dyskinesia, and this time I waited in the doctor's office until we were both sure it was over. Afterwards, I was no worse for wear other than bruises on my arms and legs, a couple of sore spots on my face, and an all-over body soreness from getting a week's worth of exercise in fifteen minutes. It was a frightening experience, but I think the most frightening thing about it was my realization that for many Parkinson's patients, this is an everyday experience that goes on for years, as a side effect of long-term exposure to levodopa. It's another reason that research into the cause of PD is important, so we can stop using treatments that end up being worse than the disease itself.

19

Exploration

Discovering that I had a degenerative, incurable disease threw a harsh light on my values, prejudices, and beliefs, both conscious and unconscious. It shook my confidence and caused me to question my basic sense of self. And, it created a desire for self-assessment and evaluation: "What have I done with my life? What do I have left to do? How long do I have? What should I do with my time? What do I really believe? Why am I here?"

In other words, it made me a particularly irritating conversational partner, and I drove away a fair number of people for a while by being unable to have a normal conversation. I tended to stifle friendly interchange.

"Hey, it's good to see you! How have you been? How's your family?"

"I'm fine, they're fine. How can an omniscient, omnipotent, omnibenevolent God exist when evil and pain are present in the world?"

"Umm, well... yeah. You take care, okay?"

I received an email from my father-in-law's old Army buddy and dear family friend who had recently retired from a long career as an engineer and corporate executive, and who was now a missionary in Mozambique. We had a surprising number of things in common, and we started an email correspondence that lasted for over a year. He was able to overlook the fact that I was a Texas Longhorn, and I overlooked his unfortunate affiliation with Texas A&M University, and although we were different in age and experience we shared life stories and kept up with developments in each other's lives. I learned that his wife and son had Huntington's disease, and that his family was working through the consequences and implications. His experiences helped me to understand the fears Amy had in her role as a caregiver, and my journey with Parkinson's gave him insight into the fears and challenges his wife and son were facing.

We also shared views on spirituality and the role of religion in our lives. Since I knew he was a missionary, I expected the hard sell—I was familiar with evangelical fervor from my encounter with the major in pilot training and with others since then, and I considered myself to be well armed and impervious. I explicitly (and arrogantly) laid out the ground rules: we could discuss whatever he wanted to along those lines, but I had heard it all before, and he had nothing new under the sun to offer me. I wasn't quite that terse and offensive, but I was clear that I thought the ground was well plowed, and I had a counter-argument to everything he might say to persuade me to his viewpoint. I half-expected him to say, "Well, all right then," and never to hear from him again.

His response surprised me, though. "Fair enough," he said. "I don't claim to have a lock on the truth, but I suspect you don't, either." His sincere attitude was that perhaps we both had things to teach, and he repeatedly proved his sincerity by listening as much as he talked. I gave him things to think about and he returned the favor, and we had a lively but largely academic exchange of ideas. I trotted out my list of unanswerable questions and showstoppers, and as usual I was prepared to refuse to consider arguments that weren't supported by my definition of evidence. I was prepared to resist so strongly that I almost fell over when he didn't push. Instead, he told me stories.

He told me about his life and experiences in Africa. He told me about how difficult it was for him to be a man of faith in the business world. He told me about his triumphs and successes, and about his failures and regrets. He told me what it was like for him to be both a rational, hardheaded engineer and a Christian, and how he thought the two could coexist. He told me about himself; he offered me no universal truths, proofs, or incontrovertible evidence. Little by little, he just told me his story. He was limited by the medium of email, but he didn't preach and he didn't push.

When I was growing up, I was immersed in church life. My mother and father met in the church choir. We were Methodists, and we attended church every Sunday. I remember being baptized, and my first spanking was the result of misbehavior in church. I even sang in my grandparents' church when I was about five. My rendition of "Bless This House" made them proud, but even then there was clearly no recording contract in my future.

When we moved to DC, the whole family seemed to drift away from spiritual life. My father insisted that we keep up appearances, but I had already begun to resist by the time the abuse began. I have no significant memories of church, no recognition of God's presence in my life, and no sense of external moral guidance from the time I was seven years old until well after I was married. I began with a vague sense of embarrassment at the concept of God that evolved into an unconscious rejection when the abuse was ongoing, and became a conscious, total rejection of God, religion, spirituality, and all the associated trappings as a teen and young adult.

How did I see the world? I had never tried to summarize my worldview until my friend asked the question, and I spent some of my sleepless nights trying to answer that question for myself. I called myself a scientific rationalist, and I defined that label through these contentions:

– Belief in anything without accompanying evidence is indefensible, and "evidence" has a very rigorous definition. It includes things that can be independently examined by other people, but not personal, inward experiences and perceptions.

– The best toolset we have for evaluating evidence is the scientific method. It's not infallible, because people are not infallible, but as a principle of thought and behavior it has power.

– There must be a foundation of evidence available to be tested and re-evaluated for all our beliefs, but it's not necessary to retest that evidence constantly. There's uncertainty, potential for error, misperception and misinterpretation of observations, and other risks and pitfalls, but that's unavoidable.

– The universe operates according to natural principles that may not be completely known, but which are potentially knowable. As time goes on, we have consistently discovered more about those natural principles and pushed back the boundaries of ignorance, and it appears we may eventually understand the fundamentals of the principles on which our existence is based. The discovery process is awe-inspiring and exciting, but there's no scientific evidence that it's mediated or managed by supernatural forces.

– Science, although flawed, is a fundamentally sound way of understanding our world and our place in it. Skeptical inquiry into root causes, explanations, foundations, and reasons for the things we see and experience is valuable.

– There is no credible scientific evidence of supernatural actors or effects in the world. The things that lead people to belief in supernatural forces are more easily explained by known or as-yet undiscovered natural causes. Lack of explanation is due to current gaps in knowledge, incomplete observation, or errors in perception or evaluation.

– Like the scientific method, the principle called Occam's Razor is useful for evaluating causes and evidence. It's not a belief system, it's just a tool in what Carl Sagan called "the universal baloney detector toolkit."

As a personal philosophy it's a little cold and dry, but it appealed to my need for order and logic and served to protect me from the unexplainable elements of life. When I dug deeper, though, I discovered attitudes that were not based on coldly logical rationality, but which were instead messy and inconvenient:

– I had a deep desire to believe that existence had meaning other than the meaning we create for ourselves. I didn't know where it came from, but if I was truthful, I had to admit it was there. I had a "God-shaped hole" in my being.

– If God existed, I was at a loss to understand His nature. He had ignored me when I needed Him most, and allowed me to suffer for no reason I could see. To be blunt, I couldn't believe in God, because if he existed, I hated Him.

– I was embarrassed by my desire for a higher purpose, and I believed that it was just a symptom of unresolved damage from my childhood history of abuse and my search for a father I could trust. It was wish fulfillment at its worst, and it was a sign of the weakness and powerlessness I dreaded so strongly.

– I rejected belief in the unexplainable. I had a sincere love for scientific, rational thought, and I thought that accepting non-rational beliefs was a slippery slope to irrationality, dogmatism, and small-mindedness.

– I believed that science and faith really were at odds, and if I had to choose, I preferred science. Faith and trust just got me into trouble, and I had made terrible mistakes in believing and trusting the wrong things. It was safer to withhold judgment in an environment of uncertainty, even one that dealt with attitudes, emotions, and values rather than facts.

My missionary friend and I corresponded about other things, but we always came back to this subject. I followed my normal pattern of asking hard questions, not to seek answers but to prove a point. He didn't rise to the bait, though. He said, "That's an interesting question; I don't know the answer" as often as he said anything else, but wasn't disturbed or embarrassed by his lack of refutations. He just kept telling me stories of his life.

I was unmoved, secure in my fortress of rationality and reason, sure I had it all figured out and afraid that I was right. I figured that the only path forward was through answers I could accept to those unanswerable, academic questions, and I both feared and longed for those answers.

I received an email from him telling me that his wife's Huntington's disease had progressed to the point that they needed to return home to Texas, probably for good. He said they both would miss the people and their work together in Mozambique, but that he looked forward to meeting me. I looked forward to it, also—even through the limited forum of email, I had grown to like and respect him, and I was eager to meet him in person. It would be the beginning of a profoundly impactful friendship and a life-changing experience for both of us.

Corey D. King

20
Things Fall Apart

I'm sure that William Butler Yeats was not writing about my home automation system, but his poem was uncomfortably appropriate. I had discovered that building a system of computer-controlled lighting and other home technologies was even more fun than flying model helicopters; not only could I chase the cat, but I could open the door as he ran in feline panic across the front hallway, and then lock the door behind him and watch him with the security cameras as he stalked around the yard, looking for a way back in. This is a hypothetical example; I haven't actually done it. I'm just pointing out that it's possible.

However, when a home automation system goes bad, it's much worse than just picking up a few parts off the floor and patching a small hole in the wall. After spending months of sleepless nights watching the shadows, listening to the whispers, and building a smart house, I found myself embroiled in a home automation Chernobyl. Without realizing it, I had built a house of electronic cards, and it only took one simple failure for almost all of it to come tumbling down.

My interest in home automation began after a discussion with a colleague at work. His description was fascinating, and it had all the right elements to capture my attention: cool electronic gadgets to buy, the need to take things apart and put them back together again, a reason to buy new tools, and the remote possibility of a workable system when I was finished. He sealed the deal for me when he showed me his home system from his office computer and told me that if he wanted to, he could turn the lights on in his master bathroom from where we sat. If you feel the need to ask why this is necessary, I can't help you.

I was particularly prone to influence, since I had realized that my scuba diving days were over and I was in search of a gadget-filled, equipment-intensive new hobby that didn't place my own life or someone else's at excessive risk. Coincidentally, we had this discussion just a few months after I had started taking a dopamine agonist, so without knowing it, I was just itching to become obsessively involved with some new activity. Life isn't all Fudgsicles and helicopters.

The next eighteen months were filled with online shopping trips, replacing perfectly functional light switches, power outlets, and junction boxes with computer-controlled equivalents at ten times the price, and vastly over-engineering my home network just for fun. I was both proud and ashamed of the fact that I had as many terabytes of data storage as I had pairs of Vibram Five-Finger shoes (another brief but intense obsession).

Then came the control software, the security cameras (eight of them, to keep tabs on the cat), the electronic door locks, the touchscreen control panel, the energy management system, the motion sensors, and the computer-controlled landscape lighting and garage door. My friend had warned me that this would happen. I wish I could blame it all on the medication, but it might have happened anyway.

I eventually gained some knowledge and expertise, but I never took the time to go back and correct the mistakes I made during the early installations. So, when the lights in the kitchen began to inexplicably flash whenever we opened or closed the garage door, when any light in any location in the house turned on or off, or when I locked the doors at night, I begin to suspect something was wrong.

Any competent network engineer can quote the mantra of

network troubleshooting: "check the physical layer first." Except for that bit of wisdom, you never really know where to start; the hardware guys always blame the software, the software guys blame the hardware, and everybody claims, "… it must be a distant end problem." I had no one to blame but myself, since I was both the hardware guy and the software guy, and the most distant my end could get was Amy's home office. So I flipped a coin and, ignoring the mantra, decided to troubleshoot the software first. I might as well have flipped a coin that said "idiot" on one side and "moron" on the other.

For someone who is not a professional software engineer, software maintenance is like pulling on the loose strings in a sweater. You just can't resist, but you soon end up with a pile of yarn at your feet. The software infrastructure I had built over a year and a half was soon in strings all around me, and the kitchen lights kept flashing.

So I flipped my coin again, and decided the problem had to be power line interference. Off on another wild goose chase I went, unplugging things all over the house to see if the lights in the kitchen would stop flashing. No luck. By this time I was desperate enough to try the first thing that I should've tried—I replaced the switch that was causing the problem. Magically, the kitchen light stopped flashing, but unfortunately the kitchen light was now the only one in the house that was still working.

Home automation hobbyists use an acronym to describe the maturity of their systems: WAF. It stands for "wife acceptance factor," and it's a measure of just how much nonsense your spouse is willing to put up with before she throws a shoe. Amy was the soul of restraint for the entire time that I was working on this little project of mine, because when it works it's actually pretty cool. I only occasionally heard her walking around the house muttering, "…can't turn a damned light on in this entire place, and I need a keyboard to flush the toilet. Wish he'd just go back to work…"

The Home Automation Incident used up a large portion of Amy's goodwill. She made it known that she was done, that the lights needed to work reliably, and that there was no need, ever again, for the house to speak to her. I think I've got it fixed now; just one more little tweak…

After I was diagnosed, things periodically fell apart in other ways, and not just with my home automation system. I had "long, dark nights of the soul," and occasionally wallowed in self-pity. Parkinson's disease is a movement disorder, but movement problems are only one part of the physical and mental problems it brings. Depression is also a very common symptom of PD. It's a result of the neurotransmitter malfunction that characterizes the disease, and is different than being sad or having a bad day. For PWPs, clinical depression can erode quality of life as much as any of the motor symptoms, and it can be life threatening.

PWPs are at risk for other psychological problems as well, including anxiety, panic, bursts of anger and aggression, paranoia, and delusions. Parkinson's apathy is not as well known, but is just as disruptive, and I began noticing it in myself as I lived with the disease.

Parkinson's apathy isn't depression. It's an inability to start activities or projects, to maintain motivation, and to finish actions, accompanied by a pervasive feeling that nothing matters. I began to have trouble returning phone calls, sending e-mails, attending meetings and volunteer activities, exercising, and having a social life. Every action was exhausting, including making the bed, washing the dishes, or doing a load of laundry. At the end of the day I would often find tasks that I had started but never finished. I felt like I was wading in molasses; every thought and movement was an effort, and it all seemed pointless. I could be cajoled into motion, but I would coast to a stop.

An inescapable sense of numb hopelessness began to invade my thoughts. I often had to force myself to stay active and connected, and I still do. Some days I win, and some days I have to resolve to try again tomorrow.

Apathy is as common as depression for a PWP, but it doesn't get as much notice. It contributes to our tendency to become socially isolated. It looks like disinterest in maintaining contact, and coupled with other communication and speech problems and lack of facial expression, it can make a PWP a "hard interface." It also contributes to frustration and conflict with family members and caregivers since it can look like laziness or a lack of willingness to help. The understanding that it's just another part of the disease isn't much comfort to anyone.

The physical and mental impacts of PD continued to plague me. It was abundantly clear to me how dependent I was on PD medications, and now on DBS. If either were to disappear, my life would become very difficult. I also had a growing recognition that my condition was not going to get better. None of the treatments and therapies had the slightest impact on the underlying disease; at best, they masked the symptoms. I knew that a positive attitude could be a weapon against the disease, but I also knew that no matter how positive I remained, I wasn't going to win against PD. What was the use?

These thoughts and feelings may have been the result of the flawed electrochemical interaction of neurotransmitter chemicals and the billions of neurons in my brain, but it felt to me like my soul crying out for answers and a reason to hope.

I ignored obligations and responsibilities and neglected relationships while, as Amy's grandmother once phrased it, "I sat and stewed on my stool of do-nothing." And I asked, "Why?"

Why me? Why this? Why now? What had I done? I asked the air, not expecting an answer and sure that there wasn't one. I wanted to hold someone or something accountable. And, as usual, all I heard was my own voice. It hadn't occurred to me yet that if I was going to ask, perhaps I should listen for an answer.

Corey D. King

21
Mice, Men, And Mortality

I had always looked forward to the Christmas holidays. When I was young, the anticipation and excitement were almost too much to bear, and my brother and I would "practice for Christmas morning" to ease the tension. Practicing entailed getting into bed fully clothed each afternoon leading up to Christmas Day, pretending to be asleep, and then whispering to each other, "Do you think it's time to get up yet?"

We would draw out the suspense for as long as possible, and then jump out of bed and race each other to the Christmas tree in the living room. He always won; he claimed it's because he was older and more agile, but I still think it was because he cheated and wasn't shy about tripping me.

As an adult, I began to look forward to Christmas as a welcome respite from the demands of work life, a chance to spend time with my family, and in later years, an opportunity to try new ways of celebrating the holidays, like food poisoning while scuba diving in Cozumel and broken bones while skiing in Park City. I even looked forward to going back to work after the holidays were over; the "fresh start" newness to old tasks and responsibilities made even the most difficult jobs more bearable.

The Christmas after I retired was the first time in nearly thirty years that I didn't go back to work afterward. The holidays felt like watching the movie *The Return Of The King*, the concluding episode of the Lord of the Rings trilogy—an enjoyable experience, but every time you think it's reached the end, it hasn't. Over, and over, and over…

I thought that a perpetual vacation would be a relief; during the most stressful, difficult years of my work life, I fantasized about never having to work again. When it became a reality, it made me uncomfortable. Although I had hopes that one day I'd be able to retire early, I wanted to hit the finish line at full speed, leaning forward and "dipping for the tape" as I once did running the 220-yard dash. John Steinbeck had it right about best-laid plans, though, even if he stole the idea from my distant kinsman Robert Burns (or from Psalm 33, depending on who you ask).

I still counted myself fortunate, though. Unexpected disability is one of the leading causes of mortgage foreclosure and bankruptcy. Parkinson's is also notorious for contributing to relationship problems, fractured families, and divorce. Amy and I had certainly weathered a few storms and had our fair share of water slopping over the transom, but we were still seaworthy. Also, Amy, in true Texas frontier-woman style, had learned to shoot. She said it was to be able to protect me in the future if she needed to; it's possible that she only wanted to keep me polite and humble. It worked.

One of the best decisions we made as a couple was to find a financial advisor we trusted, and to listen to her. She advised us, at a time in our lives when we were absolutely sure we were invincible, to hope for the best but plan for the worst and buy long-term care and long-term disability insurance policies. Her advice could not have been more on target, even though I chafed at the idea of spending money for such a thing when I was obviously so healthy. Having taken her advice will keep my Parkinson's diagnosis from causing financial catastrophe for our family. Although our lives are now radically different, disability insurance will keep us from near-term financial ruin, and long-term care insurance will prevent my eventual need for professional care from bankrupting Amy when the time comes. Things could be much worse. This time, Burns and Steinbeck were wrong.

I was still finding new ways that PD intruded on my life, like the disruption of my sense of smell. Typically, a PWP's ability to sense odors, and consequently the ability to taste more than just the basics, fades away. Loss of the ability to smell can be one of the first symptoms of the disease. In my case, however, my sense of smell went temporarily insane for several months not long after my initial diagnosis, after having been largely absent for many years. For six months, I constantly smelled a pervasive, horrible odor that I could not escape. I even imagined the odor when I was asleep, a combination of rotting fish and burning plastic. The phantom smell was bad enough to make me actively sick to my stomach several times a day.

We tried everything we could to mask or eliminate the smell: chewing gum, breath mints, air fresheners, candles, and unscented laundry soap. Nothing worked. I can advise, however, that if your spouse ever suggests that you put peppermint essential oil in your nostrils to combat a foul odor, you should back away with your fingers in your ears. I've only recently stopped sneezing, crying, and smelling peppermint-scented burning plastic and rotting fish.

PD can also cause digestive system slowness and difficulty swallowing. The resulting combination of severe heartburn and choking when eating and drinking can be disconcerting and dangerous, and for more than a year I slept sitting up in a chair to keep from waking up choking. A combination of medications and diet changes eventually let me sleep in a bed again, but sleep often eluded me for other reasons.

On one occasion, after a dinner that didn't settle well, I again lay awake all night. Even my wonder drug for gastric reflux was ineffective, and the heartburn burned through. At about 5:30 AM, I thought I felt well enough to try to sleep. After only a few minutes of dozing, though, I woke up choking. It had happened before, but this time was different. I was coughing and wheezing, but also unable to catch my breath. Amy tried to help me to relax and calm down, but I was caught in a vicious cycle. Stress makes all Parkinson's symptoms worse, and not breathing is stressful. In this case, the stress triggered a bout of dyskinesia. Again I found myself getting a week's work of exercise in just a few minutes, but this time while not breathing.

After claiming several times that I really was getting better, and a short battle with my mother-in-law (Amy didn't get her fortitude by accident), I arrived at the emergency room where they did doctor stuff and determined that I was coughing and not breathing well. After x-rays, an EKG, chest listening and thumping, and a couple of hours of calm breathing, the episode passed and they let me go home, with stern warnings not to fail to breathe regularly or there would be consequences.

For a brief, irrational time, I thought I might die. It was an odd realization for someone who's lived half a century and once considered himself to be indestructible, but my mortality slapped me in the face. It's one of those unpleasant, "mustn't touch it" topics, but PD is life limiting. Asphyxiation from choking, aspiration pneumonia, acute injuries and complications from falling, dementia, and depression can all reduce life expectancy. Ultimately, life itself is life limiting, and PD symptoms are treatable with exercise, medication, and surgery. The fact remains, though, that there is not yet a treatment that significantly changes the rate of progression or course of the disease.

I understood that no one knows when his or her own end will come, and that each of us could be hit by a bus or a falling safe at any moment. However, the likelihood is that I won't have a Wile E. Coyote experience, but that I'll live out my days with Parkinson's and probably die from it. That realization made me impatient with foolishness, meanness, stupidity, and cruelty, and with bad choices and bad judgment, especially my own. We all have so little time, and we waste so much of it.

Realizing, at long last, that I was not immortal moved me to reconsider important philosophical questions. I was an analytical thinker, and answers and reasons were important to me, but these were some of the most critical questions in human existence. Why am I here? What do I do next? How do I keep going? I had made an informal career of asking questions such as these, as if there was something virtuous in asking. There is a difference between asking questions and seeking answers, though, and I was beginning to see that asking without really seeking was a waste of time. I realized that my lack of faith in a transcendent reality was the safe, fence-sitting approach. If I didn't commit to anything that couldn't be rigorously justified, I was less likely to be wrong, embarrassed, ridiculed, hurt, or shamed. Sadly, I was also less likely to see the fullness and richness of life with a higher purpose.

Discovering I had an incurable, degenerative disease brought "meaning of life" questions into sharp focus, and I began to realize that I was unsatisfied with my conclusions, and with the basic, non-rational beliefs on which I had built them. But, I had no idea what to do about it, and I had never had a sense of being guided by a spiritual force or a sense of revelation. I prayed, but all I heard were my own thoughts and the sound of my own breathing. I felt trite and foolish, and like I was grasping at straws, abandoning my rationality as soon as things got tough.

I also began to fear that PD was having effects on my judgment and decision-making ability. How could I know what was real and what was fantasy? Can the cognitively challenged have real faith, or as some have said, is all faith a form of mental illness?

Near despair, I gave up trying to figure it out. To my surprise, that turned out to be the right answer.

Corey D. King

22
Disobedience

Before I learned I had Parkinson's, I was a scuba diver. I loved everything about diving: the sense of community and camaraderie among people with a common passion, the technical and scientific character of the knowledge required to do it well, the complexity and variety of the equipment, and the freedom I felt while I was diving. Whether I was in the gin-clear, eighty-two-degree water of Cozumel with 300 feet of visibility, or in the forty-five-degree blackness and near-zero visibility at the bottom of a Texas lake, I felt at home. Even in my frequent vivid dreams of flying, I was wearing scuba gear.

I probably didn't have to stop as soon as I did, but I was safety-minded and conservative. I didn't want to hurt a dive buddy or a student in the classes I helped to teach, and I didn't relish the thought of drowning because my PD symptoms suddenly reappeared at just the wrong time. I searched for something to replace diving, and I mourned the loss.

Through a complex series of circumstances and events, I began pistol shooting. Although it's a counterintuitive sport for someone with Parkinson's to adopt, it's surprisingly similar in unexpected ways to scuba diving. There is a community of like-minded enthusiasts who share knowledge and help each other. It can be dangerous, but with caution, training, and experience, the danger is controllable and manageable. It requires a specialized body of knowledge, but is accessible to almost anyone willing to put in the time and effort to learn. And the equipment, for a gadget geek and someone with an engineering mindset, is endlessly interesting. There's always something new to learn and discover.

About a year after I began shooting in small, local competitions, I found myself on a plane with my Aggie friend Gene on one side and a very large man and his fiancée on the other. We were all on the way to Las Vegas, them to get married, and Gene and I to head out into the Nevada desert for a four-day defensive handgun-training course. We planned to learn defensive handgun safety, gun handling, and marksmanship techniques, but we agreed we would be satisfied if we merely avoid shooting the wrong things, including each other.

It's actually not quite that bad. Although I experience many of the major motor and non-motor symptoms of PD during the course of a typical week, they don't usually happen at the same time, and I'm able to squeeze off a shot or two during the lulls. And, I have the luxury of unloading and putting the gun down if I'm shaking, stiff, or clumsy; it doesn't generally come upon me without warning. There's always plenty of time to shout, "Hit the deck!" and toss the gun away like a hand grenade.

We had planned the trip for several months. We collaborated and argued about firearms, accessories, ammunition, and range time. We spent innumerable hours discussing the merits of John Moses Browning's masterpiece (the Model 1911 .45 ACP semi-automatic pistol), the pros and cons of pistols made from Tupperware, and the meaning of life and our place in it. And now we were leaving the civilized world behind, on our way to the badlands to learn to shoot with proper adult supervision.

My large seatmate, who was now wearing a panicked look and beginning to sweat as we approached Vegas and his impending wedding, was growing larger by the minute. He was already getting premium value from his ticket price by taking half of my seat as well, and was busy trying to acquire the other half. I discovered something new, however; Parkinson's dyskinesia could be an excellent defensive tool. The more he encroached, the more I thrashed. I considered making noises, but thought that might be over the top.

I enjoyed telling people I was a shooting enthusiast. I liked their tolerantly amused expression until they realized I was serious, followed by their intense desire to know exactly where and when my next shooting excursion would be. I had advised them to avoid Nevada for the next five days.

When I was first diagnosed, I was tempted to decide out of hand that there were some things I shouldn't do. There are, of course: teaching scuba classes, tightrope walking, diamond cutting, and being a tattoo artist come to mind. But there are other things, like shooting, that I can do, with a sober, realistic approach, the right preparation, and the willingness to wait for the right time. PD is a thief, and I don't want to let it take things that I can still hold onto for a while. I had begun by "fighting back," but I was beginning to believe that was the wrong metaphor. Perhaps the right approach was less direct confrontation and more civil disobedience. PD may have power, but I could still refuse to allow it free rein. PD wanted me to sit at home. NO, I'm going to go shooting in Nevada with my friend. PD wanted me to sleep all day. NO, I'm going to the high school to talk about computers with smart, eager young people. PD wanted me to resign to my fate and give up hope. NO, I'm going to hold on and find new reasons for hope. PD wanted me to stop exercising and sit in front of the computer. Well, okay, but I'll do better next week. No philosophy is perfect.

During my week in Nevada, my way to question PD's authority over my life was to learn to clear a room and shoot from cover. It's not likely I would ever need to use those skills since being a Navy SEAL numbered among the things I probably shouldn't do, but if needed, I would be ready. And, I loved thumbing my nose at Parkinson's.

We arrived in the southern Nevada desert after a leisurely dinner on the outskirts of Las Vegas and a pleasant moonlit drive. As we settled into our hotel room and ran a few errands around town to gather supplies for the week, we discovered that there is no path between two points in the entire town that doesn't pass either through a casino or past a fireworks stand. I had been to Vegas on business a number of times over the years, so I expected the slot machines at the airport and in the grocery store. The roulette table in our hotel room was a surprise, though.

We rose early the first morning, packed guns, holsters, accessories, sunscreen, bottled water, Gatorade, and food into our rental car, and headed twenty miles across the desert to our 6:30 AM check-in at the training facility. As the sun rose over the mountains, we were greeted by our first glimpse of the landscape where we would spend the next four days.

"I thought we were in Nevada. How did we get to the far side of the moon?" said Gene.

"Oh, it's not that bad," I replied. "Look, there's a dead cow. You'd never see that on the moon. At least it's nice and cool; only sixty-five degrees. It probably won't get much hotter than that." Stupidity often sounds like optimism.

We arrived at the facility slightly before the appointed time and waited briefly in a line of other students for the staff to open the gates. At the exact moment the clock hit 6:30 AM, we entered the facility after being greeted warmly at the gate. This was our first exposure to both the precision and professionalism we would experience throughout the week.

As directed, we headed to the sign-in area to check in for our class and have our guns and holsters checked for safety. Since they didn't yet know about my steel-trap mind, the sign-in staff thought it best to write the number of my assigned range on my hand with a Sharpie. They then verified that our guns were neither too small nor too large, our ammunition would probably not detonate prematurely or with unexpected fanfare, our holsters covered our triggers, we weren't smuggling concrete or peanut butter in the barrels of our pistols, and we were otherwise prepared to be instructed. We then headed to the classroom to receive our official welcome and to sign paperwork saying that, regardless of what happened in the next four days, no matter who was at fault, irrespective of which body parts were affected, and with no consideration of intent, true culpability, or gross negligence, we were solely at fault now and for all time. I signed without reading. If there's a war in the Mideast now, I think I agreed, it's my fault.

We then headed to Range 1A, where we met our range master and his team for the first time. They were all dressed alike: crisp short-sleeved gray uniform shirts, bloused black fatigue pants, boots, and baseball caps. Sharp, professional, and squared away, they were also each friendly, approachable and genuinely welcoming.

At this point, I spoke privately with the range master and explained to him that I had Parkinson's disease, but that I could usually tell when I was having problems that would impact my ability to participate. He nodded his understanding and said, "Safety is a very important part of this course, but we'll keep an eye on you as we do for everyone, and you just take things at your own pace." My remaining concerns faded into the background.

We spent the day going over the basics: the Four Rules of Firearm Safety, the rules of the range and the facility, range commands, chamber checking and magazine checking, and other safety-related subjects. We actually didn't fire the first live round until the afternoon, which was fortunate. I learned that I had been doing almost everything wrong, and I had a significant amount of unlearning and bad-habit breaking to do.

The day ended with a lecture on the moral and ethical issues associated with deadly force, and I was once again struck by the thoughtfulness and serious deliberation that had gone into this course. These were not gun nuts gleefully popping off rounds in the desert. They were instead professionals with a deep understanding of the awesome responsibility inherent in choosing to use firearms for self-protection and sport, and a recognition that this is a controversial subject even among well-intentioned, intelligent people. Thoroughly exhausted, we headed back to town for an evening of pistol cleaning and rest.

We spent the second day practicing and learning to draw correctly from a holster, and to re-holster without shooting ourselves. Among many other things, we also learned the value of dry practice and the Three Secrets of Handgun Marksmanship. I had thought there was only one secret: shoot enough rounds and eventually you'll hit the target. Again, I was wrong.

We learned quickly. My new vocabulary now includes timeless nuggets such as "tap, rack, flip," "chamber check and mag check," tactical reload," and the popular "finger straight, look and move, check, lock, strip, rack rack rack, insert, rack, point in." It's not what it might sound like.

PD decided to reassert itself on the third day of class. I had hoped but didn't really expect to avoid a "bad day" during the week, and I awoke with the familiar, stiff, slow, shaky feeling and clumsy, shuffling gait that greets every morning. As occasionally happens, though, my morning handful of pills only brought nausea and disorientation, and no relief. I knew I wasn't safe to handle a gun, so I went to class and just watched that morning. I began to feel better by the afternoon, but my bad day brought me up short.

Who was I fooling? What was I doing here? I had PD. I wasn't going to recover, and I would never be any better at shooting or anything else than I was at that moment. Why bother? Why waste my time? I really just needed to get on the plane, go home, sell the guns, and get realistic. Feeling low and discouraged, I talked with Gene, who was also exhausted and dealing with his own challenges. Together we decided to stick it out for one more day, the last day.

I awoke on the last day dreading a repeat of the prior day's challenges, but thankfully, both Gene and I felt much better. PD is capricious and unpredictable, but that unpredictability cuts both ways. We arrived at the facility and spent the morning practicing and preparing for the final test scheduled for that afternoon. After we had practiced for several hours, though, the range master gathered us together and told us he had a surprise.

"We're going to have a competition this morning. You'll be competing against each other in a single elimination, man-on-man tournament that simulates one of the threat scenarios we've discussed —a multiple adversary hostage situation." Oh boy, I thought. As they used to say in Strategic Air Command, here was an "opportunity to excel." I resolved to try to apply what I had learned and make the best of the situation.

The scenario involved three targets made of differently colored steel armor plating. Competitors competed in pairs; each competitor had their own set of three targets that they were required to shoot in the proper order, while in direct competition on the same range. The first target was a gray man-shaped steel silhouette placed fifteen yards from the firing line, with a small white-painted steel square mounted on an axle next to the head of the silhouette, which would flip away when struck. The gray silhouette represented the hostage, and the small white square represented a hostage-taker standing behind the hostage with only a portion of his head showing. The two other targets, placed at twenty-five yards and painted blue and red, represented two other adversaries. The goal of the competition was to first shoot the white square and flip it away without striking the hostage, and then to shoot the blue target and the red target in that order, before your opponent did the same thing. Whoever finished first without hitting the hostage won the round. If both competitors hit the hostage, both were eliminated. If it sounds easy, try it in 100-degree heat wearing a concealment vest and presenting from a concealed holster.

The competition proceeded, with some shooters doing well and some less well. Gene raised the bar when he stepped up to the line and hit all three targets in order with three well-placed shots, well before his opponent, to the cheers of the class.

My turn finally came. I was part of the last pair in the first round. We stepped up to the line and I tried desperately to remember what to do as I heard, "Shooters! Firing drill. Load, chamber check, mag check, and return to the holster." My training kicked in and I didn't even think as my hands automatically moved through the drill we'd been taught over the last three and a half days. I heard, "Ready, fire!" and I smoothly (for me) swept my vest to the side, presented my 1911 .45 ACP from the holster, pointed in at the first target while snapping off the thumb safety, established the right sight picture as I removed the slack from the trigger, focused on the front sight, pressed the trigger to a surprise break, and trapped the trigger as I heard a "ping" and saw a blurry image of the white target slap back. Without consciously thinking about it, I moved the sights to the blue target, reset the trigger, and repeated the process, and again with the red target. I heard the instructor say, "when you're satisfied with the condition of your weapon, return to the holster," so I executed a tactical reload and re-holstered. It was only then that I discovered that I had won the round. I was so shocked I nearly soiled myself.

As luck would have it, I was paired with Gene for the second round. In a repeat of the first round, we both fired three shots and both connected three times for a perfect round. His red target fell about a tenth of a second before mine did, though. He eliminated me from the competition, and although I would have loved to have beaten him (he's an Aggie, after al), I was as thrilled for him as I would have been for myself. After a bye and another perfect round, he won the competition and received the Man-On-Man Competition Challenge Coin. If I had to lose, that was the way to do it.

We both went on to take the final test and finish the course. Neither of us was the highest scorer, but we weren't the lowest, either. We both had areas for improvement, but we were both safer and better shooters. And I answered or reaffirmed some of the questions I asked myself on the third day: Why bother? Because although I can fail, I cannot fail to try. Why waste my time? It isn't a waste. It is a refusal to curl up and die. Who am I fooling? No one, including myself. I have PD, and I don't expect it to just go away.

I hope for a cure, but I don't anticipate one in my lifetime. However, my willingness to be disobedient to PD can't depend on the hope for a cure. I continue to work as I can to help find one, but I also get up every day with the hope of learning something new, of meeting and overcoming challenges large and small, and of trying to go just a little farther every day than I think I can.

I struggled to come to terms with Parkinson's disease and to live without surrender, but that was not the most important struggle before me. The radical disruption PD brought to my life stripped me of the carefully crafted defenses I had built, and showed me how vulnerable I was. I believed I had control of my life; my sense of control was an illusion. I believed I had all the answers; I was asking the wrong questions. I believed that I could hide from the big questions and ignore the voids in my life behind a wall of reason and rationality; I still felt something important was missing. And I believed that the wrongs that had been committed against me gave me leeway to silence the still, small voice that I pretended not to hear inside me.

God, Whom I had ignored, denied, derided, disproved, hidden from, argued against, and rationalized away, would not be silenced. He found me, and quietly showed me I was wrong.

23

Revelation

Gene grimaced as I asked my question. I had noticed that he often did, and I wondered if he knew it. I suspected that I had begun to tax his patience. We were talking about the Bible (the book of Hebrews, to be exact), and it was making both of our heads hurt.

"I'm not getting how Jesus could have been both fully divine and fully human," I said. "Some sort of quantum state, like Schrodinger's cat, maybe?"

When Gene returned home from Africa, we resumed the discussions about faith that we had begun by email. I reiterated that I was unashamedly without belief, and Gene reiterated that he was unashamedly of deep belief. For a time, it appeared that we were simply incompatible on the subject. Gene even told me, "You're not my project; you're my friend. If you don't believe what I do, so be it. We can still talk about other things and we can still shoot." That was fine with me, too, but we still continued to talk, and I continued to ask questions.

I talked with him about both my academic and emotional objections to religious faith, and he listened without arguing. I ran down my list of "unanswerable questions," discussed passages from the Bible and pointed out the logical and factual errors, talked about religious scholars and philosophers I had read, and expounded about Russell's Teapot, Pascal's Wager, invisible pink unicorns, blind watchmakers, irreducible complexity, tornadoes and 747s, monkeys and typewriters, and other arcane subjects. Gene listened, and admitted at one point that, although he had been a missionary for many years, he had never heard some of the things I talked about. He didn't refute any of them, but instead continued to tell me about his experiences. After a particularly taxing conversation on one afternoon, he asked me, "If you're so sure you're right, why are you still asking questions?"

His question brought me up short. I had described myself to believers for years, and to Gene when we first met, as a "failed seeker." As I considered his question, it occurred to me that I used the description to both distance myself and to claim kinship. I wanted to believe, but I also wanted someone else to do the hard work. I wanted to be convinced, but only by someone who could first pass my test. If they could, I wouldn't have to take the risk of being wrong and, more to the point, of being disappointed yet again.

I went to visit Larry, the friend who had originally asked me how PD had influenced my theology, and who then had paid for it by reading the hundreds of closely spaced, tightly reasoned pages of my answer. He spent the weekend with me, and he had arranged a dinner with a group of guys he had met that he thought I would like. They were similar in a few ways; they all lived in the same city, they all had two legs, and they all professed faith in God. The similarities ended there, though—they talked, argued, disagreed vehemently, agreed more vehemently, called each other names, got mad, got glad, and thoroughly enjoyed each other's company. And no two of them believed exactly the same things. I heard as many views as there were people in the room, ranging from what I recognized as fundamentalist to surprisingly liberal viewpoints. I was astounded, and encouraged.

One of the guys asked me if I could describe why I didn't believe in God. I started down the laundry list, and began to recite the manifesto from memory. He listened patiently for a while, and then stopped me gently.

"No, I didn't ask what the reasons for not believing in God are. I asked why YOU don't believe in God. What are YOUR reasons?"

I started to protest that those were my reasons, but then I stopped. It was a fair question. I had spent years gathering other people's arguments as ammunition to defend my unbelief. Stripped of those things, what were my reasons?

Slowly, I stammered, "I've never felt like He was there. I've asked for His help, and he hasn't given it to me. I've prayed, and He hasn't answered. I don't feel anything."

The guys around the table nodded, and one spoke up. "Me, either. I've never had the experience of God's presence."

I said, "How can you commit your life to something you don't even know is real?"

"It's not about feeling; it's not as if you put your faith coin in the machine and you get your happy feelings in exchange. It's about choice. I choose to believe. It made sense to me after I'd chosen, but the fact that it makes sense didn't make me choose."

Later, discussing the evening with Larry, he agreed. He also thought I was trying too hard to force God to fit into my box. He suggested that God might have plans of His own, and maybe I should see what they were instead of dictating them.

I was thoroughly confused and despondent. I had spent my whole life figuring things out and controlling outcomes and events with knowledge. It was all I knew how to do. I was never going to think my way to God, and I was never going to get there any other way. I gave up, again, for what I thought would be the last time.

I went home and continued to visit with Gene. I loved him and his family, and I treasured my time with him. For six months or more, I visited him once a week and we would shoot, go for walks, go to lunch, talk, and enjoy each other's company. We also studied the Bible and talked about faith.

I figured it could do no harm. I wasn't seeking any longer; I had given up. I continued to read and study with him; it was interesting, and the stories illustrated principles I could agree with. I began to read on my own, and I found still more to agree with. The inconsistencies and flaws that I perceived were still there, but as I read and studied, they began to take on less importance.

Amy had taught a confirmation class at our church when our

children were young, and she had shared some of the content with me. There were several kinds of truth in the Bible, she said. She talked about six kinds of truth: moral, historical, scientific, symbolic, proverbial, and religious. I remembered our conversation, and when I encountered one of my Biblical "sticking points," I tried looking at it from the perspective of another kind of truth, instead of coming to a full stop.

I kept asking questions during my weekly visits with Gene. Slowly, without fanfare, blasts of trumpets, or fireworks, I realized that I had stopped asking to show how smart I was, and that I was asking to seek answers. The transition was slow and almost imperceptible, but I had reached a tipping point. I still had doubts, uncertainties, and questions, but I was looking at them from a different perspective. I didn't know when, how, where, or why it had happened, and I couldn't explain it, but it was true.

I believed.

24

Resolution

Recently, a good friend died. His death was completely unexpected; he left behind a large and loving family, and literally thousands whose lives he had enriched. He was a man of deep faith in God, and he lived his principles wherever he went, not like a coat he could take off when it was inconvenient, but deep in his bones, an inseparable part of who he was.

He always seemed to have a new spin or an interesting view, and he had a remarkable ability to get deeply involved in the details and then suddenly step back and look at the big picture. He didn't let the minutia bog him down—he just kept going and arrived at the solution when others couldn't even see the path.

His faith in God was as much a part of him as his big feet and booming voice. It came from his family first, from many generations back, but as an engineer and successful businessman, he was never one to accept a conclusion without examining the logic. I did the same thing, but we had different backgrounds and experiences, and I came to a different conclusion. I was focused on examining the notes and couldn't hear the music all around me. I'm starting to hear the music now.

I believe. After a lifetime of asking questions, not to get the answers but to show there were none, I believe. After repeatedly proving to myself and to others that God couldn't exist, and even if He did He didn't care, I believe. Even though I can't explain it and it's not rational, I believe. Even though I'm afraid that people important to me will not understand and will worry that PD is taking over my rational mind, I believe. After fighting it, wishing I could, and giving up countless times for almost forty years, I believe. I'm a little late to the party, but I believe.

I'm still working out the details, but the music is there. It's faint at times, but I hear it. I may never be able to play in the symphony, but I finally hear the music.

I haven't given up my respect and regard for critical thought and scientific inquiry. I don't suddenly reject thousands of years of steady social and scientific progress, nor do I deny that there is beauty in rational discovery and, as the physicist and Nobel laureate Richard Feynman put it, "finding things out." There's no need to.

I have instead broadened my world with a recognition that the God I rejected, but who never rejected me, speaks with many voices, uses many tools, and is a master of many kinds of truth. My world is not diminished; instead, it is bigger than I imagined, and the missing pieces are starting to fit together. I'll always be a questioner and seeker of deeper truth; I have that freedom. But, the minutiae don't bother me as much anymore. I don't care how many angels can dance on the head of a pin.

Why do I believe? Because it feels right and because I choose to. I didn't arrive here through rational analysis, but through a wholly personal experience that I can describe, but not explain. I can't provide a methodology for coming to faith, or for falling away, for that matter. All I can say is, "This is what happened to me."

What do I believe? That's a harder question. I have a sense that almost all of us, even the devout and learned believers, will eventually find that we had most everything wrong. When Paul told the Corinthians, "For now we see through a glass, darkly; but then face to face. Now I know in part; but then shall I know even as also I am known," I think he knew of our tendency for misinterpretation and error. However, when I consider the multiple voices, the many tools and methods, and the varied ways of expressing Truth that God can employ, I am surprised to find that a very old creed that I first learned long ago but that I still remember expresses the core of what I believe:

> I believe in God, the Father Almighty, maker of heaven and earth;
> And in Jesus Christ his only Son, our Lord;
> Who was conceived by the Holy Spirit, born of the Virgin Mary,
> suffered under Pontius Pilate,
> was crucified, dead, and buried;
> The third day he rose from the dead;
> He ascended into heaven, and sits at the right hand of God the Father Almighty;
> From thence he shall come to judge the quick and the dead.
> I believe in the Holy Spirit, the holy catholic church, the communion of saints, the forgiveness of sins, the resurrection of the body, and the life everlasting.

There is much here open to interpretation, disagreement, ridicule, or rejection. I know that better than most—I did all those things. Nevertheless, the essence of my belief lies here, in The Apostle's Creed.

My journey is not over—the most recent segment has barely begun. I recently learned that the Veterans Administration has decided that incidents during my period of service in the Air Force are the likely cause of my PD, and they have determined that my disability is service-related and that I am unemployable. That's not what Amy and I hoped for when we set out from Austin on a journey now in its twenty-ninth year, but according to one great philosopher, "you can't always get what you want."

My struggle with Parkinson's disease will not be easy, and I know there may be times when I question my newfound faith and rage at the God who has given me so much. I can only hope and pray for wisdom and strength if that time comes. I know God can take it, though—He's taken much worse from me.

I don't know why I have PD; I don't believe it's a punishment or a test, but I do believe there may be a purpose. In any case, there is no one to blame or to direct my anger toward. I don't know why my father did the things that he did, and I don't know why God allowed it to happen. The only person who carries responsibility has been gone for almost fifteen years. What my father did to me was inexcusable but not unforgivable, and I have forgiven him; not for his sake, but for mine. He was not simply an evil man who caused me pain and anguish. He walked his own crooked path, and probably dealt with pain and anguish of his own that I know nothing about. I'm still angry at him for what he did, and for the harm it's caused me and my family, but I'm no longer tormented by it.

There is always the possibility that Parkinson's disease will be cured tomorrow, next week, or next year, but I choose to live my life exuberantly and with purpose whether that happens or not. I choose to disobey PD's control over my life. I choose to love my family and friends openly and unselfconsciously, and to continue to learn, grow and stretch for as long as I can. And I choose to make God central in my life, in spite of doubts, uncertainties, and unanswered questions.

I choose to believe.

Part II

Stumbling Toward Victory

Living In Defiance Of Parkinson's

Corey D. King

Introduction to Part II

I wrote *Walking The Crooked Path* in 2013, four years after I was diagnosed with early-onset Parkinson's disease at age 47. In that book, I not only publicly struggled to come to terms with my diagnosis, I struggled to put a traumatic childhood into context, and to make some sense of the arc of my life up to that point. It was an ambitious undertaking, and I wrote less about Parkinson's disease than about my personal response to hardship and my emerging belief in God after four decades of agnosticism. I was more surprised than anyone else. A few readers who were expecting a book full of practical tips on living with PD were disappointed, but I received positive feedback as well, and not all from friends and family.

I have lived with my Parkinson's diagnosis for seven years now (only a short time; this is a slow-moving train, and for many it doesn't arrive at the final station for twenty or more years), but seven years is long enough for me to have developed a viewpoint about living successfully with it. This book, *Stumbling Toward Victory*, is a collection of essays about my way of fighting Parkinson's disease, and about my attempt to live honorably with or without Parkinson's.

I write to make room in my cluttered brain. These ideas pop into existence, and unless I write them down they compete for space with more urgent matters, such as where I put my car keys or whether I paid the electric bill. I hope there is something in here that makes you chuckle, makes you think, or even makes you angry. However, this is not a checklist for living well, and it may not work for you. It doesn't even work for me all the time.

I didn't invite Parkinson's into my life, and I don't intend to live peaceably with it. It's not welcome here, and while I can I intend to resist it, rebel against it, sabotage its attempt to ruin my life. With God's help and the support of family and friends, I intend to live in defiance of Parkinson's disease. It can't have me; I claim victory.

Corey D. King

Know thyself, know thy enemy.
A thousand battles, a thousand victories.
Sun Tzu

The horse is made ready for the day of battle,
but the victory belongs to the Lord.
Proverbs 21:31

1
Risk Management

One of the greatest discoveries a man makes, one of his great surprises, is to find he can do what he was afraid he couldn't do.
--Henry Ford

To be yourself in a world that is constantly trying to make you something else is the greatest accomplishment.
- Ralph Waldo Emerson

Amy glowered, frustrated and upset. I pretended to be unfazed, but my Parkinson's-ravaged body and brain betrayed my turmoil. I writhed in the passenger seat of my truck, fidgeting like a three-year old with pinworms. I am not fond of Amy's anger, but for the past several weeks I had been powerless to avoid it.

"I just want you to be safe, and to keep you around as long as I can." Her voice quavered, and tears welled in her eyes. "Can't you understand that?"

"Yes, I want that, too. We don't agree about the definition of the word 'safe,' though, and I am not going to sit in a chair and watch the world pass me by." My voice was as shaky as my hands were, both from the emotion of the conversation and from the effect of stress on my whole body. "I want to be with you as long as I can, but the length of my life isn't the only thing that's important to me."

Amy released her seatbelt as soon as we passed through the front gate of our neighborhood. For our entire married life, I've been able to judge how angry she is by how far away from the house she removes her seatbelt. She was royally pissed.

"Fine. Do whatever you want." She opened the door of the truck as we rolled to a stop in the driveway and disappeared into the house, slamming the door behind her.

I stayed behind and thought. Amy and I have been married for over thirty years, and I have learned that it's a bad idea to keep after her when she's thrown out the "No Trespassing" sign. I was also upset enough that I was having trouble walking.

The discussion had been about my driving, and the effect Parkinson's disease has on my reaction time, coordination, and judgment. I will stop driving someday. That day is not today, but it's a matter of contention between Amy and me when that day will be. My Parkinson's symptoms are slowly getting worse, and she's concerned that before too long I'll be a danger to myself and others behind the wheel. I disagree, of course. I think I have plenty of time, and my good days still outnumber my bad days.

I want to live my life with brio, a word that a trusted counselor taught me. It means "audacious confidence." Panache. Chutzpah. I don't want to give up before I am forced to, but I also don't want to be foolish or put others or myself in danger. Amy and I want the same thing; we just disagree about where to draw the danger line.

We both eventually cooled down, and I didn't spend the night in the passenger seat of my truck. In a subsequent, less passionate discussion, we agreed to use objective evidence. I'll shoot until the range safety officer says I'm not safe, or until I don't feel safe, whichever comes first. I'll drive until the professionals that run the driving simulator at the hospital say I'm no longer safe, and I'll take a driving test once per year.

American teenagers for almost 100 years have known the sense of freedom and independence that driving a car brings. Giving up driving won't just be giving up another piece of mobility; it'll be giving up a large chunk of my freedom and capacity to be independent. It's going to happen, but not today.

The confounding factor is that my judgment will become less reliable over time, and I will rely on Amy to make decisions for me. I don't think either of us is eager for that day. It's not because I don't trust her to make the right choices, but because in "handing the keys" to someone else, either literally or metaphorically, I'll be giving up another piece of ground to Parkinson's, dropping back to another fallback position on this armed retreat.

The good news is that I couldn't have a better partner when the time comes to relinquish the keys. A friend (let's call him "Larry," because that's his name) once told me that when I first saw Amy, I saw a beautiful, smart girl that I immediately knew I wanted to marry. However, God saw a woman of character, tenacity, and sharp mind that would be right for this journey with me. I hope and pray that when I finally hand over the keys to the partner God chose for me, it will be without recrimination and excessive wailing. Today is not the day, though.

Not long after our driving discussion, I went on a trip to Washington, DC. On my return flight, we were delayed on the ground at Reagan National Airport while the pilots and maintenance team diagnosed a problem with the aircraft. The maintenance crew thought they saw a wire hanging from the wing, and the pilot told us he wanted to check it out. I was already exhausted, but I thought the pilot had made a prudent decision and I hauled out my iPad and began writing.

After an hour, the pilot made a short announcement. "I just wanted to give you a little update. It wasn't a wire. It was a piece of caulking that we use to fill a gap where the flap joins the wing, and I guess it looks like a wire. They just cut it off and everything's fine, so we'll be on our way. Sorry for the delay, and thanks for choosing Grabass Airlines." (I made up that last part.)

Shortly after we took off and passed 10,000 feet, the cabin pressure dropped suddenly. I yawned and wiggled my jaw, equalizing the pressure in my ears as easily and unconsciously as during my diving days, and I saw everyone sitting around me doing the same thing. I glanced out the window at the wing, and saw the spoilers on the top surface of the wing pop up. Spoilers only have one purpose - to change the shape of the wing so it doesn't lift the plane. It's disconcerting to see the spoilers deploy at 12,000 feet, and we descended rapidly and leveled off at 5,000 feet.

The pilot then made another announcement.

"Folks (they always call you "folks" when something's wrong - it's supposed to be soothing), we're having a little problem with the cabin pressure and we don't know why. We've run our checklist up here, and it's telling us that we need to land the airplane. We're headed to Dulles Airport, and we'll just land there and see if we can figure out what's wrong."

Okay, maybe a little too much information, but good to know. He continued.

"Since we've declared an emergency, you'll see fire trucks and emergency vehicles waiting for us on the taxiway. They're just there to check our brakes after the landing. Since we're going to be landing heavy, they want to make sure our brakes haven't overheated and caught on fire."

Wow, that's way too much information, I thought. Had he actually used the words "fire" and "emergency" twice EACH, while we're still in the air? Yes -- yes, he had. I think he must have been sick during airline pilot charm school.

We landed, and were indeed met by trucks with flashing lights. Serious men and women swarmed over the landing gear and checked the underside of the plane. I know this because the pilot told me.

"Folks (there it was again - not out of danger yet), they're checking to see what the problem might be. The good news is that our brakes are fine. They're looking now to see if we might have had a tail strike. I'll let you know more when I get it." No doubt, I thought.

A tail strike occurs when the pilot drags the back of the plane on the runway during takeoff or landing. Sparks and damage ensue, and it makes the flight crew use words like "emergency" and "fire," sometimes more than once. The pilot was admitting over the intercom that he might have dragged the back of the airplane on the runway for a thousand feet during takeoff, emitting a shower of fire like a roman candle and breaking things that we might need at 36,000 feet. After another hour, he made it all better, though.

"The maintenance team has been over the aircraft, and they can't find anything wrong with it. I'm not sure what happened, but I hesitate to just take off, since we might have to come back here and do this all over again." Yes, hesitate -- please. At least he didn't call us "folks."

After yet another hour, he gave us the scoop.

"Well, after considering the situation, I've decided not to accept this aircraft. There's another one here, and they may be able to give us that one. We'll let you know as soon as possible - we'll taxi to the gate now. We've got meal vouchers for everyone, so that the condemned can eat a hearty meal before we leave again." (Again, I made up that last part.)

As he started the engines and we began to taxi, the cabin crew played the arrival video.

"Thank you for flying with Grabass Airlines…"

The entire cabin erupted in laughter.

I spent that night in a hotel in Herndon VA, in a Grabass Airlines-provided suite, enjoying the rest and relaxation. I returned home the next morning - on another airline. Life is risk, and in my view, a good life is partly about managing the risk and living with brio. There's no need to be stupid, though.

This is my seventh year of living with a diagnosis of early-onset Parkinson's disease. In those seven years, I learned about the disease well enough to talk about it publicly, and occasionally ease the fears of a newly-diagnosed fellow person with Parkinson's. I swallowed roughly 45,000 pills, and replaced my deep brain stimulation system battery three times. I allowed God to find me (I didn't find Him; He wasn't lost), I saw both my children grow into remarkable adults, and Amy and I together learned we can endure any hardship, overcome any challenge.

And I learned a few things about myself.

I discovered that defiance comes more easily to me than I expected; that resistance is not futile.

Parkinson's disease is progressive, degenerative, and incurable. It needs a better strategy if it wants to defeat us, though. It must sap our will to resist. It must corrupt our joy in living, and steal the love we feel for our friends and families, the gratitude we feel for the good times, and the grim satisfaction we feel for successfully crossing the wastelands of pain, stiffness, tremor, and confusion between the good times.

Parkinson's disease won't kill me, and I refuse to live my life in fear of the suffering it can inflict. I choose instead to scream in its face, to dare it to do its worst, to pit my minimal strength combined with the awesome power of friends, family, and God against Parkinson's, to live with brio, chutzpah, panache.

I choose to live in open defiance of Parkinson's disease.

Corey D. King

2
Alpha And Omega

Being deeply loved by someone gives you strength, while loving someone deeply gives you courage.
- Lao Tzu

Sometimes even to live is an act of courage.
   - Seneca

The first time I kissed Amy was in the spring of 1984. I was a senior at The University of Texas at Austin and an Air Force officer candidate, and I lived with a group of other Air Force ROTC cadets in a house in far south Austin. I was looking forward to graduation, commissioning, and pilot training, unencumbered and free to navigate.

We rented the house from our Air Force ROTC instructor, a captain who had been reassigned at the beginning of my last year in college. The captain had shepherded us through the Professional Officer's Course and knew our strengths and weaknesses, and should have known better than to rent to us. I blame him for the misfortune that befell his house that last year.

The house was not exactly pristine when we moved in. The good captain had a huge black dog named Bjorn who was flea-infested and indiscriminate about his excretory habits. It took six bug bombs, a whole box of industrial-size garbage bags, and a hazmat suit to make the house fit for human occupation. We actually improved living conditions in the house, briefly. It wasn't difficult - an occasional pass with a leaf blower and periodic sessions with a bow and arrow in the back yard to control the rat population in the woodpile did the trick. We even cleaned the pool once or twice during the fall semester, usually after parties to make sure there were no bodies in the deep end.

However, all our good housekeeping was undone during Christmas, when my other roommates and I abandoned our roommate Barry. The winter of 1983 was the coldest I had ever experienced in Texas, and I spent the holiday in Dallas. On Christmas Day the low temperature was 6° F.

In a choice between a six-pack of beer and a gallon of antifreeze, beer usually wins for a college student. I had plenty of water in the radiator of my car, but only because water was free. My radiator froze, and the engine block cracked. I didn't return to Austin as quickly as I anticipated after Christmas, because I needed to stop every five miles on the drive from Dallas to add oil and water to the engine. It wasn't an inconvenience, since I was already stopping to add power steering fluid, brake fluid, and transmission fluid.

The unprecedented cold snap also gave Barry a few challenges as our unwilling home caretaker. The pool pump, filter, and plumbing froze and shattered, as did several of the external water spigots around the house. Everything would have been fine if the weather hadn't warmed up again. Barry came home from wherever he went during the day to find that most of the pool had migrated to the front yard, and several new fountains were spraying festive jets of water from unusual locations around the house.

Barry, an emerging military leader and responsible young college student, responded as you might imagine. He found the water shutoff valve, closed it, and left to spend the rest of the holiday someplace else. I happened to be one of the first of the roommates to return from Christmas break. Always the keen observer, I noticed after a stop in the bathroom that the water was turned off in the house. It took me somewhat longer to realize there was both no Barry in the house or water in the pool, but I leapt into action. I found the valves to isolate the pool pump, used a little duct tape after that failed to produce results, finally called a plumber that was willing to bill us (poor, dumb, trusting plumber - the last of his clan), and then, when we had running water again, washed my hands of the whole mess.

There should have been a leader someplace in our group of college-educated almost-officers who could have taken control and solved the problem. There wasn't, and by the time of our spring break party we not only still had a broken pool, but we also had a swampy, stinking mess in the bottom of the pool that was spawning new life forms.

Amy and I met only weeks before I invited her to our party. We were sitting on the edge of the concrete hole that was formerly our pool, talking about everything and nothing. I was already hooked and suspected that I was done looking even before I started, but I had no idea if she felt the same way. Sometimes I still don't. I think she likes it that way.

Our conversation reached a comfortable lull, and we both lapsed into silence, with nothing but the screams and raucous laughter of the other party-goers and the gentle bubbling of the science experiment in the bottom of the pool to interrupt the quiet. I don't know who leaned toward whom first - we'll say it was me, because I'm telling the story. We met in the middle, aligned noses after a few feints and false starts, and...

I had been kissed before. The first time was when I was about five years old, by Susie who lived down the street. Although I had a crush on her, I vowed there would be no more of that nonsense. It was undignified and unsanitary. My attitude changed with age.

There can only be one first kiss with the love of your life. I won't describe it - if you've been there, I don't need to, and if you haven't, you wouldn't believe me. That kiss is not the reason we are still married thirty years later, but it's among the top ten reasons.

First times are important. The first time to ride a bike, drive a car, drink a beer, hold your newborn son or daughter; they're milestones, and they shine in memory.

Last times are also important. I've done things that I once loved for the last time, like skiing the backcountry at Breckenridge, drift diving in Cozumel, running on the beach in Maui, or climbing a ladder to install an antenna. When I'm doing something I enjoy, I occasionally wonder whether it will be the last time.

Several years ago, I ventured into the desert with my friend Gene to take a defensive handgun class for the first time. I returned twice, each time thinking, "this may be the last time." I am happy to be wrong so far, although it gives Amy indigestion and headaches. She worries about me, and not without cause - I did fall though the ceiling in our bedroom only five years ago, trying to wire the house with network cable.

When I meet someone extraordinary, they don't always look as I expect. An instructor at my second handgun training course, a crusty old bast... ahh, gentleman who was a former military diver, demolition expert, firearms trainer, wielder of pointy objects, and who saw nothing wrong with jumping out of a perfectly functional airplane, was working with me.

On the first day of the class, I told the range master I had PD. He thanked me for the information and asked a few questions, but was unconcerned. Word apparently spread, though, because I received extra attention for the first few exercises, mostly from the instructor we'll call CB (for Crusty Bast... ahh, Gentleman).

The point of the "one ragged hole" exercise was to shoot a series of rounds through the same hole in a paper target to demonstrate that we understood the concepts of good handgun marksmanship. It sounds impressive to say we were shooting at targets 100 meters away, so we'll go with that. Too much honesty damages a good story.

When it was my turn to shoot, CB approached me and asked how many times I had attended a course there. I admitted to one previous experience, and he said, "Badass, huh? You think you can do this?"

Instead of spouting the string of excuses, caveats, and conditionals that immediately came to mind, I said, "Sure, I can do this. Where do you want the hole?"

He smiled. He probably used the same expression to scare adversaries in combat before dispatching them. It was not a pleasant sight. He said, "Center of the target will be fine."

My first shot was indeed center of target, but my second shot was six inches lower. He snorted and said, "I thought you said you could do this. Don't jerk the trigger; press it back and make the shot."

Stress usually makes Parkinson's symptoms worse, but apparently stung pride counteracts the effect. I put the next three rounds through the same hole as the first shot. He said, "That's better. I may even let you keep that fancy pistol. Keep going."

I made my ragged hole a little bigger with the next three

rounds, and then jerked the next one towards Egypt. CB shook his head and said, "You know, you have an obligation not to waste every fourth shot. Work on it." He then put a hand on my shoulder and said, "You're doing fine. We're not going to take it easy on you, though."

The more I thought about that three-minute interaction, the more I was impressed by the wisdom, compassion, honesty, and practicality CB showed. He said more in three minutes about what it means to have a chronic disease in the real world than I've been able to say in the last seven years. Yes, it sucks to be sick, but the standards don't change. Yes, eventually I won't be able to shoot, but today I can. Yes, my body and mind are failing, but so are everyone else's. No, I'm not the best shooter here, but I am here.

I'd never before been inclined to see God in my interactions with other people. On that day, I saw God in a craggy, crusty old Navy master chief who spoke plainly and let me know there were no kitchen passes available today, but he was aware of the challenge.

Among those with degenerative illnesses, death may be the ultimate taboo subject. Everyone dies, but thinking about it is perceived as pessimistic and morose by almost everyone, and unfortunately perceived as a lack of trust in God's providence and grace by many people with faith.

I'm not afraid of death. However, I am afraid of ceasing to live while I'm still alive, of merely existing without purpose. That's why I am compelled to live as well as I can, while I can. I wish it had not taken the Parkinson's alarm bell to create my sense of urgency. Every day is a fresh opportunity, though.

The people that I am blessed to know make my life worth living and give it purpose. I only knew CB briefly, but he changed me and I'll remember him for the rest of my days.

In the Bible, the apostle Peter said if we want to love life and see good days, we need to do some things with our lips and some with our lives. He was referring to our relationships with other people. I can live a good life only if I focus on the people in my life, and I can't just talk the talk; I need to walk the walk as well.

Living well isn't about adventure and new experiences, although they're fun. It's about CB and others like him. It's about talking with my children, and being amazed at how much they know and what good people they are. It's about going to a support group meeting and sitting with someone who needs to talk, or who I need to listen to. It's about watching a movie with Amy, laughing at all the same dumb jokes, and making up new dumb jokes. And it's about discovering that Amy has been waiting prayerfully for almost thirty years for God to get my attention, and finally being able to share that part of our lives.

The Native American Shawnee chief, Tecumseh, had a unique insight on living and dying well. He said:

So live your life that the fear of death can never enter your heart.
Trouble no one about their religion; respect others in their view, and demand that they respect yours.
Love your life, perfect your life, beautify all things in your life.
Seek to make your life long and its purpose in the service of your people.
Prepare a noble death song for the day when you go over the great divide.
Always give a word or a sign of salute when meeting or passing a friend, even a stranger, when in a lonely place.
Show respect to all people and grovel to none.
When you arise in the morning give thanks for the food and for the joy of living.
If you see no reason for giving thanks, the fault lies only in yourself.
Abuse no one and no thing, for abuse turns the wise ones to fools and robs the spirit of its vision.
When it comes your time to die, be not like those whose hearts are filled with the fear of death, so that when their time comes they weep and pray for a little more time to live their lives over again in a different way.
Sing your death song and die like a hero going home.

To live honestly, without fear or regret, in the service of your people, giving thanks and being grateful to God to the end; a difficult standard but a worthy goal.

3

He Ain't Heavy

No greater love hath a man than he lay down his life for his brother. Not for millions, not for glory, not for fame. For one person, in the dark where no one will ever know or see.
- J. Michael Straczynski

That's a terrible idea - what time should I be there?
- Unknown

My brother Ken and I stopped traveling together for several years while we both focused on other concerns, and when we were both ready to start again, we headed to Nevada together for his first and my third shooting class. We went to Front Sight, a firearms training institute in the desert southwest of Las Vegas, where we attended a four-day class in handgun safety and defensive handgun techniques.

Amy was supportive, as usual. She asks more questions than in the past, but my answers were acceptable. No, we didn't intend to shoot each other. No, I didn't intend to gamble, drink, or consort with questionable people (except Ken). No, I didn't intend to take a side-trip to Area 51 and visit my gray-skinned, three-foot tall space friends.

Ken taught me skills and talents as we grew up together that have served me well in my adulthood, and a few that I might have been better off without. He is not shy about sharing his knowledge with me (even, and perhaps especially, when he doesn't have any), and some of my most memorable and formative experiences were due to either his active participation or his noteworthy absence.

Our family mythology states that I raised myself. I was the youngest child by about six years and mercifully, my parents were focused on other concerns by the time Ken left home. I was not left completely to my own devices, though. I had Ken's example (both real and imagined) to fall back upon.

Ken and I are similar in many ways, but the family mythology placed us in different roles. He was the rebellious, gifted athlete but poor student that everyone liked, and who could sell icebergs to the Inuit. I was the quiet, serious nerd boy who preferred books to people, and who never met a standardized test he couldn't ace.

Neither Ken nor I fit into the molds that were created for us. Ken definitely is a gifted athlete, but is also one of the smartest people I know, and is both an excellent student and insightful teacher. I'm agnostic on whether he can sell air conditioners in Alaska, but he was able to convince me of almost anything when we were younger. He was rebellious and non-compliant as a teenager, but it was a survival response to the experience of growing up in our family. And, I have heard rumors that not everyone likes him, although I've never seen objective evidence.

On the other hand, I am every bit as brilliant as I am reputed to be (and modest to a fault), but I'm not quite as serious as we all thought. I am an excellent test taker, and also outstanding at cheating and getting away with it. I am also very good at surrounding myself with talented, capable people, which is why my own children turned out so well. Marry wisely, and the rest is easy.

I love telling stories about my brother, but the Aesop's Fable approach to growing up with Ken misses the "I can't believe we lived through that" nature of the experience. I could talk about the two separate occasions when my parents went on extended vacations and left Ken in my care. He complained about my cooking both times; I was not yet thirteen, and he was seventeen. I could talk about the occasions when he took me on dates with him when he was in high school, because he liked me and he thought his friends would too. I could tell a story about my first six beers (it involves Ken, a long weekend, and the phrase, "here, take this and leave my friends alone.") I could even talk about the night we ended up at a biker wedding reception and drank several hundred dollars worth of Kamikazes without actually being invited to (we ended up in a taxi, I was carrying the leg of a broken bar stool, and Ken kept muttering, "I'll be ok – I'll just meet you at the pier"). I could tell all these stories, and more, but I'd hate to create the right impression.

Ken taught me to hit, kick or catch every type of ball known to Americans. He taught me that the way people look has nothing to do with the way they feel. He taught me to play pinball, to throw a newspaper at 3 AM, to laugh instead of scream. And though I doubt he knows it, he helped me survive the darkest times in my life so far, because I believed that he would survive, and if he could maybe I could too.

So, after a long traveling hiatus, we headed to the desert for a little brotherly bonding amid fire, smoke and hot metal. Before departure, I reminded him that I have a brain implant; he reminded me that his knee implant is completely manual, and he doesn't need batteries. I pointed out that I have a degenerative, incurable disease; he said, "Oh? Just the one?" I mentioned I would be bringing 210 pills and 24 syringes with me, and he said, "Well, at least you'll have something to eat. I may need to fast all week."

We're not competitive at all.

Corey D. King

4

Come And Take Them

What do we say to the Lord of Death? Not today.
- George R. R. Martin

Shall I tell you what the real evil is? To cringe to the things that are called evils, to surrender to them our freedom, in defiance of which we ought to face any suffering.
- Lucius Annaeus Seneca

According to legend and history, King Xerxes I of Persia at the Battle of Thermopylae in 480 BC demanded that the Greek Army lay down their weapons and surrender in the face of the overwhelming power of the Persian Army. Outnumbered by about 20 to 1, the Greeks might have been forgiven for complying with the demand. Certain death awaited the 7000 Greeks, Thespians, Thebans, and a few others, and their deaths might have faded unnoticed into history if it had not been for King Leonidas of Sparta and The Three Hundred.

The Spartans were born for war. From about 650 BC to 371 BC, they were the preeminent military power in ancient Greece. Their society was focused on military training and excellence. Their women were as tough and dedicated as their men, and enjoyed a level of equality unprecedented in the classical world. Their entire culture embraced the virtuous military values of duty, honor, and sacrifice, and so when Xerxes demanded that Leonidas and his force of 300 hand-picked Spartan warriors lay down their weapons and surrender, he responded, "μολὼν λαβέ (MOLÒN LABÉ)!" which translates roughly as "Come and take them!"

Leonidas, The Three Hundred, and most of the assembled Greeks at The Hot Gates were slaughtered by the Persians, but The Three Hundred inflicted heavy losses on the Persians and significantly delayed their progress toward Athens. Leonidas' defiance was a rallying cry to the Greek Army, and in subsequent land and sea battles the Greeks halted the Persian invasion, and Xerxes lost most of his 150,000 troops.

My brother Ken and I didn't succumb to hordes of Persians in a valiant but doomed last stand at Thermopylae. We did complete our four-day class in defensive handgun techniques at Front Sight Firearms Institute in Nevada, though, and took our rightful place in history.

The class was not trouble-free. My main physical problem during the course was bradykinesia (slow movement – one of the many joys of Parkinson's), which is usually not helpful in a gunfight. However, you can't miss fast enough to win, so speed isn't always an advantage. They also say that "slow is smooth and smooth is fast," so it stands to reason that I should have been the fastest shooter in the class. Not hardly, although I may eventually get an award for being the shooter with the best dancing rhythm. Dyskinesia, a side-effect of long-term use of Parkinson's medications, is sometimes mistaken for really bad dancing. It comes naturally to me, because I'm a really bad dancer in the best of circumstances.

As it always does, Parkinson's intruded randomly on our fun. On the last day as we were preparing for the final test, I began to sway to the dyskinesia waltz, and not only did my accuracy and speed diminish, but my balance, coordination, and safety suffered. As the episode of dyskinesia worsened, I decided it was time to stop shooting, and I dropped back to the shaded area at the rear of the range to rest and recuperate. I was armed with a weapon I wasn't carrying on my last trip to Front Sight, though; an injectable rescue drug for PD. My self-administered injection was the riskiest thing I did during the entire trip; I was much more apprehensive about safely hitting my thigh from six inches with a tiny needle than hitting a paper target at fifteen yards with my 1911. The injection worked its magic, and in half an hour I was ready to get back into action, just in time for the test and the man-to-man shooting challenge.

The man-to-man challenge is a single elimination contest. The goal is to shoot a set of targets in head-to-head competition before your competitor does, and to avoid shooting penalty targets. The first finisher in each pair proceeds to the next round of competition; hitting a penalty target is cause for immediate elimination

With over forty people in the class, about fifteen minutes elapsed before the range master called my name. Unfortunately, I saw my brother fall to the competition after shooting a clean round with three well-placed shots, beaten by only a tenth of a second. We commiserated, and I promised to avenge his honor if I had the opportunity. Secretly, though, I remembered when he was teaching me to play soccer, and he kicked a soccer ball at me so hard that it knocked the breath out of my unborn children. Younger brothers have long memories, and I fleetingly thought, "serves him right, dammit."

On my first round of shooting, I took several unplanned practice shots, and then dropped the three scoring targets while my opponent was busy destroying all the penalty targets, the landscape, and an unsuspecting lizard or two with dozens of shots. I was still slightly dyskinetic, so I did a little dance to honor my first round victory, bowed accidentally to the class, and sat down to wait for my next opponent.

On the next round, I beat the unfortunate fool who had damaged our family honor, and avenged Ken. I bowed to him and danced a jig in celebration.

For the third round, the field had narrowed considerably, and there was no competitor for me to shoot against. The crowd was feeling gladiatorial, though, and instead of allowing me a bye, they forced me to shoot the course with no opponent. I dropped the scoring targets with three careful shots, amid cries of, "not that one!" and "miss, miss!"

My fourth round was against a friend that Ken and I met in the class, one of another pair of brothers with a similar sense of humor. I dropped the targets with four shots, and finished ahead of our former new friend. The crowd began to turn in my direction, sensing there was an underdog event in the making, and I received an enthusiastic round of cheers.

My final round was against Connor, a finely-chiseled mountain of a man who was polite, professional, and had a plan to shoot everything he met. Our range master introduced us to the slavering crowd like a couple of prize fighters, and the crowd cheered and screamed for us both. I turned down the volume on my electronic ear protection and waited.

"The range is set. Ready…fire!"

I missed with my first shot, but scared all the paint off the target. Connor connected with the penalty target, and emptied his gun in rapid-fire frustration. I glanced to the right and saw him standing with his pistol slide-locked, looking disgusted. The competition was mine to lose – all I had to do was to drop my targets without hitting the penalties.

Three trigger presses, three pings. The scoring targets dropped, and I won the competition. No one was more surprised than me, except for everyone else in the class and all three instructors. Ken swears he knew all along. I believe him, because he's not only a great brother, he's my friend. He's had my back for over fifty years, and he is one of a small group of people I trust with my life. He also beat me in the final skills test, so he could afford to be magnanimous.

I won bragging rights and a Front Sight Challenge Coin. I won't go down in history as anyone noteworthy, but I'm pleased with myself anyway, and the experience reminded me of a valuable lesson for those of us with challenges and threats to face (a list that includes everyone): attitude can change everything.

Another Spartan story underlines the lesson. Philip II of Macedon, after invading southern Greece and accepting the surrender of numerous city-states, send a message to the Spartans: "If I enter into your territories, I will destroy ye all, never to rise again." The Spartan Council merely responded, "If."

Later, as Philip continued his campaign of conquest in Greece, he sent another communique to the Spartan Council, asking if they preferred that he enter their territory as a friend or as a foe. Their response: "Neither." Deeply intimidated, Philip never invaded Sparta. Neither did his son, Alexander the Great.

μολών λαβέ! Nuts! Damn the torpedoes, full steam ahead! We're surrounded – that simplifies things. Here I am. Either with your shield or on it. Come and take it.

When faced with overwhelming odds, when things seem hopeless, when outnumbered, outgunned, outmatched – attitude makes a difference.

Resist. Defy. Disobey. Rebel. Persevere.

Corey D. King

5

Fantastic Plastic

Heroes are made by the paths they choose, not the powers they are graced with.
- Brodi Ashton

Heroes may not be braver than anyone else. They're just braver 5 minutes longer.
- Ronald Reagan

I loved building airplane models when I was young. It thrilled me to see the aircraft's graceful shape emerging from a pile of plastic parts, and in my imagination I would strap into the jet I was building and slip the surly bonds of earth. I logged hundreds of hours of flying time during these flights of fancy. It was clearly a fantasy, though; I was never airsick and never caused the aircraft to spin unintentionally.

I was an untutored and unskilled model builder. I didn't have any modeling tools, so I borrowed knives from my mother's kitchen drawers. Not only were they not well-suited to the task, the small thefts didn't endear me to my mother. I could afford very few paint colors and supplies, so everything was either black or white, and usually ended up a mottled shade of gray, because the only paintbrush I owned was about a foot wide.

My biggest limitation was my lack of patience. I became so impatient to see what the finished model looked like that I skipped whole sections of the instructions, didn't paint anything, got more glue on the outside of the aircraft than on the seams, and often found later that I had glued critical parts to the seat of my pants or my forehead in my haste to see the wondrous aerodynamic beauty pictured on the box. My models never looked like the box, but I had hope.   My situation is different now, and I've started building models again. With an additional 45 years under my hat, I am more patient. I can buy more than one paintbrush and two colors of paint. The models are different, too. It's now possible to spend more on a model of a fictional spacecraft than on a nice dinner for two at Ruth's Chris Steakhouse.

There is a downside; model-building isn't a social activity. I understand there is something called a "group build." I'm not sure what it is, but I think it's wholesome. There's an upside too, though - a model of an F-35, an Me262, or a P-51D is much less expensive than many of my other toys, and I don't have pangs of guilt and regret after going on a wild paint-buying spree. The people I meet in modeling stores all have interesting stories, and my standard poodle Izzy doesn't mind keeping me company and sleeping on a chair while I build a model. She is a dedicated companion, but she doesn't approve of gunfire, and doesn't even want to be in the same county during my trips to the range.

Building models gives me a sense of accomplishment and competence that's important for anyone, and it's good for my mind and my hands (although less so for my backside). Building models keeps me thinking and interested in learning, but it also has a more important purpose.

My neurosurgeon (now, there's a phrase I didn't expect would ever apply to me) was recently honored for his achievements at a dinner, and I was honored to be asked to speak on his behalf. He implanted the electronic system in my brain that, along with medication, keeps me functional, and I hold him in very high esteem.

I spoke about his skill, his self-effacing humor, and his ease in the operating room, and recounted some of the highlights of my implantation surgery and three battery replacements at his hand; all boring and uneventful, just as he promised.

Then I gave him a model I had built of an Air Force fighter jet that coincidentally, I helped to design as a young engineer fresh from college. Without his skill and commitment as a surgeon, I would not have been able to build an F-16 model, much less walk to the podium and tell him what he had done for me. I was thrilled, and I think he was, too. His thank-you letter explained that the model sits in a place of honor on his young son's bedroom shelf, as an example of what daddy does and why it's important.

I build models because I can, but I can only because of people like Arnold, and Eric, and Tony, and Kathy, and Maria, and thousands of others who have given their lives and talents to people like me. I try to live in defiance of Parkinson's after their example.

Corey D. King

6
The Grace Of God

If Heaven exists, to know that there's laughter. That'd be a great thing.
- Robin Williams

Always remember you are braver than you believe, stronger than you seem, smarter than you think, and loved more than you know.
- Christopher Robin, *Winnie The Pooh*

When I learned of Robin Williams' death, I had no intention of writing about him. I was familiar with portions of his professional presence, but I have no right to express a viewpoint about how he lived his personal life. His death still strikes too close to home.

I learned, however, that he was a person with a form of Parkinson's disease. He was was still in the early stages of Parkinson's with Lewy Body Dementia, but I know that severe depression is often an early symptom. His private battles with depression over the course of his professional life, as well as his attempts to self-medicate with drugs and alcohol, were possibly the result of Parkinson's disease. But in the end, I don't know anything about him. I don't know his anguish, and I don't know what horrible tortures caused him to end his own life.

I have heard Robin Williams both vilified as a coward and celebrated as a hero. He may well have been either; at one point or another, we all have the capacity to be both. The facts that he had Parkinson's disease, and that he struggled with depression, alcohol and drug dependencies, and that he committed suicide, don't make him either coward or hero. I don't know what those facts make him, but I know that I feel kinship with him regardless. I'm probably not entitled to it, but I'm probably not entitled to the kinship that I feel with everyone who has Parkinson's disease.

We undoubtedly are all different; we come from different backgrounds, we've had different experiences, and we're not all as publicly visible as Robin Williams, Michael J. Fox, Muhammed Ali, Linda Ronstadt, or Davis Phinney. We do all share one thing. We are all fighting an intractable enemy. Not all of our battles end the same way, though.

Amy occasionally tells me she doesn't know whether she's talking to Corey or to Parkinson's. I understand how horrifying that must be for her. To not know whether you're interacting with the person you've been married to for 30 years, or with some alteration of that person changed by an implacable disease, must be unsettling.

Where do I stop and where does Parkinson's start? Where does good judgment and personal responsibility end, and disease begin? When do I cease being responsible for my own actions? When do I become someone other than me? I don't know, even though Amy and I are already discussing whether I can be left alone safely, and how much longer I should be allowed to drive a car. I do know that, even though Parkinson's continues to steal from me, I am still me. I suppose one answer is that as long as I can still ask, I'm still me.

Robin Williams committed suicide, and had Parkinson's disease. I don't believe that the disease led to the behavior that ended his life, but I don't know that for sure. What I do know is that for me, it feels horribly wrong to label Mr. Williams as weak-willed or cowardly for having taken the path that he did. I also think it's wrong to condone his choice: "Of course he committed suicide; who wouldn't when faced with such a future?"

When I was first diagnosed with Parkinson's, every conversation with someone I had not seen for a while was burdened by the news of my diagnosis. I remember telling a friend and dive buddy about my unwelcome discovery, and being shocked speechless when he suggested that I might want to take one last dive while I still could, and just keep going down. I couldn't then and still can't fathom the thought of throwing away all the goodness and love that lies before me over fear of pain or disability.

I feel terrible that a man who was so wonderfully talented and who made me laugh so many times felt such anguish that he believed his only option was death. Was he responsible for that decision, or was he absolved by mental or physical illness? I don't know. I don't know what he was thinking when he made that final choice. I believe, however, that as long as we can ask the question, we remain responsible. And I also believe that God wants us to keep asking the question for as long as we can.

Mr. Williams made me laugh more times than I can count, but he only made me cry once, as a character in a movie called The Fisher King. His character was a tortured soul reaching for greatness, but failing - he played the role of the damaged, wounded Parry with such sincerity that I've remembered how sad I was then for almost 25 years. I'm sad to know he was drawing from life experience for the role, and I hope and pray for peace for his family, and for him.

What do I tell people that ask what I think about Mr. Williams' death? That I don't know anything about him - I never met him or talked to him, and I'm not entitled to judge. If they're someone I am close to, though, I tell them that I wish he had known at that instant, as I do right now, that he had the love and support of family and friends, and there was purpose and power in his life, and that he was not alone. I know those things were true for him. It's not up to me, though. I'm sad he carried the burdens he did. And I'm sad he set them down, and is no longer with us.

Corey D. King

7
Fear, Lies, And Self-Preservation

There are two ways to be fooled. One is to believe what isn't true; the other is to refuse to believe what is true.
— Søren Kierkegaard

The senses deceive from time to time, and it is prudent never to trust wholly those who have deceived us even once.
- Rene Descartes

Having Parkinson's disease sometimes feels like riding a roller coaster for the first time, and not being completely sure they've finished building the damned thing. I hate roller coasters even under the best of circumstances, and not knowing if this ride will end where it started, or if the tracks will end before we get home and we'll go flying into the void, adds to the fun. I know many people love both roller coasters and suspense. Have my portion - I've got enough nausea and uncertainty, thanks.

Chronic disease attacks the core of your self-image. I think that most people, and maybe men in particular, would prefer to see themselves as strong, self-sufficient, competent, reliable, and perhaps above all, unafraid. Life tries to flip each of those characteristics on its head, but chronic disease seems to flip them all at the same time.

At one time or another, we all tell ourselves lies just to survive the day, and we sometimes even believe them.

"Afraid? Me? Nahh - I actually LIKE rattlesnakes."

"No, thanks, I don't need any help. I meant to fall off the curb."

"Ask directions? Are you KIDDING? My middle name is Magellan."

"I've been skiing since I could walk, thanks. And no, that's not a tree branch sticking out of my head; I'm just having a bad hair day."

The lies we tell ourselves help us maintain the "me" picture in our own minds. With some, the lies are small and inconsequential, because the truth and the fantasy are close enough to require only minor scaffolding. Some lie to themselves about almost everything, and the true unfortunates don't even know they're lying.

I think that a chronic incurable illness steadily makes our fictional self-image more and more implausible until one day, we're unable to believe the fiction, and the universe shifts around us. It's jarring to realize that you're not physically strong any longer, nor self-sufficient, nor competent at anything you choose to be, nor reliable, nor fearless. Even if you never actually were any of those things, the fiction dies hard.

On some nights, I'm afraid to go to sleep because I know I'll wake up choking and unable to breathe. Even if I take the right medications on schedule, carefully plan the timing and content of my meals, and don't eat anything at all past 8 PM, sometimes I still feel the burning at the back of my throat and the foul, bitter taste in my mouth that presage the worst of my nights. If I lay down to sleep, I'll wake up coughing and choking in less than an hour, with the added downside of scaring the daylights out of Amy, Izzy, and Skitter, the stray cat who recently adopted me. So, I sit up and wait for a better day tomorrow, and until daylight returns I think about the universe shifting around me.

I don't know with certainty and I never will, but the evidence indicates that the chronic, degenerative, incurable disease that is a part of my life was caused by exposure to toxic chemicals during my 10 years of military service. The Federal government (notoriously difficult to convince) agreed immediately when they looked at my case.

I'm not who I used to be, but maybe I never was. I can't bench-press 300 pounds or run the quarter-mile in 50 seconds anymore, but one of those is a lie anyway. I'm not an island of rugged self-reliance, but I have more friends and better relationships now, and I'm better for it. I can't ski or scuba dive anymore, but I can still build a nice F-15D in 1/32 scale if you give me a month, and shoot the wings off a fly with a .45 under carefully controlled conditions. I can't run a business anymore, but I'm fortunate to be volunteering for a non-profit organization with great people who let me do what I can. And I'm not a steely-eyed, square-jawed fearless missile-man rocket scientist, but with faith, family, and friends, my fears are manageable, and I can still spit in Parkinson's eye.

And for better or worse, I'm still me.

Corey D. King

8

Tinfoil Hat And Matching Shoes

After everything I've been through, the last thing I'm going to apologize for is my paranoia.
- Richard Finney

Cure sometimes, treat often, comfort always.
- Hippocrates

I'm fascinated by secrets and conspiracy theories. I spend too much time on YouTube and fringe websites watching videos and reading about aliens, secret underground bunkers, shadowy government programs, black helicopters and men wearing black suits, and other, even more unsettling topics, as if the foregoing wasn't weird enough.

I've been a science fiction fan since almost before I could read. I love the sense of wonder science fiction brings. Science fiction gives me the sense that the universe (both the parts that we understand,

and the parts that we don't) ultimately makes sense, and although we will probably never understand everything, there's a chance that we could someday.

The best science fiction feeds our thirst for hope and nurtures our desire for explanations. At my most lucid, I don't believe the things that I read in science fiction, but I still sometimes wish they were true. As Jedediah Nightlinger said in the John Wayne movie *The Cowboys*, "...if it isn't true, it oughta be."

As a Christian with Parkinson's disease, hope and faith figure strongly in my life. I could not survive each day without the hope that tomorrow will be better, and the faith that with God's help, I can go on whether it is or not.

The phrase "with God's help" is a new part of my lexicon, and I still sometimes struggle to reconcile it with my skeptical nature. I do think that we are all caught in the struggle between our greatest hopes and our deepest fears, and at such times we have a tendency to believe the most outlandish things.

Everyone is entitled to believe what they choose, and sources of hope and faith are widely varied. However, some of those beliefs are harmful. I think that some people affected by a chronic, incurable disease such as Parkinson's tend to believe that a cure is just around the corner, and will suddenly emerge like the sun after a thunderstorm if we stay vigilant.

We breathlessly exchange snippets of information gleaned from the Internet about previously unknown treatments, therapies, positive research results, or breakthroughs. Our conversations often contain an undercurrent that the medical establishment is conspiring to keep these emerging treatments from us but that the truth is out there if we can only find it. In the time since I've been diagnosed, I have seen this phenomenon with Coenzyme Q-10, coconut oil, stem cell therapy, the disease-modifying potential of rasagiline, forced exercise, cinnamon, glutathione, curcumin, and medical marijuana, to name just a few.

I'm aware that there are people who are itching to tell me I'm wrong, that one or more of these treatments or something that I haven't mentioned is truly the secret to success, and that all that I'm doing is diverting people from the search for the truth. So be it.

I think that we have to evaluate claims about cures or new therapies using a technique that Carl Sagan once described as "the baloney detection kit." It's not rocket science; it basically says that claims require evidence, and extraordinary claims require extraordinary evidence. It does not eliminate the possibility of a revolutionary breakthrough and it does not limit the potential for hope and faith. It does keep us from being drawn in by the most egregious of the snake-oil claims, and gives us armor in our battle to get through the day.

What do I suggest, as an alternative? I try to live each day fully regardless of whether or not a cure is imminent, finding things to do that are valuable and useful, with my eyes on the horizon and not on my own feet. Every day, I try to exercise and learn something new. I tell my wife and my children that I love them every day, and I tell my dog and cat that I love them about every 15 minutes because they're here more often. I take my medications as prescribed, and I check my DBS battery level occasionally. I have hope for the future and faith in God, my family, friends, and doctors. And about everything else, I'm skeptical.

I'm no more closed off to the possibility of a miraculous cure tomorrow than I am to the possibility that aliens actually exist and they live in my guest bedroom. I just think it's not likely. In the words of an old business colleague, "Fascinating, if true."

We are all entitled to find sources of strength and hope where we can, without anguish, despair, and pain. There's enough of those in the world. The sources you rely on are a choice - choose wisely.

Corey D. King

9

A Cure Any Day

If we knew what it was we were doing, it would not be called research, would it?
- Albert Einstein

Learn from yesterday, live for today, hope for tomorrow. The important thing is not to stop questioning.
- Albert Einstein

Before I was diagnosed, Parkinson's was just another of the many rare diseases that I knew very little about. Tourette's - isn't that the one where people have outbursts of foul language? Huntington's - runs in families. Essential tremor - Kathryn Hepburn. Parkinson's - old people who shake, and Michael J. Fox.

Seven years, roughly 45,000 pills and three DBS batteries later, I know more, but still very little. The reason is simple - no one knows what causes PD, and although we are getting smarter all the time, a cure is not imminent. Even if there were a "eureka" moment somewhere tonight (I envision a lone researcher, working feverishly in a darkened lab illuminated by a single desk lamp. She swirls a test tube and the contents turn red instead of blue. "That's it!" she shouts. "Call the NIH!"), by some estimates it would be eight to fifteen years before the magic bullet hit the street.

The process is not necessarily broken, either. It takes a long time because careful science takes a long time, and careful science protects lives more often than revolutionary cures do. The alternative is being surrounded by zombies, alone in New York City with only your German shepherd, hunting deer from the driver's seat of a Mustang Cobra, like Will Smith in the movie I Am Legend. Or, on a much more somber note, the alternative is another Vioxx; another Fen-Phen; another thalidomide.

Bringing a new treatment to people who need it takes time so we don't inadvertently kill people while we're saving them. From my limited perspective, the problem is that there isn't anything going into the research pipeline that may eventually come out the other end in 15 years. I recently asked someone well-positioned to know if there any prospects for a cure in the next 5 to 10 years. He didn't even speak; he just shook his head.

Awareness doesn't actually have any effect. Awareness of Parkinson's, Huntington's, essential tremor, dystonia, or any of a host of neurological disorders that we don't understand will do nothing to solve the problem if it's not accompanied by action. Awareness is self-soothing – it provides the illusion of having an impact on events without the necessity of actually having an impact. "Yes, I am aware that there is genocide going on in Somalia. Terrible. Pass the roast beef, would you, please?"

Awareness is valuable when it is followed by action. Walk or run in support of research, and form a team or obtain sponsors. Comfort a friend who needs it, and instead of saying "let me know if you need anything," ask, "Can I bring you dinner on Thursday? There's a new exhibit at the McNay - would you like to go with me on Saturday?" Learn and be aware; then teach. Then, come together and act.

Money and research are important, but connectedness and community are just as important. Money and research will eventually enable us to find a cure. Our connectedness will help us get through this night, and the next. We may not be close to a cure for PD; on the other hand, there may be one discovered tonight. In the US alone, however, there are more than 1 million people with PD who will get out of bed tomorrow and use the gift of life as well as we can. We can't rely solely on the hope for a cure. There's too much living to be done to wait for the phone to ring.

Corey D. King

10

Blessings Like Stars

Decision determines destiny.
- Israelmore Ayivor

Never underestimate the power you have to take your life in a new direction.
 - Germany Kent

I once feared for the future. None of the fears I envisioned have come to pass.

Amy and I are not destitute and living in a refrigerator box under a bridge, although some are, through no fault of their own. I have not bankrupted us through compulsive gambling or uncontrolled spending, a real concern among people with Parkinson's who take certain medications to control their symptoms.

There are diseases worse than Parkinson's - I don't have them. I did not have a bad experience with brain surgery; on the contrary, I owe my life and continued ability to function to the expertise of a very skilled and dedicated neurosurgeon and his team, to an extraordinarily gifted neurologist, to one of the best medical assistants anywhere who I am honored to also call a friend and colleague, and to a host of other healthcare professionals without whom I simply could not live.

I have not dived into a pit of depression, either from the effects of the disease or from the reasonable and normal response to incurable illness, although many have. I have not become isolated and marginalized by PD, and I have not become irrelevant. I can't do some things, but I can still function, and my days are still filled with joy and satisfaction. I can no longer hold down a job, but I'm doing worthwhile volunteer work with great people. They do the work, and I show up and take the credit. It's a great system, and I wish I'd discovered it years ago.

I have not lost my friends and family or driven them away. I have the best friends anyone could ever hope for (some of them I have known for over half my life, and some are new, but all are extraordinary). I'm so proud of my children that I talk about them to everyone I meet, and it's not about what they do, it's about who they are. They make good choices and are genuinely good people, and I even like their friends; even, and maybe especially, the Aggies.

And Amy...

She's a gift from God.

And I had nothing to do with any of it. I don't deserve any of it. I can't claim that my blessings are the result of exemplary behavior on my part, any more than I can claim that tragedy only happens to those that deserve it or that someone is always at fault if you look hard enough. It may be fashionable, but it isn't true.

All I can be sure of is that we spend too much time deciding who to hate, and pointing fingers at what's wrong, and not enough time marveling that anything is right, much less that so much is right.

Focus and attention determines reality - we are all free to choose how we respond to the things that happen to us. Sometimes, it's the only thing we actually are free to choose.

Viktor Frankl, an Austrian author, neurologist, psychiatrist, and survivor of the Holocaust, one of the most horrible events in human history, put it elegantly:

"Everything can be taken from a man but one thing: the last of human freedoms - to choose one's attitude in any given set of circumstances, to choose one's own way."

Freedom to choose - either to focus on what's wrong and be consumed by it, or to raise your eyes, focus on what's right and be elevated by it. The choice seems clear to me. As a friend of mine loves to say, "So, how's that working out for you?" I regularly have to remind myself that if I've made a choice that's not working out, I can choose again.

I can't choose not to have Parkinson's disease. I can choose not to wring my hands about it and spend my days moaning, or as my niece Kelli puts it, "contemplating my misfortunes on the Tree of Woe."

There's no doubt that Parkinson's causes suffering. I don't intend to send the message that I am unconcerned about the pain and misery this disease causes. On the contrary, my days and nights are an almost constant battle against pain and misery.

One of the weapons that works for me, though, is to give no ground to Parkinson's. I will not give it a minute of my time and energy without a fight, and I certainly won't allow it to choose for me how I feel about my life.

Not every day, hour, or minute is good. There are fewer good times than there used to be. Barring a miraculous cure, I will not prevail against this disease, regardless of how much of a positive attitude I maintain. I don't care - I'm not going to capitulate.

One of the gifts I received from my military background (other than Parkinson's disease, of course) and from my later training in personal defense was an understanding of "the combat mindset." The combat mindset, simply put, is a commitment to never giving up, never throwing in the towel, never deciding that the fight is lost.

Winston Churchill described the combat mindset this way:

"…never give in, never give in, never, never, never, never—in nothing, great or small, large or petty—never give in except to convictions of honour and good sense. Never yield to force; never yield to the apparently overwhelming might of the enemy."

Others have expressed the concept in other ways:

"It does not matter how slowly you go so long as you do not stop."

"Never confuse a single defeat for a final defeat."

"Fall seven times, stand up eight."

"Courage is not about having the strength to go on; it is about going on when you don't have the strength."

"Be on your guard; stand firm in the faith; be courageous; be strong."

"So do not fear, for I am with you; do not be dismayed, for I am your God. I will strengthen you and help you; I will uphold you with my righteous right hand."

We all die; it's how we live that matters. Michael J. Fox, the actor, Parkinson's patient and advocate, and one of my personal heroes, has a unique view on living well with Parkinson's, and it applies to all of life regardless of the challenges we face:

I didn't choose to have Parkinson's disease, but surrounding that one non-choice are a million choices I can make.

If that's not freedom, I don't know what is.

11
Common Valor

I am fated to journey hand in hand with my heroes and to survey the surging immensity of life, to survey it through the laughter that all can see and through the tears unseen and unknown by anyone.
- Nikolai Gogol

Heroes are ordinary people who make themselves extraordinary.
- Gerard Way

Davis Phinney is a Tour de France stage-winning cyclist and athlete who was diagnosed with early-onset Parkinson's disease when he was 40 years old. Rather than resting on his laurels as a world-class athlete and successful sports commentator, public speaker, and journalist, he established the Davis Phinney Foundation in 2004.

The primary mission of the foundation is to help people with Parkinson's live well today. Their main activity is the Davis Phinney Victory Summit, a one-day seminar that includes presentations by researchers, clinicians, physical therapists, professionals, caregivers, and patients. The goal is to empower people living with Parkinson's to enhance their quality of life.

In 2015, the Davis Phinney Victory Summit came to San Antonio for the first time, supported by a very large number of of local organizations, clinicians, and medical practices who help people fight back against Parkinson's. Organizations like the World Parkinson's Congress and the National Parkinson Foundation were there, as well as pharmaceutical companies and medical device manufacturers critical to the fight to live well with PD.

I've been fortunate to work with one of those groups, the SA Moves Foundation. SA Moves is a non-profit foundation created by a group of physicians, Parkinson's advocates, and medical professionals who were kind (or crazy) enough to ask me to lead them. SA Moves is chartered to provide educational programs for patients, care givers, and medical professionals involved in caring for people with Parkinson's and other movement disorders.

However, I have never had a conversation with a foundation. I have never had a heart-to-heart chat with a corporation, shaken hands with a consortium, or gotten a hug or a pat on the back from a society. The organizations that made the Victory Summit so successful for the almost 700 people who came are essential, but they are made of people, and it's the people and the web of relationships that we create with each other that make it all work.

I was fortunate enough to meet Davis Phinney and shake his hand. I joked with him that several people had asked me if I was him, and a few had asked if I was his brother. He said he was flattered, and he hoped I was too. We agreed that we were a couple of good-looking guys, which seemed more ego-preserving than agreeing that we were similarly ugly. Davis Phinney is an icon among the cycling community and among PWPs, but he's also just a nice guy who goes out of his way to put you at ease and who is easy to talk to.

At the Summit, I spoke with people who were newly diagnosed and who were scared, and I spoke with people who were deep into the advanced stages of Parkinson's and who were scared. I reestablished acquaintance with people I had not seen for a few weeks, and people I had not seen for years. I talked with people who I had never met before, and people I have known for 20 years. I taught some; I learned some. I joked with people, and I was struck to the core by stories of suffering that would make Job pale. I told people how much their example means to me, and I was blessed to have a few people tell me I was a source of inspiration and comfort to them. And throughout the day, one thought kept recurring to me; how lucky, how fortunate, how blessed by God I am to be in the company of such heroes.

There's no question in my mind that the people with whom I spent my day that day are heroes. The people who live with PD every day; the people who provide care and support; the people who use their expertise and steady hands to ease suffering; the people who conduct research, develop drugs and devices, and help people to understand them; the people who build organizations that fund and deliver the services that are critical to living in defiance of this abominable disease.

People with names like Tony, Claire, Maria, Sheila, Tommy, Eric, Amy, Paula, Cindy, Sean, Larry, Heather, Davis, Jo, Laura, Ken, Scott, Michael, Becky, Vikki, Robin, Arnie, Chris, Leticia, Peggy, Beth, Trisha, Patrick, Gretchen, Glenn, Kasondra, Marjorie, Kathy, Richard, Melinda, Steve, Christina, José, Patrick, Rebecca, John, George, Chris, Mary, Doug, Andrew, Karen, Robin, Philip, Ruth, Javier, Carol, Teri, Israel, Caroline, Catherine, Jean, Bill, and millions others around the world who go to war every day with PD, HD, dystonia, essential tremor, Tourette's, and other intractable, incurable diseases.

You are all my heroes.

Corey D. King

12

Cinéma Verité

All through my life, I have been tested. My will has been tested, my courage has been tested, my strength has been tested. Now my patience and endurance are being tested.
- Muhammad Ali

Life is a succession of lessons which must be lived to be understood.
- Ralph Waldo Emerson

Amy and I love to watch movies together. I would not choose the movies she chooses, and so our evening movie-watching adventures become an opportunity for my personal growth. I am not allowed to choose the movies we watch, which is an opportunity for refinement of my self-control and patience. I'm apparently partial to movies that Amy describes as "Gilligan's Island in space." She has no tolerance for such nonsense. So, we watch meaningful movies. "Meaningful" is defined as "with dialogue in a foreign language, with subtitles in a different foreign language, with characters that are indistinguishable from one another discussing obscure topics." One such meaningful movie features Max Von Sydow dressed as a medieval knight playing chess with Death on a beach. I don't know why; I suspect Max doesn't either.

Documentaries are also popular during movie time. The last one we watched was entitled, *Death And The Civil War*. Historically speaking, there was a lot of death during the Civil War. There was even more death during this documentary, which was fascinating. I had no idea that refrigeration, embalming, and many mortuary technologies were developed during the Civil War to manage the huge number of soldiers killed in action on both sides of the conflict. Even more fascinating was the shift in social convention and public and private attitudes about death that occurred during the Civil War. This little aside proves I was not sleeping, and gets me off the hook.

Amy and I both have a set of movies that we call "blankie movies," named after my daughter's security blanket, which she still carries (although not while on duty) as a successful 25-year old labor and delivery nurse at a major hospital. These movies are familiar and comforting and bear repeated viewing, and we both have about 15 or 20 movies in our individual blankie movie lists. We watch Amy's together; I watch mine after she goes to bed. Not a single one of my movies is entitled *Gilligan's Island In Space*, but thirty-year marriages, like life, are not always fair.

One of Amy's blankie movies is called *Molière*. It tells the story of a French actor and playwright during the mid-17th century. Molière developed into one of the first and most successful comedic playwrights in history. He fancied himself as a commentator on serious subjects of the day, and longed to be serious-minded and sober. His serious writings were terrible, though, and he regularly was pelted with rotten vegetables when he tried to perform anything but his comedies and farces.

I write a blog about living in defiance of Parkinson's disease called "The Crooked Path." One evening, I asked Amy if she had read my last blog post, in which I tried to comment learnedly about some damn thing that was briefly important to me. She had. I asked her if she had any opinions about it, and she said, "Molière was better at humor, and came off as kind of a prig when he didn't play to his strengths. Good night, honey. Enjoy Gilligan." I have no idea what she meant, but I think she called me an ugly name.

It's easy for me to become bogged down in the solemnity of dealing with an incurable disease, and to begin to take life, and myself, too seriously. Sometimes the burden of daily management of a disease that doesn't improve becomes overwhelming, and a blankie movie helps. Sometimes, though, nothing helps, and pain, stiffness, tremors, inability to walk or talk, or confusion conspire to drain the enjoyment from life. These "off" periods, when the medications aren't working and my symptoms are at their worst, are walks through the wastelands that help to remind me how sweet the good times are, and even provide a grim satisfaction of their own.

I was a sprinter in high school. My race was the quarter mile, and I entertained the conceit that I was actually good at it until I tried to walk onto the track team at The University of Texas at Austin.

During the off-season, though, my high school track coach Randy Changuris insisted that I run on the cross country team. I did not love running those three-mile races, but I loved the ten-mile training runs even less. During cross country season, I never felt the simple joy of running as fast as I could for as far as I could - I instead felt the burning in my chest, the leaden weight of my legs, and the irritation of being passed by all the distance runners on the team, chatting and laughing with each other while I tried not to swallow my own tongue.

I occasionally succumbed to bad influences. After running out of Coach Chang's sight, I would find a comfortable spot on the route and spend the workout relaxing and chatting with other misplaced sprinters. These transgressions didn't feel right, though, and usually my fast-twitch sprinter buddies and I would slog through the workouts, praying for relief and thinking about Coach Chang's 5-gallon tank of Hawaiian Punch in the team van.

Coach Chang would often take us to a hilly spot in a state park not far from our high school on weekends for a change of scenery. These were different times, and there was no need for parental consent or volumes of documentation and permission slips - we just went. I remember Chang following us in the team van, screaming "burst the crest, burst the crest!" from the driver's seat, as we struggled up hill after hill with the bumper of the van inches from our heels. I don't think he would have actually driven over us if we had failed to sprint over the top of each hill as commanded, but he was not above letting us wonder.

I remember the pain and exhaustion of those workouts, made

worse by my conviction that sprinters didn't need distance workouts, since sprinting was all natural talent anyway. I also remember feeling a grudging sense of accomplishment for completing a workout, even if the reward was nothing more than an easing of the pain and a plastic cup of diluted, lukewarm Hawaiian Punch.

All of life's experiences are training for experiences yet to come. I had no idea that, struggling up those hills with Coach Chang on my heels in the team van, I was training for Parkinson's off-time forty years in the future; I thought I was merely staying on Chang's good side and enjoying the scenery (the girls' cross country team worked out with us, and they were beautiful to watch).

Now, as I shuffle my way through an off period, I remember enduring. I remember bursting the crest, hitting the tape leaning forward, and accelerating through the finish line. I remember the taste of Hawaiian Punch, as sweet as Amy's laughter at the thousandth retelling of a joke during a blankie movie. I don't have to remember the beauty of the scenery, though.

Amy is a distance runner.

13
That Was Then, This Is Now

Such knowledge is too wonderful for me, too lofty for me to attain.
- Psalms 139:6

Be sure you put your feet in the right place, then stand firm.
- Abraham Lincoln

I was once a confirmed agnostic. I had thought through all the arguments, and made a conscious choice to be "absent of belief in a god or gods." I joked that I wasn't all that different from my friends and family who believed in God; I just believed in one less god than they did. I also believed that I was not insufferably arrogant, and not just as smug in my arrogance as I thought those I ridiculed were. I was wrong.

I called myself an agnostic rather than an atheist because I felt the intellectual need to acknowledge I might be wrong. My comment was typically, "I might be wrong. But, I don't think so." I was comfortable with the illogic of this position, and I felt an unshakable superiority to people who believed in "medieval superstition and wishful thinking." I was deluding myself.

I was well-educated in the arguments against belief. I could talk about the Problem of Evil all day long: "How can a God who is all-powerful, all-benevolent, and all-knowledgeable exist when suffering and evil are present in the world?" I had the answer, too: "He can't. Next question."

I could point out that we were all non-believers in something: "Do you believe in Zoroaster? How about Ra? Mithra? Zeus? Eck? Surely you believe in Xenu? Allah? Buddha? Ahh, a fellow atheist, then?" I was clouding the issue, because I didn't want answers.

I was proud of my intellect, and I told myself (and everyone else) that there were no mysteries that couldn't eventually be explained by scientific inquiry. I could explain (with just a hint of condescension) that the more we learned, the less space there was for the "God of the Gaps" to exist. I prided myself on my expansive thinking, never realizing just how narrow-minded and unimaginative I was.

Not even the horror of learning I had Parkinson's disease shook me; it's just the breaks, I thought. The randomness of the Universe, the power of the bell curve. Someone has to win the lottery, someone has to have Parkinson's. There's no need to crumple now, just because I pulled the short straw. I'm not weak-minded or weak-willed. I'll just soldier on, and…what? Try not to think about it? Yeah, I'll do that.

I had decided what I thought, and I didn't want to be distracted by alternatives. I was also unwilling to consider alternatives, because of a frankly horrible childhood that soured me on the concept of a benevolent God who had a personal interest in me. "God loves me, eh? Then, where was He when I was screaming silently in the dark? Where was He when I begged Him to save me? No, I don't believe there is a God. And, I hate Him."

My friend Larry asked me a simple question. "What has having Parkinson's disease done to your theology?" He tells me he had never asked anyone a question like that before, and hasn't since. It was the first snowflake in a snowstorm that changed my life. We exchanged emails for almost three years. I wrote some of the most moving treatises against belief that I had ever read, and I was passionately convinced by myself. Larry, not so much.

Larry and God kept dropping snow on me, and when Larry introduced me to "the guys," a group of friends and fellow believers who met regularly to talk and share ideas about faith, the storm intensified. When my friend Gene joined in the discussion, the mountainside began to move.

No one convinced me; the avalanche that changed my beliefs was not an intellectual shift. I still have doubts, questions, uncertainties. I didn't think my way to belief in God by reexamining and eliminating all the arguments against God I was so skilled at delivering. I can't explain it. I wish I could; it would make my relationships so much easier. It's a wholly personal experience I can describe, but I can't give a checklist for getting there.

I didn't want it to happen, but God touched my life. He didn't give me any answers to my questions, other than the Big Question. I know He exists without a doubt now, and I don't attribute that knowledge to Larry's emails, discussions with the guys, walks in the woods with Gene, or my own chin-scratching cogitation in the middle of the night. I don't attribute it to fear of the unknown from having Parkinson's disease, or from a shift in my emotions or thinking processes as a result of the disease. I was much more comfortable with my eyes closed, but now they're open and I have work to do, learning what this change actually means.

It's always been important to me to be intellectually honest - if you asked me if I could be wrong, I'd say "Well, sure I could be wrong." This is not an intellectual issue for me, however. I tried to use my intellect to both escape and pursue God, and I was using the wrong tool.

Could I be wrong? No, not about this. I had an experience I can't explain; God touched me. I have a lot of learning still to do, but of that I'm sure.

Corey D. King

14

Halloween And The Importance of Wearing Pants

I have been driven many times upon my knees by the overwhelming conviction that I had no where else to go. My own wisdom and that of all about me seemed insufficient for that day.
- Abraham Lincoln

Fate whispers to the warrior, "You cannot withstand the storm" and the warrior whispers back, "I am the storm."
- Unknown

When I was young, I loved Halloween. Halloween gave me the opportunity to roam my neighborhood at will, seeing things and going places I visited during the day but which held a special newness and excitement at night. From the time I was seven or eight until I was twelve, I bid my parents goodbye as the sun set, and didn't show up at home again until people stopped answering their doorbells, at 9:30 or 10 PM. It was a different time – if my parents ever worried about me, I didn't know it, and my only restriction was an injunction against unwrapped candy or apples (I grew up thinking that every apple I received on Halloween had a razor blade in it, although I never heard of that actually happening to anyone). Mysteriously, all the $100,000 Bars and Hershey's Minis also disappeared from the evening's haul, and I didn't know to blame my mother until she confessed years later.

I received my first real kiss on Halloween night ("real" being defined as not followed by either a punch in the nose delivered by the lucky girl, or a chorus of "ooh, gross" from onlookers on the playground). Karen, I don't know what ever happened to you, but you set the standard until the spring of 1984.

Halloween was pure freedom to me; limitless opportunity, unknown joys, something wonderful at every door and around every corner. Occasionally I would stumble across my brother Ken and his friends, out on the town and unreachably far away in time – six years older. Ken was always good to me, but he seemed especially welcoming on Halloween, as if he knew what I was feeling.

I loved knocking on strangers' doors, and I liked peeking inside to see how they lived as much as I liked the candy they gave me. Christmas and Easter held their own charms, but to me, Halloween represented the promise of a world hidden but not threatening, of unbounded potential.

Too soon, Halloween lost its special charm for me. I still remember the feeling of roaming the nighttime world, though, surrounded by friends, feeling both that I could meet any challenge that I encountered, and that the challenges would all be small. I misplaced that confidence for a while, but a glimmer of what I felt on Halloween night helped me to endure some darker nights that followed.

Before Amy retired (prematurely, just as I did), she asked me every day when she came home from work, "So, what did you do today?" I usually gave her a short list of items and activities that are not like they once were, but are not so bad nonetheless. "I worked on an airplane model, I went to the park and crashed a quadcopter, I went to the range, Izzy and I went on a long walk, I went to the grocery store, I vacuumed the house (actually, I pushed the button, and the Roomba vacuumed the house – endlessly fascinating), I worked on a book, I wrote emails, I went to a board meeting," or whatever it was that day.

Usually, the list was just one or two items long, and almost never more than three. However, one day, although I was joking, I said, "Well, I put my pants on." I actually did put my pants on; I wasn't joking about that. However, later I realized that for more than a week, I had not put my pants on more often than I had.

My world is shrinking, but some of the shrinkage is within my control. Parkinson's disease is insidious and relentless, like a boa constrictor. Boas don't kill by crushing their prey with one mighty squeeze – they wait until you relax slightly and exhale, and then they tighten up just a little so your next breath isn't as deep. Then they wait for you to relax again, and when you do, they tighten just a little more. Eventually, you can't inhale at all. That's unhealthy, and not recommended.

I had been relaxing. Parkinson's squeezed each time I did. I avoided exercise; what was the point? Squeeze. I stopped trying to eat a healthy diet...squeeze. I lost interest in engaging with the world, volunteering or just visiting with friends...squeeze. And I stopped putting my pants on every day...BIG squeeze.

I realized I was giving up. I no longer saw the world as limitless, full of opportunity, and unbounded. I sometimes forget that faith is made to be relied upon – God is a limitless, unbounded wellspring of hope when you run out, free for the asking. So, as odd as it may sound, when things are bad I rely on God to renew my Halloween spirit. I don't really understand, but I'm confident God does. And that gives me not only the energy to keep going, but the desire to keep reaching. As Robert Browning said, "Ah, but a man's reach should exceed his grasp; else, what's a Heaven for?"

Exercise is very important for a Parkinson's patient, and I'm the first to recommend it to others. I'm not so great at living up to my own recommendations, and that is partly why I began to lose my way. I resolved to do better.

After months of hints and reminders, I finally accepted my friend Sheila's invitation to a Rock Steady Boxing for Parkinson's class. Rock Steady Boxing is an exercise program designed specifically to help people with Parkinson's fight against the physical and mental deterioration that accompanies the disease.

I have never even been to a boxing match, and I lost the only fight

I had when I was young (unless you include the time my brother Ken kicked me squarely in the right cheekbone in a play karate fight – in that case, I have lost two fights). Sheila assured me, though, that no one would either punch me or kick me in the face. One less thing to worry about, I thought. My DBS implant and I took her at her word, and I showed up at the gym, ready to punch some bag.

It took a while to get to the punching. First, there was the stretching and the rotating and the large-stepping and the bear-crawling. Wait just a minute, I thought – is this an exercise class? I get plenty of exercise with the TV remote – I'm here to hit something.

Just as my suspicion that the class was designed to be beneficial reached a peak, we stopped with the exercising and our instructor Steve handed out boxing gloves and told us to find a bag and a partner. I partnered with a kind, unsuspecting, trusting lady who was experienced in the ways of Rock Steady and promised to show me the ropes. Poor Sue. I hope she recovers.

I love velcro, but never more than while trying to put on a pair of boxing gloves when just emerging from an "off" episode. When I'm off I feel like I'm already wearing boxing gloves, so I struggled to put on the pair Steve handed me. The velcro helped enormously, and my lack of a sense of smell kept me from realizing that the wrist flaps I was tugging with my teeth were saturated with the sweat of eons.

I have absolutely no training in the manly art of boxing, but I would be damned before I would admit that to anyone. Pain is an excellent teacher, and I quickly learned to punch from the shoulder and stiffen my wrists to avoid the "accordion effect" – those Saturday morning cartoons weren't wasted after all.

We started with a left-right jab combination, moved on to a left-right jab and left hook combo, and ended with jab combos followed by uppercut combos. That's what everyone else was doing, anyway. Chuck Norris had become my spirit guide, and I was beating the crap out of that bag, freestyle. And Sue as well, unfortunately, who was caught between the bag and the wall, bouncing back and forth like a pinball caught between two bumpers (young guys, find an old guy like me and ask).

Steve dropped by and suggested I stop killing Sue, and I reluctantly agreed. I learned something else: I like hitting things, and it's hard to stop when adrenaline becomes a factor. I also learned that I feel much safer beating up people and things that can't fight back than I do taking a swing anywhere near Steve, who looked like he could not only take a punch, but could deliver one, too.

Paper targets don't shoot back; double-end bags don't punch back, either, so all my thrashing and flailing didn't really do anything but make me sweat profusely and feel like throwing up. Hey, I thought, just like Parkinson's. That thought was worth another uppercut; I missed the bag, of course, and almost caught Steve south of the border. Steve is a professional, and he has spent enough time working with my people to be on guard; he dodged, saved his huevos, and I nearly punched myself in the head. Chuck Norris, where are you when I need you?

I had a blast, and Rock Steady is now a part of my routine. I'm hoping that Sue will forgive me, drop the lawsuit, and just punch me a few times instead.

Corey D. King

15

Never Alone

Fear is the mind-killer...
- Frank Herbert

There is no illusion greater than fear.
- Lao Tzu

My mother-in-law Jeanette and my friend Gene were just married. They have known each other for nearly sixty years. Gene and Amy's father Bobby were friends in the Army, and Gene's wife Frances and Amy's mother Jeanette were also friends. Their lives and the lives of their families intersected repeatedly both before and after Amy's father died suddenly and tragically more than 20 years ago.

Jeanette lost Bobby to a sudden heart attack in 1993. He was young, only 55 and full of life and laughter, and his passing was unexpected and devastating for his entire family. Jeanette, a survivor from a family of survivors, learned to live without him, but the pain of his absence only lessened over the years and never disappeared.

Gene lost Frances, his wife of over sixty years, to Huntington's disease last year. She had been sick for a long time, and although her death was not unexpected, it was devastating nonetheless. Gene had time to prepare, but it's impossible to prepare for such a loss. Gene and the entire family miss her terribly.

Neither Gene nor Jeanette expected the confluence of events that led to their marriage. Gene became my friend, mentor, and confidante, but I had known him for less than six years. Jeanette had known him for six decades. Our extended families once again intersected when Gene and Frances returned from a long mission trip to Africa, and I saw him at least once a week for several years. Our families shared holidays and birthdays, joys and sorrows, and a fair amount of good food, and we also shared the tragedy of Frances' death, and grieved with Gene and his family.

It started small, but cascaded quickly. It was only two months from a friendly dinner that was (in retrospect) a first date to the wedding, but they had known each other for years as friends. That friendship grew into something more, and they were married on February 20, 2016.

Even at 81 and 70-something, Gene and Jeanette are still newlyweds. Rumor has it that Gene is somewhat set in his ways, and Jeanette had learned to live on her own successfully after being a widow for 22 years. As all committed newlyweds do, they're working it out, learning to live with each other, establishing new relationships and trying to manage existing relationships. It's a handful; they're overachievers, and they managed several major life events simultaneously in the space of just a few weeks. They're also building a house together with all the attendant decisions and collisions of preference and personal style. I'm exhausted just thinking about it.

They live in Austin temporarily while their house is being built, and then they'll move to San Antonio. This marriage business isn't for sissies, and they are anything but that. I'm waiting to see what they'll do next.

Amy and I visit them regularly in Austin, but not yet as often as in the past; every newlywed couple needs time to set up a household and firm up their relationship without spectators.

We visited recently, though, and spent two days with them. Gene and I went to the shooting range, and Amy and her mom went to home furnishing stores, nurseries (the plant kind; no new siblings are in the plan), and hardware stores to gather supplies to make Gene's former bachelor pad look a little less Spartan.

It was a long day, and we ended it with a barbecue. Amy and I spent the night with the happy couple, since it was too late to make the trip back to San Antonio.

I was "unwell" that night - I don't know why, but it happens sometimes. My digestive system doesn't work well even under the most benign circumstances, and we had a long day and a late dinner, conditions which sometimes conspire to cause problems for me.

I didn't get much sleep that night, and when I took my morning handful of pills, there was no noticeable effect. I was as off as I ever get (my deep brain stimulation implant keeps me from going too low), and I was stiff, shaky, and shuffling. Gene and Jeanette had seen me this way before so no one, including me, was upset.

We sat down to a sumptuous breakfast I was completely uninterested in eating. As the food began to make the rounds and morning conversation flowed, I noticed I was having more difficulty than usual with movement. I wasn't shaking or dyskinetic - I couldn't move at all, and the harder I tried the worse it got. My hands clenched into fists, and I couldn't unclench them. My legs wouldn't move. I couldn't turn my head. I was frozen in place in my chair, and I panicked.

I was once a scuba diver, and I loved the feeling of being underwater. I was a somewhat experienced diver with over 300 dives logged as a dive master, and I was comfortable in the water. I had experienced a few minor emergencies underwater, mostly equipment failures and problems with students, and I had handled them adequately.

A student once panicked during a mask clearing exercise. The goal of the exercise was for the student to remove their mask underwater, breathe for 30 seconds without a mask, and then replace the mask on their face and clear the water from it. The student choked on water during the last part of the exercise, and tried to make a dash for the surface, 40 feet away. That can be fatal, so I slowed the student's ascent by grabbing him by a chest strap and accompanying him slowly to the surface. On the way up, he thanked me by ripping off my mask, clawing the regulator from my mouth, and punching me in the throat. All in a day's work as a dive master.

The only time I remember panicking during a dive was during dive master training. The exercise was relatively simple; working with another diver, we were supposed to share air while solving a problem underwater. The problem we were solving is unimportant; the purpose was to provide distraction from the life-critical activity of breathing using someone else's equipment when mine wasn't working.

I was so focused on solving the problem we were given and so comfortable in the water that I forgot to use my equipment properly. When the exercise was over and I transitioned back to breathing from my own equipment, I choked on a mouthful of water.

In my overconfidence, I started the transition on an exhaled breath. I was already air-starved, and I struggled with my equipment. Regardless of my efforts, all I got was water. I gave my partner the "chopping hand across the throat" sign that means "I'm out of air," to a diver, and he gave me the OK sign, not understanding I was serious.

In the clear light of day I knew what to do, and I was not actually in distress. I had at least another thirty seconds before my need to draw a breath overwhelmed me. I had options, and if I had relaxed and recalled my training, I would not have reached out to my partner and snatched his regulator.

My theft of his air source was a surprise to my partner, but he calmly transitioned to his alternate air source, and we began a controlled ascent to the surface.

I remember the feeling of being sure I was going to die, as the freedom I normally felt underwater was replaced by pervasive claustrophobia. The water pressed down on me, and fear and panic closed my mind and froze my muscles. I felt the same way during my first significant Parkinson's freezing episode at Gene and Jeanette's house.

My panic spiraled out of control, but I still couldn't move. The harder I tried, the worse it became. It's embarrassing to admit, but I began to sob with fear. Once again, I felt like I was going to die, and there was nothing I could do about it.

Everyone swung into action on my behalf, though. Amy went to get my rescue injection, and Jeanette got a cold cloth to hold to my head and talked to me to help me relax. And Gene began to pray, in a calm, deep voice, with his hand on my shoulder.

I finally unfroze enough to inject myself, and the freezing episode faded away with no lingering physical ill effects. The episode scared everyone badly, though, me most of all.

In the clear light of day, on the surface and with the crisis behind me, I can see that I was in no danger, and that all I needed was medication. In the midst of the episode, though, conscious thought abandoned me, and I needed Amy, Jeanette and Gene.

I needed medication; Amy took care of that. I needed to relax so I could use the medication; Jeanette's insight and kind spirit helped there. And I needed to remember that God was with me, and that I didn't need to be afraid. God, through Gene, filled that need.

I have written about fighting back, not giving in, rebelling, resisting, defying Parkinson's disease. It's difficult to do those things alone, though. Alone, my strength fails. Alone, my fears overwhelm me. Alone, I fight for no purpose. Alone, I am not equal to the challenge.

I am not alone.

Corey D. King

16

Decent Proposal

A man's daughter is his heart. Just with feet, walking out in the world.
- Mat Johnson

The most important thing a man can do for his daughter is to love her mother.
- Theodore Hesburgh

My daughter Rebecca will be married soon. Her fiancé Chris is my son Andrew's good friend, and Chris met Rebecca through their friendship. Andrew's friend Willa is Chris's good friend also, and Andrew met her through his friendship with Chris. They're a tight-knit group, with a large circle of friends that enjoy many of the same things: hiking, camping, rock climbing, biking, good food, and good music. They are also Texas A&M graduates, which originally was an issue for me. I have since grown, and I recognize that The University of Texas is not the only university in Texas (it is the best, but not the only).

Amy and I recently vacationed in San Francisco and Yosemite

National Park, and we invited our son, daughter, and their "significant others." We started by meeting in San Francisco for two days, partly to enjoy the restaurants and sights and partly to allow me much needed rest before we headed to Yosemite. A reasonable plan, but it never works out that way.

On my "day of rest" we took a bus tour of the city, had lunch in Chinatown, went to a museum on Fisherman's Wharf, and then had dinner at a great place in Telegraph Hill. We relaxed the next day though, and only visited every church in the mission district and hiked to the park at the top of Corona Heights. Fortunately, my son took pity on me while everyone else hiked; he introduced me to Lyft, and we got a Lyft taxi to the park. He's been well raised, has good breeding, and is instinctually kind to his dad. I credit his mother.

We made the trek to Yosemite the next morning, and set up a home base at the Lodge at the Falls in Yosemite Valley. We spent the next four days hiking, riding mules though the Valley, hiking, climbing a portion of El Capitan, hiking, enjoying the scenery, and hiking.

One of the hikes was to a location above the valley called Glacier Point. From 1872 to 1968, the park caretakers and rangers performed an event called "the firefall" at Glacier Point; they built a bonfire on the edge of the cliff, and as a ranger in the Valley some 3.000 feet below shouted, "Let the fire fall!" they slowly pushed the bonfire off the cliff. It looked like a waterfall made of fire (hence the name). There was also a hotel on Glacier Point, but it burned in the mid-1960's., about the same time the Park ceased the firefall. Perhaps these two events are related.

There is a hiking trail from Yosemite Valley to Glacier Point. It's about nine miles long, and when the kids decided they wanted to hike to Glacier Point, Amy and I begged off. Amy, who is an iron woman and could have hiked up with the kids without a problem, decided to take the bus with me to the top, and we agreed to meet the kids there for lunch. Everyone but my daughter knew this was to be a momentous day, but we were all keeping the secret from her.

Chris had been planning the event for months. Chris does things right. Unlike his Yankee-trained father-in-law-to-be, he came to Amy and me and asked for our blessing before he to proposed to our daughter. He told me he planned to be in San Antonio to "help a friend," and offered to come over for lunch. I contemplated toying with him a little, but decided my humor was inappropriate and told him to come on over.

He had been telegraphing his intent for some time. I attended a concert with Andrew, Chris, Gene, and several others in Austin almost a year before. Chris and I were chatting with one of our companions before the music started, and she asked, "So, how do you know Corey?"

Chris said, "Well, I met Andrew on a bike ride, we had some friends in common at Texas A&M, Andrew introduced me to Rebecca, I fell in love with her, and Corey is Rebecca's dad. And there you have it."

I was touched by his honesty, and impressed by his courage. He seemed a little shocked afterward, though; I've never asked him whether it just slipped out, or whether he had a plan in mind. Too late now, I suppose.

He arrived at the house for our lunch at about noon, and I cooked hamburgers for us. He picked at his, obviously nervous but soldiering on anyway. I tried to put him at ease. He wasn't having it.

He was eager for the beer I offered him, though, so I ate my hamburger on the patio while he drank his beer. And another. And another. We had a great conversation, and talked about almost everything except the subject I knew he had come to discuss.

Amy had come home by this time, and it was almost 4 PM. We sat on the couch and chatted, and I finally decided to take the frontal approach.

"So, Chris, what are you going to do this afternoon? When do you have to be back in Austin?"

He gripped his beer bottle tightly, gathered up his courage, and said, "Well, I guess you know I didn't come to town to help a friend..."

"I suspected," I said, smiling.

"It can't have escaped your notice that I'm interested in your daughter. As a matter of fact, I'm in love with her, and I'd like to ask for her hand in marriage. I've come here to ask for your blessing."

Amy burst into tears. Not wanting that to be his only answer, I said, "We'd be happy to give you our blessing. I can't think of a better person for Rebecca, and we'd love to have you join the family."

There were hugs and more tears.

When we decided to take a vacation to Yosemite and invited Chris to come along, his engineer's mind went to work, and he came up with a plan. The plan was flexible enough to handle contingencies, but he intended to leave California with an answer. As the trip developed, Glacier Point became the place for the question.

Amy and I met the four of them at the top, and as we looked out over Yosemite Valley with Half Dome in the background, Chris told Rebecca he wanted to get some pictures. He asked Amy to be the picture taker, and Amy, who knew exactly what was about to happen, snapped a few preliminary photos and played along. Chris stumbled on a rock, and went to one knee to steady himself. Rebecca scolded him for being clumsy and almost pitching off the cliff, until she realized that he wasn't getting up, and had reached into his pocket.

It had been a cloudy day, but the sun came out as Chris held up Rebecca's grandmother's engagement ring. Jeanette had given it to him just for this purpose, and he had taken it to be modified and resized, making it Rebecca's own. With the glory of Half Dome and Yosemite Valley behind and below them, in the sight of God, her parents, her brother, his friend, and about fifty cheering, clapping onlookers, he asked my daughter to marry him. She said yes.

I want a lot of things, but right now I want three. I want Rebecca to have a remarkable life, full of love and happiness. I want her to have a life companion as loving, dedicated, and good-hearted as I have had. And I want to be able to dance with her at her wedding.

I'm getting all three.

17

Traveling Pains

Traveling with Parkinson's is nature's way of making you look more like your passport photo.
- Corey King

In life, it's not where you go, it's who you travel with.
 - Charles Schulz

Amy retired last year from her teaching career, helping south Texas high school students to appreciate the French language and culture. During my thirty or so years of professional life, I did lots of different things, but I never was that selfless or impervious to insult. She loves everything French, though, and was able to endure school-district politics, parents who just couldn't believe that little Johnny or Jane could ever misbehave in class, and receiving the blame for everything from failing grades to students engaging in behavior in her classroom that would result in
 a prison term on the street.

She put up with all of it for the ten percent of her time she actually taught French, and for those students whose lives she not only was able to change for the better, but who were able to return the favor and change her life as well.

She retired so we could spend more time together and do some traveling before it becomes too complex and difficult. We have been to Washington DC, Pennsylvania, Minnesota, New Orleans and Baton Rouge, San Francisco, Yosemite National Park, and everyplace in south Texas with a cemetery containing Civil War-era honored dead. We've trespassed on more private land than a person really ought to in rural Texas. We've met some nice people that way, and haven't been shot at yet.

The only major difficulty we've had so far has been going through security checkpoints in airports. Everything requires practice before you get the bugs worked out, and although I spent thirty years and over 1 million frequent flyer miles traveling by air while I was working, I usually traveled alone and without Parkinson's disease.

I have a deep brain stimulation implant to help control my Parkinson's symptoms, and I'm not supposed to go through airport metal detectors with it. I'm not sure what would happen if I did, but if there's even a small chance it involves flames and sparks, I want no part of it.

When I tell the TSA agents at the checkpoint I "have an implanted medical device," the usual response is some variation of "Huh?" However, I've received the entire spectrum of responses from "I understand. How would you like to handle it?" to "Male assist for a strip-search, and bring the BIG periscope!" A security guard in the Marrakech airport once asked me to remove the implant, and was unmoved when I told him it would be difficult and would probably kill me. He was inclined to press on and take the chance, but backed off when I asked for some towels to mop up the blood.

It's much easier to navigate the checkpoint as a team, and Amy and I have gained some expertise. No expertise comes without cost, though, and we have left my wallet, my shoes, my iPhone, my MacBook, my jacket, my cane, my belt, and my self-respect behind. That was just the first time – we're much more skilled now.

We've also tried to take things through the checkpoint that, strictly speaking, we shouldn't. I say "we" because I'm team-oriented. "I" have never tried to take a concealed weapon through the checkpoint, but "we" have.

Here's a lesson in logic: "we" minus "I" equals…any married man knows the answer is "me." It's my fault "we" tried to take a small self-defense weapon called a kubotan through airport security, because I was the one who gave the damned thing to the female half of "we," and who failed to remind said female half three times to take it out of her purse. Twice, yes. Three times, no. A clear transgression. We'll laugh about this in ten years or so. It's a shame I won't remember it.

Our travel concerns are different than in the pre-Parkinson's past, too. My startle reflex is almost like an infant's now, courtesy of PD, and sudden sounds make me jump about a foot in the air. I also have a tendency to stare, and I often have the classic "frozen face" of a person with Parkinson's. These characteristics combine in interesting ways on the street in a large city. Picture this: Amy and I are walking down the street in San Francisco or Washington DC, and I hear someone say, "Hey – Texas boy. I like those boots. Take 'em off." I jump, startled by the sound; slowly, I swivel in the direction of the voice; I look at the source of the voice with dead eyes and frozen face, devoid of emotion; I hold the gaze for 30 minutes or so.

Amy sees this behavior as provocative and offensive. I see it as a deterrent to attack. Who in their right mind would attack someone who appears to have the emotional range of an international assassin? However, "we" think it's a bad idea to behave this way, so "we" are currently engaged in an operant conditioning program to eliminate this behavior of "ours."

I've been self-reliant for most of my life, and although Parkinson's has had an impact, I'm still startled when Amy asks me, "do you need to use the bathroom?" when we're traveling. I typically say, "If I needed to use the bathroom, I would currently be using the bathroom, don't you think?"

The mere question makes me need to use the bathroom, though. It tends to reduce the effect of my haughty self-reliant indignation to rebuff her suggestion, and then rush off to find a restroom. I think she knows this; it's a little travel game we play, with the "don't eat that – it's not good for you" game and the "don't stare at strangers on the subway" game. Some games I play to win; some I play just for the enjoyment. These games are not like that.

I am truly enjoying spending time with Amy on the road, and

we're planning more trips both domestic and overseas and learning to live together under new conditions. The conditions are unusual, but all married couples who have any history to their credit have to make accommodations. And, I can still beat her in a staring contest, so I have that going for me.

18
Wobegon Days And Nights

Before you criticize a man, walk a mile in his shoes. That way, when you do criticize him, you'll be a mile away and you'll have his shoes.
- Steve Martin

Good judgment comes from experience, and experience comes from bad judgment.
- Will Rogers

I think I'm different and special. It's the baby-boomer curse – we are the generation that created a marching army of children who believe that participation deserves a trophy and that self-esteem is the same thing as self-actualization. I think the rules don't apply to me; I am a charter member of the Lake Wobegon crowd, where all the women are strong, all the men are good-looking, and all the children are above average. I hate it when reality intrudes on my little fantasy and reminds me that I, too, am prone to the same unavoidable facts that affect us all.

One night, I paid a visit the drugstore in the middle of the night.

Amy was recovering from surgery, and woke up at about 3 AM in pain. I've always had trouble when the women I love are in distress (sorry, my son, but your pain is like mine – we'll get over it. Rub some dirt on it and get back in the game).

It was not very smart of me, but I couldn't stand to see her in such pain, so I got out of bed, put on the nearest pair of pants, and crawled into the truck. I was massively "off," so it took a while, but I finally arrived at a 24-hour drugstore and took my bottle of extra strength Motrin to the checkout.

The young woman at the checkout (her name was Chrystalle, or Gristle, or something similar) rang up my purchase and waited, cracking her gum with a bored, faintly hostile expression on her face while I struggled with my wallet and dropped the bills in the floor. As I finally handed over the money, she said, "Had a few, huh?"

I replied, "No, I have Parkinson's disease."

She sneered, "Yeah, whatever. Have a nice day." I was on a mission, so I didn't rise to the challenge of a teachable moment, but her attitude and insult made an impression.

I expected to have trouble walking and moving. I expected to be unable to run, dive, and ski. Someday, I won't be able to shoot, drive, swallow, and speak and think clearly. I expect to be wheelchair-bound and bed-ridden someday.

I even expected to encounter a lack of understanding about my symptoms from many people I meet. Parkinson's is a rare disease, and even with the efforts of people like Muhammad Ali, Davis Phinney, and Michael J. Fox, PD is still "old people who shake" in the eyes of many. That's why I carry a card in my wallet that says, "I have Parkinson's disease. I may have trouble moving or speaking. Please give me time to communicate. I am not intoxicated."

I didn't really expect to have to fight both PD and the small number of people I encounter who just don't care, though. It's small-minded of me, but it makes me angry.

I get angry when people who should know better knock me down in the airport or on the subway. I walk with a cane about half the time out of necessity; but I carry it with me whenever I travel, as a sign and a warning. There are always people who have their heads deeply embedded in their own concerns, though, who see the cane, see my difficulty moving, and who knock me down anyway. Not on purpose; they just don't care enough to be careful.

I get angry when people who are able-bodied but in a rush use the disabled parking spots. I get angry when someone gives me attitude when I get on an airplane early, or pushes past me on the jetway. I get angry when a cashier becomes impatient when I struggle with my wallet, my cash, my credit card.

I don't stay angry for more than a second or two, thankfully. For every person who knocks me down, there are a hundred who help me up. For every person who uses a disabled parking spot when they don't need it, there are a thousand who don't, and a thousand who need it more than I do. For every person who is rude, dismissive, or thoughtless, there are a million who are kind, concerned, and caring.

I'm not different. I sometimes forget that although Parkinson's is my enemy, everyone is fighting something. I'm not special. People are not required to defer to me, just because I have a problem. Everyone has problems.

I live in defiance of Parkinson's disease, but I have to remind myself that it's no one's fault, and no one deserves my anger because of the disease. On the contrary, I have more reason to be grateful than most, because I see the best in people much more often than I see the worst.

Chrystalle, I have Parkinson's disease. It's ok; it scares me too sometimes. You have a great day.

Corey D. King

19
Claiming Victory

…for the Lord your God is he who goes with you to fight for you against your enemies, to give you the victory.
- Deuteronomy 20:4

When I despair, I remember that all through history the way of truth and love have always won. There have been tyrants and murderers, and for a time, they can seem invincible, but in the end, they always fall. Think of it--always.
- Mahatma Gandhi

It's interesting to me how differently people react when I tell them I have Parkinson's. It's noteworthy and sad how often they tell me about an aunt, uncle, cousin or parent who had PD. Some have no idea what it is, and are interested. Some have no idea and are not interested. And some respond with, "Oh. Ohhhh…," as if I had just told them I had an alien living inside my chest, but it wouldn't be making an appearance until they were safely gone.

Occasionally, I meet someone else who has PD, and hasn't

wrapped their head around the concept yet. That happened in Hawaii several years ago, while I was touring a sugar plantation. The receptionist was a nice, matronly sixty-something Hawaiian lady who was taking tickets with her left hand, hiding her right hand in her lap with a classic PD pill-rolling tremor. I handed her my ticket, smiled, and said, " I think we've got something in common."

I don't know if she thought I was hitting on her, but she guardedly said, "What?"

"I have Parkinson's disease, too," I said.

It's a risk, because sometimes I'm wrong. Even if I'm right, people can perceive the comment as an invasion of privacy. I try not to offend, but sometimes it's worth the risk.

"You do? You're so young! My doctor just told me last week, and I'm scared," she said.

We talked for about an hour, and I think she felt better afterward. She was burdened with misperceptions about Parkinson's, and her fear had filled the gaps in her knowledge. I felt better, too.

I am not the same person I was before I discovered I had Parkinson's disease. I don't know all the ways I have changed; there are changes I probably can't see because the disease has changed my ability to see. Those changes are better identified by others.

I can feel that I've changed in some ways, though. I am more outgoing. I enjoy people more. I would never have talked to my new Hawaiian friend ten years ago. I would have excused it by saying I didn't want to violate her privacy, but the truth would have been that it was my own privacy I was concerned about. I would have never spoken or written publicly about such deeply revealing and emotional subjects as I have in the last seven years. I was too reserved for that.

I rely on other people more. I don't see my reliance as weakness. It's survival. I'm slower in almost every way. I think slowly, I move slowly, and the pace of life is slower. I'm less driven, and the things that drive me are different. I was career-focused; that boat has definitely sailed. Money was both a security blanket and a scorecard. Money could not protect me from PD, and I no longer use it to keep score; I don't even play that game any more.

Improving the quality of my life and the lives of others motivates me now. I'm driven to do as much as I can while I can with the people I love, and to try not to be selfish and crass in the process. I hear the clock ticking loudly, though.

When the end of my time here finally comes, I hope I'll meet it with no regrets, having lived well in God's eyes until the last moment, with memories full of family and friends, happiness, and hard times well-met. I hope I will have defied Parkinson's power to cause despair, that I will have fought the right battles, resisted where and when I should and made peace where I could.

And I hope I can claim victory.

Corey D. King

Part III

Seeking The Way Home

Facts, Faith, and Finding Peace

Corey D. King

Introduction To Part III

It's 3:30 AM, and I need to write. I don't know why. Perhaps it's because I can feel the ability to express myself slipping away, and I still have something to say. Perhaps it's because I want you to read, and say "aww, he's still in there." Perhaps I actually do have something useful to say, and God (or the Universe, or Whoever) wants me to say it. We can decide later - I'll finish writing, and hopefully you'll finish reading.

In the past, I sought as much feedback as possible on my writing (preferably positive). Like most people, I dislike criticism, and at very least I don't want to inflict an unpleasant experience on friends and family who might feel obligated to read what I write. This time, however, I'm avoiding early feedback, both for self-protection and as a courtesy to those of you I usually ask to read early drafts. It's not that I don't care about feedback. It's simply that feedback doesn't matter this time. I have some things to say; hopefully, they'll come out right. If not, they're coming out anyway.

I was not an engaging writer before Parkinson's disease. I was clear and precise, a technical writer, but the most effusive praise I received was that I wrote "just like a textbook." I wrote for ease of understanding, but I was more comfortable avoiding messy emotions or topics without clear answers. I was like that in person, too - interesting, but a little distant.

Parkinson's disease has shaken something loose. I may not be a better writer, but I write about better subjects. I may not be a better person, either, but I think my priorities are better than they once were. I don't pretend to have any special insight, nor do I have any expertise as a philosopher. I violate many of the rules of writing for a popular audience, and this may be nothing more than an exercise in vanity. It's possible that Parkinson's is affecting my judgment and perceptions, and I should stop writing before I alienate people. I can't, though - I may stop publishing, but I know I won't stop writing until either my mind or my hands stop working. I'm interested to see which lasts the longest. I hope it's my mind.

We have a journey ahead of us. During our trip, you might agree or disagree; you might be angry; you might laugh; you might cry; you might even decide to stop reading. It's okay. I usually write for you, but this one is partly for me.

I'd like to think I have evolved over the last few years. I have certainly spent time walking in the wilderness and turning over the rocks. I'll try to tell you what I've found, and what I think it means for me. Maybe it will mean something for you, too. And, although I don't know precisely where we'll end up, it'll be a helluva trip.

1
A Recipe For Truth

fact
fakt/
noun: fact; plural noun: facts
a thing that is indisputably the case.
"It is a fact that Austin is currently the capitol of the state of Texas."
synonyms: reality, actuality, certainty; truth

o·pin·ion
ə'pinyən/
noun: opinion; plural noun: opinions
a view or judgment formed about something, not necessarily based on fact or knowledge.
"My opinion is that chocolate ice cream is better than cabbage."
synonyms: viewpoint, outlook, attitude, position, perspective, persuasion, standpoint

be·lief
bə'lēf/
noun: belief; plural noun: beliefs
a conviction based on cultural, personal, or religious faith or morality
"My beliefs prevent me from serving in the military and using a gun."

I was diagnosed with early-onset Parkinson's disease almost nine years ago, and I've been retired from professional life for seven years. Occasionally the time weighs heavy on my hands. I volunteer for several Parkinson's foundations and I have pastimes and hobbies that keep me occupied, but I still seem to find ways to cause trouble.

Writing lets me keep my mind active and keeps me engaged with the world, but it's no substitute for face-to-face interaction. Personal contact is not always possible for me, but I've made a personal choice not to complain excessively about my limitations. I have had a good life, full of love, happiness, wonders, and challenges, and I will continue for as long as God allows.

I am full of opinions that I don't mind expressing, and I think I'm entitled to them. I don't have the arrogance to pretend that they are anything but opinions, though. I've lived a fascinating life, and I've seen enough to make me less confident in my viewpoint, rather than more confident. I often write about my opinions on my blog, The Crooked Path, and they're not all about living with Parkinson's.

We live in interesting times. There is sound and fury o'plenty, but much of it signifies less than nothing. Expressing strong viewpoints publicly is fashionable, and doesn't require any knowledge - after all, in our egalitarian culture, stupidity and ignorance are as valuable as wisdom and knowledge. Everyone gets a trophy, and every opinion is of the same value. The rub is that not every topic is amenable only to opinion - troublesome facts interfere. That's just my opinion, though.

For instance, it's my opinion that our current president is doing a rather poor job. My opinion is based on my personal interpretation of the facts. The facts are not up for discussion, but my interpretation might well be. My opinion that the President is rude and boorish didn't just fly out of my backside - it's based on my observation of his behavior. You're free to interpret his actions differently, but you are not free to claim his actions didn't occur.

Similarly, my opinion that he is failing as chief executive didn't emerge from thin air. We can look at the same facts and come to different conclusions, but one of us is failing to grasp the concept if we resort to "alternative facts."

Let's consider a non-emotionally-charged example. The speed of light in a vacuum is approximately 2.9979×10^8 meters per second. Dissenting opinion about that fact doesn't change a damned thing. You're free to opine as an "alternative" that it's twelve furlongs per fortnight, but your opinion doesn't alter the speed of light. Some things are objectively true.

Unfortunately, most things are not. Our collective problem, in my opinion, is that we fail to make a distinction between fact, opinion, and belief. Instead, we think everything is opinion-based or influenced by belief.

Consider global climate change (erstwhile called global warming). It is either true that the climate is changing as a result of human activity or it isn't. It's possible that the climate is changing in entirely natural ways we don't understand; it's possible that we are headed for catastrophic changes that have nothing to do with human activity; it's possible that humans are destroying the planet and it's too late to do anything about it. Other scenarios are also possible.

However, this is a scientific issue, not a political or religious question. The time for non-scientific opinions and beliefs is after scientific truth is established. Unless we're qualified to have them, our opinions and beliefs about scientific facts associated with climatology, chaos mathematics, and predictive simulation are about as important as our opinions and beliefs about the existence of gravity.

We used to teach critical thinking in our schools, and I remember learning about logical fallacies in junior high. I received an assignment to send a letter demanding an explanation for logical fallacies in a selected company's product advertising. I sent my letter to the American Tobacco Company, accusing them of a false dilemma for claiming "Tareyton smokers would rather fight than switch." Are there no other alternatives, I asked? In response, they sent me (a thirteen-year old junior high school student) a carton of cigarettes.

Today, false dichotomy is everywhere, and the "if you're not one of us, you're one of them" sentiment runs rampant. Speaking bluntly, I think our current president is a dangerous idiot, and I am flabbergasted by how many people believe this means I must be one of those "other people" - you know, leftist commie pinko flag-haters. I'm sorry to burst the bubble, but there are more than two diametrically opposed viewpoints on this subject. I didn't want anyone to win the last election. I nearly voted for Kinky Friedman, and only because Lincoln, Kennedy, Johnson, and Reagan are dead.

Many Americans have trouble distinguishing between fact, opinion, and belief, but we're clearly not the only ones. I'm sitting in my living room in Texas with my dog snoring companionably beside me and the cats fighting in my lap, so I feel fairly safe in expressing the opinion that Kim-Jong Un has a funny haircut. It's only my opinion, but expressing it and other more serious opinions about his emotional and mental stability would likely get me executed in Pyongyang.

As I write this, North Korea is threatening to detonate a hydrogen bomb above the Pacific Ocean. Hopefully the threat is just bluster, but if it's not, we may be facing global nuclear war. If we destroy ourselves, I think it will be a direct consequence of our collective inability to sort fact from fiction.

Fact, opinion, and belief must work together to create and implement Truth, with an intentional capital. Alone, they are impotent. Together, they are the foundation upon which Truth rests.

Facts form a baseline for our world view and tie us to our physical reality. Opinions tie us together as a thinking species and bring our social and cultural values to life. Beliefs tie us to the Infinite, and are the bridge between our material world and the mind of God.

We're not free to choose our facts. They emerge from our observations of the world and each other, or torn from the fabric of the universe by the human power of the scientific method. However, we are free to choose our opinions and beliefs. We're not obligated to be reasonable when we do, and there is often no discernible link between reality and our opinions and beliefs.

It's fashionable to exempt opinions and beliefs from evaluation, analysis, and criticism, in the name of inclusion or tolerance. Nature admits to no such exemption, though. I am perfectly free to form the opinion that gravity is an evil global conspiracy and to act on that opinion by walking off a cliff. I am also free to hold the belief that when I do, the Supreme Being who created the universe will keep me from falling to the rocks below, like Wile E. Coyote. Give it a try. You'll likely find that Nature has a different set of rules.

To further complicate matters, "facts" are not always factual. It was once accepted as fact that the Earth was at the center of the universe, evil spirits caused mental illness, cats caused the Black Death, and, stomach ulcers were caused by anxiety and stress, as well as many other supposed facts superseded by a deeper understanding of the natural world. Clearly, a heathy skepticism about facts, opinions, and beliefs is required. We have our work cut out for us.

We must think critically, seek facts and truth with a small "t," face those truths without flinching, and trust our own minds. We must form opinions based on facts and the best of our beliefs, and then learn to communicate well enough to find common purpose. And we must be open enough to identify beliefs that bind us together, and not focus on those that divide us. We could start with "love each other as you love yourself, and love God (or Whoever), with your entire being." I'll bet that idea exists in some form wherever Truth exists.

So, why does this rather academic discussion hold any importance to me? What difference does it make?

Unavoidable facts govern my life. I have Parkinson's disease. There is no cure, and none of the current research indicates a cure is imminent. Parkinson's disease is progressive and degenerative. I will never be employed again. I will never ski, dive, or run again. I will continue to experience pain and disability. I will slowly become less able to communicate, to swallow, to move, to think. I will eventually die, probably from the effects of Parkinson's.

These facts don't tell the whole story, though. They help to form my attitudes and viewpoints. I am fortunate to have a wonderful wife and family that loves and supports me. I see life as precious, even more so under the conditions I face. My challenges are no worse than anyone else's. There is more happiness than despondency in my life; more joy than despair; more love than indifference. I still have things to share. I can still participate, and sometimes lead. I have a good life, full of meaning and purpose.

I also believe that all of our lives have meaning. I believe we are here for a reason. I believe the universe behaves rationally according to natural laws, but did not occur by accident. I believe we are not the only intelligent species here, and I hope I live long enough to have evidence. I believe that "we see through a glass, darkly," and that we often miss the point.

I believe God exists. I believe our campfire stories, superstitions, and industrial mega-religions do not reflect the intent and mind of God. I believe that God is largely unconcerned about rules, and is amused by the rules that we have created and imposed on ourselves in God's name. And I believe that God has a plan for my life. I believe I may not like it and I will never see it clearly, but that's no excuse for not trying.

This is my Truth: I have Parkinson's, I am happy, and I have a purpose.

Corey D. King

2
Method In The Madness

To mistrust science and deny the validity of scientific method is to resign your job as a human. You'd better go look for work as a plant or wild animal.
— P. J. O'Rourke

I do not feel obliged to believe that the same God who has endowed us with sense, reason, and intellect has intended us to forgo their use.
--- Galileo Galilei

Dilbert: Evolution must be true because it is a logical conclusion of the scientific method.
Dogbert: But science is based on the irrational belief that because we cannot perceive reality all at once, things called "time" and "cause and effect" exist.
Dilbert: That's what I was taught and that's what I believe.
Dogbert: Sounds cultish.
— Scott Adams

I love science. I don't understand most of it, but I love science nonetheless.

Science satisfies two needs for me. First, it helps to explain the nearly incomprehensible complexity of the universe. It's comforting to know that the same basic principles that describe the behavior of black holes and the shapes of galaxies are in operation when I trip and fall. Astronomer Carl Sagan famously said, "we are star stuff," referring to the fact that all the heavier elements in our bodies and our world were created inside stars and distributed through the universe in colossal supernova explosions. If Carl was right (and you know he was) not only am I star stuff, I am just like a black hole. That's reassuring on days when my legs aren't working, and I fall on the way to the bathroom. I'll take any reassurance I can find.

Second, science shows me the wonder in the universe. Did you know that if you stretched out all the DNA in your body in a single long string, it would reach from the Sun to Pluto? Not just once, but seventeen times? Did you know that, in our galaxy alone, there are likely over 100 billion planets similar to Earth? And that there are over 100 billion galaxies just like the Milky Way visible from Earth? Or that a single solar flare releases 100 billion times as much energy as the first atomic bomb? I did, because of science.

I recently traveled with Amy to The University of Texas McDonald Observatory near Fort Davis, Texas, and had a chance to talk to the working astronomers about their work. One of their most fascinating research projects is an effort to find habitable planets orbiting other stars. The physics, engineering, and technology required to conduct this awe-inspiring research, not to mention the basic fact that we can actually find other Earth-like planets in the vastness of space, just using our brains and bits and pieces of our own planet, are part of the reason I believe God must exist.

Sir Francis Bacon, the 17th century philosopher, jurist, and statesman. was was one of the first to claim scientific knowledge was best gained through observation and inductive reasoning. He thought that by carefully observing the world, and then making and testing guesses about the source of those observations, we learn how the world works. This method of learning is called the scientific method, and it forms the core of rational thought in the modern world.

So, how does the scientific method work? First, we observe. We look around. We use our senses to gather information about the world around us. The sky is blue, but clouds are white. My son looks like Amy, but my daughter looks like her grandmother.

Second, we think of interesting questions to ask about the things we observe. Why does the sky look blue? Why do children have characteristics in common with their ancestors?

We next make a guess, called a hypothesis, about the answer to our question and the reason the answer is true. In developing hypotheses, we're trying to build a general rationale that explains our observations, but also is consistent with other observations and hypotheses. Then, we use our hypothesis to make predictions we can test.

We then gather data, often through reading, discussion, or experimentation, to gather additional observations. Biases can influence our experiments, and not understanding and protecting against them can change the outcome of the experiment. There is no point in conducting an experiment if Nature is not allowed to speak uninterrupted through the results. She will tell us the truth if we learn Her language and listen.

When all the experimentation is complete, we heave a collective sigh of relief and then buckle down to the really hard work: interpreting the data, deciding what answer Nature has given us about our research question, and then deciding whether our hypothesis is true or false.

The process of evaluating your own hypothesis is a little like deciding whether or not to punish your child. It may have been well-intentioned, but if it's wrong, it must be disciplined. As Richard Feynman, the Nobel laureate physicist, science advocate, and bongo player said, "It doesn't matter how beautiful your theory is, and it doesn't matter how smart you are. If it doesn't agree with experiment, it's wrong."

Now that the hypothesis has been evaluated, the real fun begins: creating or modifying theory. In common parlance, a theory, a guess, and a wild-assed guess are the same thing. Not so in the world of science. A scientific theory is a well organized, internally consistent, testable explanation of some facet of the behavior of nature. Some scientific theories approach the solidity of fact, and some are less certain. To a scientist, a good theory carries weight and stature, and has survived multiple attempts at falsification. Good theories not only explain existing experimental observations, they are able to predict observations for experiments that have not yet been conducted. The best theories are beautiful and "elegant"- simple and straightforward. Bad theories are replaced over time by better theories.

Newton's Laws of Motion are an example of a good theory. Isaac Newton, one of the greatest intellects in human history, observed objects moving in a variety of situations and conditions, sat down with his brain and his pen, and wrote one of the most amazing scientific works of all time, *Principia Mathematica*. Within its pages, he developed a set of three laws to describe motion of objects under general conditions.

Newton's laws have stood for 330 years, sufficient to spread us over the Earth and take us to the skies, deep under the ocean, and to the moon. Newton's laws apply under almost all conditions a human can experience, and they precisely predict the motion of every thrown rock, baseball, artillery shell, missile, or skydiver ever to have existed. They are not complete, though, and another genius 250 years later helped us understand more fully.

Albert Einstein was a German-born physicist who lived in the late 19th and early 20th century. He was a patent clerk in the Swiss Patent Office when, thinking about Newton and the motion of objects, he realized that Newton's 17th century laws of motion were not consistent with James Clerk Maxwell's 19th century equations that describe electric and magnetic fields. The cases where Newton's predictions are not correct are outside the realm of common experience, but not outside the reach of Einstein's imagination. He wrote a paper in 1905 containing his insights, entitled "On The Electrodynamics of Moving Bodies," and fundamentally changed our understanding of the universe. Einstein added new insight to Newton's theory of motion and expanded the range of conditions over which we can make predictions, but he did not discard Newton's work; he augmented it with deeper knowledge.

As time goes on, we make fewer and fewer revolutionary changes to our understanding of the universe. We typically do not discard one theory in favor of another; we simply make changes to existing theories and incorporate new understanding, insights, and observations. The scientific method enables us to "stand on the shoulders of giants" like Bacon, Newton, Maxwell, and Einstein without discarding the work that has gone before.

It's popular for non-scientists to claim "well, it's just a theory" when arguing with scientists, as if the theory in question was the product of a long night of drinking followed by an early morning burrito buffet. This is the wrong way to influence a scientist. The theory in question could have been the product of hundreds of thousands of hours of careful work by research teams around the world, and might have been independently validated hundreds of times. You may as well claim that their pocket protector is ugly. Because scientists are people, they sometimes make mistakes, but by and large science itself is amazingly self-correcting.

Sometimes science runs afoul of culture. A common example is the battle between the scientific community and the Church over the structure of the solar system. Nicholas Copernicus (mid-15th to mid-16th century), Johannes Kepler and Galileo Galilei (early 17th century) were convinced that our solar system was structured differently than the Catholic Church's interpretation of the Bible claimed. The Church resisted adoption of the scientific theory which placed the Sun at the center of the solar system and persecuted its proponents, although this theory fit the experimental observations better.

The heliocentric theory was not a new concept. It had been proposed long before the Church existed, as early as 220 BC by Aristarchus of Samos in ancient Greece. However, it was contrary to then-current Biblical interpretation, and was banned by the Church as heresy.

Galileo was tried and convicted twice for attempting to promote the idea that the Earth was not the center of the universe. He remained under house arrest over this issue until his death in 1642, although the real reason might have been the fact that he essentially called Pope Urban, the head of the Catholic Church at that time, an idiot.

To save his own life after his second conviction, Galileo was forced to renounce his claim and say the Church was right and he was wrong. According to legend, he figuratively thumbed his nose at the Church after his conviction as he was leaving the court. He had just been threatened with death for his idea that, instead of remaining motionless, the Earth moved around the Sun. He publicly stated the Church's position: all other celestial objects moved in a comic dance around a stationary, eternal Earth at the center of the universe. However, unable to completely turn away from the facts, he muttered as he was leaving the court, "Eppur, si muove! (And yet, it moves!)"

Amazingly, the Church remained largely silent on the issue from the days of Galileo until 1822, when the Vatican issued an edict that books that contained scientific discussion of the heliocentric theory were "no longer banned," and not until 1992 was there an official statement by a sitting Pope in support of Galileo.

A more modern example of the capacity of scientific theories to create conflict is the debate over Charles Darwin's theory of evolution by natural selection. There are few scientific theories that have been more exhaustively scrutinized, analyzed, attacked, and derided than Darwin's theory of evolution. The theory of evolution by natural selection provides a mechanism that explains the vast diversity of life on Earth, without resorting to nonscientific explanations such as intelligent design. Although it's not my purpose to explain Darwin (Richard Dawkins does a better job than I could do in his book *The Blind Watchmaker*), the basic idea is simple.

The theory goes like this: there is a process (genetic mutation, unknown to Darwin at the time) that causes random changes in the inherited characteristics of organisms. Some of those changes make an organism more likely to survive in its environment, some less. On average, organisms with non-beneficial mutations die or compete less effectively for resources, and organisms with beneficial mutations survive to reproduce. Over time, these beneficial mutations aggregate, and gradually a new organism emerges, better able to survive and compete in its environment.

The theory does not address the origin of life, nor does it claim that "monkeys turned into man." It does nicely explain the vast diversity of life on Earth, though, and why life exists in every possible ecological niche.

Is Darwin's theory of evolution by natural selection complete? Perhaps not, in the same way the Newton's theory of motion is not complete. Does it explain and predict? Yes, within its limitations. Is there a better theory that explains all this one does, and is testable? No, there is not, if we limit ourselves to scientific theories.

So why isn't intelligent design an equivalent theory? In my view, the short answer is because by the same definition, it's not a scientific theory. The idea behind intelligent design is ancient, and appears to have originated with Socrates. It began as a theological argument for the existence of God called the teleological argument or the argument from design, or any of a half-dozen other names over the last 2400 years. The argument basically states that life (or the Earth itself or the universe) is too complex to have emerged by chance, and must have been created by a sometimes identified and sometimes unidentified "intelligent designer." By its detractors, the argument is sometimes called the argument from incredulity or "I don't understand it, so God did it." There is emotional energy tied up in this 2400-year old discussion, and it sometimes emerges in snide comments and sarcasm.

Proponents of intelligent design have made an effort in the last thirty years or so to divorce the concept from its theological/religious origins by intentionally not referring to the identity of the designer. The unintended consequence has been to put religious creationist thinkers in the same camp as proponents of ancient alien theories and "X-Files" mythology. In addition, intelligent design supporters have postulated several pseudo-scientific arguments against evolution by natural selection. Let's look at two of them; irreducible complexity and the argument from probability.

The idea of irreducible complexity holds that there are systems and mechanisms in living creatures that are so complex that removing any part of them results in a non-functioning system. The idea proposes that these systems and mechanisms must have been created as a whole by an intelligent designer, rather than developing over time by means of a random series of mutations. Examples of irreducible complexity often include human DNA, the cascade of chemical reactions that causes blood to clot, the human eye, and the "molecular motor" that drives the propulsive motion of a bacterial flagellum. Remove any part of these systems, and you don't have a less capable system; you instead have a completely nonfunctional system that can't support life, according to the idea's promoters.

Unfortunately, the concept of irreducible complexity also reduces to "I can't imagine how it could have happened, so it must have been supernaturally designed." There are plausible evolutionary pathways for each of the examples cited, but proponents of irreducible complexity tend to reject them out of hand. Once again, arguing against strongly-held beliefs with rational, fact-based arguments fails, because the original proposition and the refutation talk past each other.

The argument from probability is similar, and suffers from a simple misunderstanding of the mechanism of evolution by natural selection.

The argument goes like this: the sequence of evolutionary steps required to create a new, viable species, or even a biologically viable change to an existing organism, is so highly improbable as to be effectively impossible. It would be more likely for a tornado in a junkyard to spontaneously assemble a 747 airplane.

The argument fails on the assumption that evolution operates all at once, instead of by many small steps over a long time period. Each small change is viable and results in a new generation of organisms with the new characteristic. If evolution worked like a junkyard tornado, the argument might have some merit, but it just doesn't work that way.

When I was an engineering graduate student, I was also married, the father of our first child, and an Air Force first lieutenant. We were not poor, but we were definitely austere, without extra funds for recreation. I was overjoyed when one of my fellow students gave me a copy of a computer game for my brand-new IBM PC-XT. Occasionally, after the day's studying was over and Amy and my infant son were in bed, I relaxed with my bootleg computer game.

As every computer gamer knows, the best (and usually only) way to win is with strategic use of the "save" function. I saved the game whenever I successfully completed a challenge or achieved some other milestone. Then, whenever I inevitably caused my own death in the game, I could revert to the saved game instead of beginning the game again. By saving my successes and ignoring my failures, I successfully reached the end of the game very quickly.

This process of exploiting successes and ignoring failures is precisely how evolution by natural selection works. Evolution "saves the game" by passing on successful genetic mutations to the next generation through reproduction; unsuccessful mutations are ignored by death or poor competition for resources. This process, called the "evolutionary ratchet," prevents losing ground by saving every positive change that makes an organism more likely to survive; hence, it's described as the "survival of the fittest." This common saying does not refer to individual organisms, but to genes. Organisms live and die, but the genes that result in more survivable organisms are preserved to be passed along during reproduction.

The "junkyard tornado" that builds a 747 in one pass is highly unlikely, to be sure. It's a straw man, though; a distraction, similar in likelihood to winning a computer game without saving, in one sitting, the first time you play. It just doesn't happen that way.

There is a huge body of thought behind the development of

scientific inquiry. A similar effort has gone into arguments that seek to logically prove the existence of a supernatural supreme being. My view is that it's wasted effort, but it's not my effort, so who am I to say? My personal experience is that one can not be rationally argued into belief - it comes from a different source.

People have been trying to resolve this apparent conflict between science and religion for as long as they have both existed. All the attempts are flawed to a greater or lesser degree. For instance, Steven Jay Gould proposed that science and religion do not serve the same function, ask the same questions, or provide the same types of answers. His contention is that they exist in "non-overlapping magisteria," or completely separate areas of inquiry. There is some merit to the idea, but now the argument is where the dividing line should be drawn. You just can't please some people.

Intelligent design may be a philosophy, or an explanation, or a world view, or a belief, but it is not a scientific theory, because some of its elements are, by definition, supernatural and not available for independent examination. That doesn't necessarily invalidate the argument, but it does mean that natural selection and the argument from design are not comparable because they are not the same type of beast. You might as well do a performance comparison between a bicycle and a Shakespearean sonnet to see which one serves as a better source of nuclear power. They just don't compare, and the test makes no sense.

By the same token, some of the more recent theories in physics that attempt to unify quantum field theory and general relativity into a grand "theory of everything" may not actually be scientific theories either, because there is currently no way to test them. An emerging theory of the origin of reality, called m-theory, postulates the existence of the "multiverse," an infinite number of universes of infinite diversity. M-theory is elegant and predictive but completely impervious to testing. These theories are closer to philosophy than science, according to purists who claim that theory without experimental evidence is worthless.

It is entirely possible that Whoever (bear with me - I am not trying to be offensive by using that term; I am, however trying to keep religious conflict and sectarianism out of the discussion, at least for now) created the entire world just a little more than 6000 years ago, populated it with everything we see, and placed "evidence" for us to find that makes us believe that evolution is true, as a test of faith. It's also entirely possible that Whoever created the universe a little over 13 billion years ago, set the initial conditions to have it evolve in the way it has, and also takes a personal interest in each of us and "knows when every sparrow falls." It's possible that Whoever created the universe, set the initial conditions, and was called to do something important and is no longer involved. It's even possible that there is no Whoever, the multiverse emerged as a result of unguided natural processes, life is meaningless except for what we make of it, and there is no grand plan and never has been. Many other scenarios are possible, but these are not scientific questions, because there is no hope of ever testing or observing the results of tests based on these questions. Expressing discomfort with an idea is not the same as refuting it.

We have looked around, asked some interesting questions, developed and tested a hypothesis, and made judgments about either an existing theory or (if we're really lucky, really smart, or both) we've created a brand new theory with our name on it. We're done, right?

Sorry, no - the scientific method is not "one and done." It's a repetitive process that builds on past work and suggests new questions to ask. We continue until we answer all the scientific questions there are, or until we die.

The scientific method is an enormously powerful tool to help us understand our place in the world, but it's not the only tool. From a personal perspective, five years ago I had no interest in the impact of opinion or belief on the truth, because it was clear to me that science produced truth. I think I was wrong - science does not produce truth, it produces facts. My sense is that science is best when concerned with the structure of the universe, but less successful with meaning and value. For that, we need other tools.

I am a scientist at heart (well, actually I'm an engineer at heart, the distinction being that a scientist learns how things work, and an engineer makes things work). However, I've learned to appreciate the fact that most people aren't compelled by science. Opinion tends to be formed more by relationships and culture than fact, and people are amazingly adept at ignoring facts if they do not fit with their opinions and desires.

I've also learned that the axle on which the world turns is belief.

Every belief cannot be factually correct. That's generally not the way to start a conversation, though. Acknowledging that beliefs are mostly non-rational and seeking common ground anyway is a better approach.

My beliefs have changed over the last few years. Even claiming that "I have no beliefs" is a belief system of sorts. No one is belief-free; I believed in the power of rationality, and the effectiveness of science at answering questions. I started asking different questions, though, and found that science by itself didn't measure up. Rather than giving up on science or ignoring the issue, I added to my toolkit.

Corey D. King

3
We All Have Them…

Opinion is the medium between knowledge and ignorance.
— Plato

Too often we… enjoy the comfort of opinion without the discomfort of thought.
—John F. Kennedy

You are not entitled to your opinion. You are entitled to your informed opinion. No one is entitled to be ignorant.
— Harlan Ellison

I had an online conversation recently. I use the word "conversation" advisedly, because a real conversation is more than an exchange of information. It involves facial expression, body language, tone of voice, and other verbal and non-verbal cues that can communicate as much as the spoken element of the conversation. Communication is possible online through email, text message, and other newfangled methods that make my head hurt, but these are not truly conversational. It's a risky form of information exchange due to the potential for hurting feelings and missing the point, both of which I managed to do.

I like arguing, especially online. I can control the intensity of the discussion and disengage if I'm uncomfortable, and I can engage at my own pace and make sure I like what I've said before I hit the "enter" key.

I'm not usually given to personal attacks. I like discussion, and I have a personal philosophy that an unexamined and unsupported opinion is of no value. That doesn't mean that I think the person who holds an unsupported opinion is of no value, but that distinction is occasionally lost, especially online.

I was browsing through one of the social media platforms (in the interest of fairness, I won't say which, but the name begins with Facebook), and I saw a post from a friend. This friend is a real flesh and blood friend - she and her husband have been to my house. My friend had made a completely noncontroversial post about a topic of current interest, and the first response she received was "bullshit!" Oh, boy, I thought. Game on. I swung into action, carrying my sword, atop my white stallion, ready to do battle for truth, justice and the American way.

I struck the first blow, asking which of the responder's strongly held beliefs or opinions led the conclusion that this response was appropriate, helpful, or even civilized. I should have realized by the lack of a coherent response that I was in an unnecessary battle with an unwilling opponent, but I wanted unconditional surrender.

I thought we were still discussing ideas, and I hope I would have never done in person what I did next. I went into "slice and dice" mode and deconstructed the argument step-by-step, showing how foolish it was (and how smart I was). If we had been sitting together over a cup of coffee instead of separated by untold thousands of miles, I hope I would have noticed body language, tone of voice, and the trapped, "deer in the headlights" expression, and I would have backed off. As it was, I was too enamored with my own argument, my righteous sense of justification in defending my viewpoint, and my self-congratulatory defense of a friend who had not asked for my help and did not need it.

Someone I didn't even know had an opinion about a subject I knew something about and couldn't defend it, so I destroyed them. I didn't even realize how emotionally invested this person was was in the discussion until the end, when they responded with a rambling, nearly hysterical outpouring of pain, loss, and despair, and I finally understood I had been cruel.

Objectively speaking, I still think my adversary was wrong. I think a person is obligated to defend their publicly expressed viewpoints. I draw a distinction between opinion and belief, and I think a person's opinions should be based on fact, even if their beliefs are not. Not everyone agrees with me, but that's the fun part, isn't it? Let's get in the ring and mix it up! How arrogant, how lacking in empathy could I be?

Opinions create powerful emotional responses, and our difficulty in talking about them is a major source of conflict in the world. We will always have differences of opinion, even if we work with the same facts. We almost never work with the same facts, though, and we almost never draw exactly the same conclusions from even the same facts.

There are over seven billion of us now. How do we talk to each other and get anything done? Certainly not by doing what I did.

Ideas are important, but you cannot communicate effectively with someone you've just bludgeoned. There is a difference between winning an intellectual argument and destroying an opponent, and in the heat of the moment, I lost that difference. It's not sufficient to have strength of conviction, or a grasp of the facts. Wisdom, compassion, and a sense of which battles are important need to be present, also.

Some enemies need to be defeated. With a certain compassion and remorse, perhaps, but defeated completely nonetheless. Some battles are existential. Against tyranny, oppression, hatred, and enslavement; certainly. Against a foe who would steal my freedom to think and act, kill my family, take my liberty; without doubt. This was not one of those battles.

Some battles are won with might and power; some are won with sympathy and compassion. I chose incorrectly this time. Hopefully, I'll choose differently next time.

Corey D. King

4
Faith

Optimism is the faith that leads to achievement. Nothing can be done without hope and confidence.
— Helen Keller

Life is full of happiness and tears; be strong and have faith.
— Kareena Kapoor Khan

Faith is taking the first step even when you don't see the whole staircase.
— Martin Luther King, Jr.

My first introduction to proof was during high school. The school district where I lived prided itself on its progressive educational approach, and the mathematics curriculum was one of the shining examples. I was a student in an experimental math program called "Unified Math," a survey course that didn't follow the standard progression of math subjects typically taught in high school. Instead, I learned a little bit of everything, from symbolic logic and topology to analytic geometry and calculus.

During my senior year, we spent several weeks on the proof of mathematical theorems. I remember a comment my teacher made: "In mathematics, half a proof is of no value. The outcome of mathematical proof is that every doubt becomes impossible." It was not until years later that I discovered he was paraphrasing one of the greatest mathematicians of all time, Carl Gauss.

I was full of doubts as a teenager. Perhaps that's why I was so attracted to math and science - there were answers there, and they didn't change or waver. Making "...every doubt become impossible..." was irresistible. Everywhere I turned I found doubts, except for math and science.

There is no such certainty in most of life. Why do bad things happen to good people? Why do bad people so often prosper? Why is there such seemingly needless pain and suffering in the world? Why are we here? Where do we come from? What is our purpose?

There are as many answers as there are questioners, with no certainty that any answer is correct. There are no proofs for most of life's important questions, so what are we to do? How do we get through the day without answers, when doubt is not only possible but pervasive?

Professor and philosopher of science John Lennox said, "Faith is not a leap in the dark; it's the exact opposite. It's a commitment based on evidence... It is irrational to reduce all faith to blind faith and then subject it to ridicule. That provides a very anti-intellectual and convenient way of avoiding intelligent discussion."

However, evolutionary biologist Richard Dawkins criticizes faith by focusing on faith claims that conflict directly with scientific evidence. He describes faith as "belief without evidence; a process of active non-thinking." He has publicly stated that faith and religious belief are practices that corrupt our understanding of the natural world. He asserts that faith allows anyone to make a claim about nature that is based solely on their potentially distorted personal thoughts and perceptions. He contends those claims are exempt from testing against nature, have no ability to make reliable predictions, and are not subject to peer review.

These two views are at extreme ends of the spectrum, and I think they're both wrong. Lennox implies that coming to faith is a rational act, and Dawkins all but says that faith, by definition, is completely irrational. In my experience, examination of the evidence is necessary, but not sufficient. I came to believe that God exists by examining the evidence, certainly. However, the evidence was not enough. At some point, a leap of faith is required to bridge the gap between evidence and belief. You have to choose, and not choosing is a choice.

Faith is not like mathematics - there is no incontrovertible proof, no single, crystalline answer that makes every doubt impossible. I think faith is more like engineering; there are a small number of elegant, beautiful solutions, a larger number of satisfactory solutions, and a huge number of ugly non-solutions that don't fit and don't answer the question.

I also think that faith and religion are at best distant cousins. In many ways, organized religion is like a bad engineering solution; it's a Rube Goldberg collection unnecessary parts, preconceived notions, and misapplication of bits and pieces that happen to be lying around. How else can you explain the fact that, by some estimates, there are over 4200 different religions in the world, or that there are between 40 and 40,000 different denominations of Christianity, the world's most popular religion? They can't all be right, but some are probably more right than others.

Realizing how little I really know and how wrong I've been before finally tipped the scales for me. When I learn something new, I'm reminded of the abyss of my own ignorance. It's arrogant to claim that we (or I) know everything there is to know. Perhaps there is a Gauss, Copernicus, Bacon, Newton, or Einstein not yet born who will have insights that radically shift our understanding of the Universe and our place in it. In my view, it is too soon and there are too many unanswered questions to claim we know how it all works.

Lord Kelvin, the renowned Scottish mathematician and physicist, said in 1900, "There is nothing new to be discovered in physics now. All that remains is more and more precise measurement." Less than a decade later, quantum mechanics and general relativity changed our basic understanding of the physical world, and new insights continue to emerge. Who's to say that a similar revolution in thought will not further integrate our knowledge of the world, and help bind together fact and faith? It's far too soon to close the door on our understanding.

Corey D. King

5

The Last Of Human Freedoms

I'm sorry, Dave - I'm afraid I can't do that.
— HAL 9000, *2001: A Space Odyssey*

I've seen things you people wouldn't believe. Attack ships on fire off the shoulder of Orion. I watched C-beams glitter in the dark near the Tannhäuser Gate. All those moments will be lost in time, like tears in rain. Time to die...
— Roy Batty, *Blade Runner*

There is an explanation for this, you know.
— Ash, *Alien*

For the past three years, I've been trying to write a novel. It's not going well.

I received excellent constructive criticism from a fiction-writer's workshop and have read every how-to book I can find, but I'm not a novelist yet. I may never be - I'm running out of time. With the Parkinson's triple threat of physical deterioration, cognitive deterioration, and apathy, I may run out of airspeed before I get this beast off the ground.

According to my critics, I explain more than I should. I try to describe my fictional world in its entirety, instead of only revealing the necessary bits a little at a time.

"You have to let your readers experience your world through the eyes of your characters. And keep the action going - every chapter needs to add to the action. Oh - you also need to come up with characters who are interesting and three-dimensional, and you can't be too obvious about where you're taking them. But don't be too cryptic, and don't use big words or arcane technical concepts. Be sure it's new and fresh, too. Not too short, not too long..."

Well, crap. I started with about 80,000 words, and I've now edited down to roughly zero. I hate my main character, and he's got terrible taste in friends, so I hate all the other characters, too. And I'll be damned if I can get any one of them to tell me what happens next.

This master work is intended to be a science fiction novel about the emergence of artificial intelligence, and the epic battle between Good and Evil that results. I'm trying to make it as technically feasible as possible, so I'm researching photonics, quantum computing, Godel's Incompleteness Theorem, strong AI, nanotechnology, machine-brain interfaces, the future of hacking, the nature of consciousness...

Sorry, I fell asleep for a moment. Therein lies the problem. The basic concept is interesting to me, but I'm perhaps the only person in the world who thinks so, and even I get bored by the details. This may be too hard for me to do, but never say quit, right? Positive mental attitude and optimism will carry the day.

Except when it doesn't. A positive mental attitude didn't keep me from vomiting my way to the untimely demise of my Air Force flying career, and it isn't going to turn me into Isaac Asimov. Nor does it keep me from having Parkinson's disease.

Positive attitude is a valuable resource, necessary for navigating the pitfalls of life. In my experience, it does not make all things possible, though. It does not change the reality of my life. Misunderstanding the role that optimism plays in managing adversity is dangerous, in the same way that misunderstanding the purpose of prayer can be dangerous.

I've observed people who use prayer as an "order delivery

system," praying for an expected outcome like they were submitting an order to amazon.com. That approach may work for some, but not for me. Admittedly, I am not a sophisticated believer with decades of experience, but I don't pray for a change in my circumstances or for God to magically intervene on my behalf. It seems arrogant to expect God to respond to a prayerful entreaty with, "You know, I never thought of it quite that way before. You're absolutely right. I'll take the disease away immediately. And, just as a show of good faith, next Wednesday's winning lottery numbers are 4-8-15-16-23-42. Talk to Me tomorrow, and I'll give you the Powerball number."

Instead. I pray for strength, wisdom, or understanding - tools I can use to deal with the reality in front of me. I don't have (and never have had) a perception of personal communication with God. God doesn't talk to me, and I have no sense of a personal relationship. Just the act of praying gives me clarity, though, and maybe that's a sort of communication. My attitude may not be theologically sound, but I'm a work in progress, and I haven't made much progress yet.

I don't expect a positive attitude to change my situation any more than I expect God to find me a parking spot when I ask. Optimism doesn't change my circumstances; it does, however, give me the strength to live with my circumstances, and that makes all the difference.

One of my personal shortcomings is a tendency to take on too much, and then to feel overwhelmed. I do it now in my work as a volunteer, and I did it during my professional career.

My first civilian job after leaving the Air Force was with a small defense contractor, Trident Data Systems. I joined Trident as an engineer, and within five years I was a vice president. I was smart and capable, but no one is that good. The company was growing and changing rapidly, and I was caught in the whirlwind. I couldn't say no, mostly because I was flattered to be offered yet another opportunity to step into a promotion I wasn't experienced enough to handle well.

I decided to put my head down and bull my way through. With a positive attitude and a sense of optimism, I figured I would be fine. I was wrong. My positive attitude didn't give me the business sense I lacked or experience at handling problems I had never seen before, and I made some egregious mistakes.

Trident was primarily a defense contractor and worked for NSA,

CIA, and other shadowy three-letter organizations doing shadowy, secret things. We employed some of the best network and computer experts in the world at a time when computer security, virus protection, and hacking were exploding in the commercial world, so we decided to start a commercial security consulting business to augment our government contracts.

After a painful and chaotic two years, I was tasked by our corporate headquarters with shutting down our commercial operation, which was bleeding money. I stepped up, as I always did (and as was expected), and walked directly into a buzz saw. Over a two week period, I fired forty-six people, one by one, some of whom I had hired less than a year before. I felt personally responsible, and insisted on bearing the burden alone.

If I had more experience, I would have been able to temper my positive attitude with a more careful skepticism, and I might not have taken the understandable anger and hurt feelings expressed by those I fired so personally. I also would like to think I would have suggested to the executive team that they spring for a couple of airline tickets and come solve their own damned problem.

Battle scars are useful. They are reminders of errors in judgment, and they warn against repeating those errors. There is also a certain pride in displaying them, as evidence that you've been there and survived. There are some of the forty-six I fired that still carry a grudge, but they all carry their own scar tissue and war stories about the experience.

My war story is about the proper role for positive attitude. In short, attitude doesn't change a damned thing. Hope is not a plan. A positive mental outlook is a poor substitute for a good weapon, plenty of ammunition, and something solid to hide behind.

On the other hand, attitude changes everything. It provides the strength to keep going when you're tired, hurting, and afraid. It reminds you of the reason you're there, and suggests that maybe you've been called, that you are the best one to stand in the gap and take the punishment. Attitude lets you take one more step, last one minute longer.

I may not finish my novel. It's possible, however, that I'll wake up tomorrow knowing what happens next, and I'll be able to write it down.

Attitude is nothing. And it's everything.

6
Counting Up

Unhappy is he to whom the memories of childhood bring only fear and sadness.
— H. P. Lovecraft

Whenever I think of the past, it brings back so many memories.
— Steven Wright

Nostalgia is not what it used to be.
— Simone Signoret

I try to recognize and be grateful for the many victories that happen every day of my life, instead of focusing on the negatives. I sometimes wake up in a foul mood and have difficulty living this simple philosophy, but every day is a new opportunity to try again.

This year, I turned fifty-five years old, and I realized that I graduated from high school thirty-seven years ago. Thirty-seven years. Four hundred forty-four months. A little over 13,500 days. There was a time when I couldn't even imagine being thirty-seven years old, but here I am with just a little less than six decades of living under my belt, and I've been out of high school for thirty-seven years. If I repeat the number enough, it might seem smaller - "thirty-seven, thirty-seven, thirty-seven."

Nope.

I've known my friend Marty for almost forty years. We were teammates on our high school track team, and Marty's mother was a wizard with a Super-8 camera. I'm not sure how she did it, but at every major track meet and school event, she was there with her camera, not only capturing Marty's successes and antics, but documenting the high school careers of dozens of Marty's friends. I am fortunate to have been the occasional subject of her wizardry, although she always seemed to favor the few times that Marty beat me in head-to-head competition, and miss all the hundreds of times when I beat him (the nice thing about memory is that it requires neither accuracy nor honesty - the truth is, Marty and I were evenly matched, although it's taken me 40 years to admit it).

Marty is the owner of a treasure trove from our past - the collection of Super-8 movies that he and his mother crafted together. Marty obviously inherited some of her artistic wizardry, because he digitized some of these films and set them to music, and he periodically shares them and takes his classmates on a journey four decades into the past. He recently completed the film of our high school graduation from Seneca Valley High School in Germantown, Maryland, in the late spring of 1980. Thirty-seven years ago.

I don't often travel back there - it was not my best time, and although my memories no longer torment me, they're not quite toothless. I hardly remember what it was like to look at the world through seventeen-year-old eyes. I look at the grainy images of myself and I want to warn that stupid kid about what lies ahead, to keep him from making the mistakes that lie in his future, to avoid hurting the ones he loves, to sidestep inexperience, bad choices, bad luck.

I want to tell him that regardless of what he has already endured, life has more in store. I want to advise him to keep his eyes open and learn all he can, because he has work to do. I want to whisper in his ear that it's best to ask, and not tell, the love of your life to marry you. I want to let him know that anniversary gifts shouldn't have power cords. I want to warn him about the importance of the "thank you" bite when he is offered his new bride's sautéed red peppers for the first time. I want to tell him which doors to open and which to leave closed, which battles to fight and when to retreat, and that nothing really matters unless it's your family, your friends, or your faith.

I want him to know the wonders he'll see; the midnight sun and the aurora borealis, the blaze of a nighttime rocket launch and the golden fire of a reentering Space Shuttle, the horizon from the cockpit of a military jet after the instructor steps out and says, "don't bend my plane," the night sky over the desert when you have work to do and secrets to keep.

I wish I could tell him about the face of his beloved wife, illuminated by firelight. I want him to know that both his children will be beautiful, regardless of how they will look to him in the delivery room. I want to ease his fears that he will be just like his father - he won't. I want him to be sure his children will survive his mistakes and thrive - they will.

I'd be keeping him from becoming who he should be if I told him any of these things, though. He'll live through it all. He'll tell his own kids someday, "adversity builds character," but he won't tell them until they're grown that he heard it from Calvin's dad in the "Calvin and Hobbes" comic strip before he learned it himself. It's hard to believe the grinning kid with the Farrah Fawcett hair was me, but Marty's videos don't lie.

Now, fifty-five years down the road and thirty-seven years past high school, I can look back and be proud of my life. I am proud of my children, who ignored me when I was wrong, listened when I was right (most of the time) and are great people in spite of my mistakes.

I'm also proud of my thirty-two years and counting with Amy. We have thrived (mostly) and survived (occasionally), and raised two great kids together. In all that time, she has only bounced one shoe and one nasal aspirator off my head in the heat of anger. She claims one of them was an accident, but the story keeps changing. She is the love of my life, and I'm so very fortunate to have found her. I suspect I had Help.

I can also look forward and be optimistic, as strange as that may sound. Parkinson's is not pretty, and the easy part is already behind me. But there are still things to learn, things to teach, new experiences, laughs, and love ahead. There are also challenges ahead, but I think I'll be ok, with all that I have going for me.

At one time, optimism irritated me. I don't have the luxury of an arms-length, jaded, cynical assessment any longer. Optimism and a positive outlook are a choice, and they are also essential weapons in my arsenal for getting through the day. I'm fortunate that those feelings are sincere and authentic in me.

I have Parkinson's. I also have a great life, full of meaning, purpose, and people who make all my challenges worthwhile.

7

Good, Better, Best

Life is an incurable disease.
— Abraham Cowley

Survival can be summed up in three words - never give up. That's the heart of it really. Just keep trying.
— Bear Grylls

The best monsters are our anxieties given form. They make sense on the level of a dream - or a nightmare.
— Victor LaValle

Since I was diagnosed with Parkinson's, I occasionally struggle with the knowledge that, on average, I will never again feel as good as I do right now. There are variations, of course - some days are good, and some are not. Some days are good enough that I feel a little guilty. I retired from professional life in 2011, two years after my diagnosis and just a few months after my deep brain stimulation system was first implanted. On my best days, I sometimes feel as if I've been playing hooky from school for the last six years, and I should get serious and get back to work. It doesn't last, though. In an hour or two, Parkinson's reasserts itself, and I remember again why I retired.

I have a recurring nightmare. I find myself in a huge classroom. I realize that I am late for a final examination because I couldn't remember where to find the classroom. I recognize the classroom and the people in it, but I haven't been there for a long time. With a sinking feeling, I realize that I haven't studied for the most important test of my life. If I fail, I will never get another chance.

I am late enough that many of my fellow test takers are finished and some are gathering up their things and leaving. I find my seat, open my test booklet, and read the first question. It's in French. I don't speak French. Desperate, I flip through the booklet, trying to find a question I can answer. I finally find a math problem - with relief, I begin to work the problem. My pencil breaks in half. The alarm bell rings. The whole class begins to laugh and jeer. I discover I am naked. My teeth fall out, and the professor clips a huge rubber band to a hook on the harness I am suddenly wearing, and pulls a large wooden lever set into the floor. The rubber band slings me through the skylights in the ceiling (did I forget to mention the skylights?) and screaming, mostly naked, holding the stub end of a broken pencil, toothless, and panicked, I rocket up into a gray, stormy sky. After an eternity in ballistic flight, I crash down in an asphalt parking lot littered with broken glass, and roll into the door of a building. I look around - I find myself in a huge classroom.

And so on.

I spend most of my conscious effort trying to have a "good day." Why do I feel guilty when I do? All of us with chronic diseases that are sometimes not apparent have our own way of managing usually well-intended comments about our state of health. In a small number of cases, the real underlying message is skepticism. If the disease is so unpredictable, and sometimes I look better than other times, isn't it possible that I'm just malingering?

"You look great! It's almost as if you were normal!"

"Uhh...thank you?"

"You seem to be feeling much better - I'm glad you're recovering."

"Yes, I'm having a good day today."

"Every time I see you, you look stronger. Are the doctors sure you have PD?"

"No, it's all a giant hoax, designed to bilk society of valuable resources. You and a small number of other mouth-breathers are the only ones not in on the joke. I'm sorry, did I say that out loud?"

I don't want to have this damned disease, and I also don't want to whine about the fact that I have this damned disease. So, what do I do? I keep marching forward, and I work to be grateful for the good days. There are fewer than there once were, but every one is a blessing.

For the first time in twenty-five years, I am riding a bicycle. This past spring, Amy suggested we rent bicycles and go riding on the Mission Reach in San Antonio. I told her she was crazy. Did she not remember I had Parkinson's? We went anyway, since she is both more persistent and smarter than I am.

It took a while, my balance was terrible, and I had to stop several times, but the sun was out, it was cool and breezy, and I had the most knowledgeable (and beautiful) tour guide anyone could hope for. I was sore the next day, but we kept going back. My balance is better, and I love the feel of the wind on my face. I just bought a bicycle, and now I'm the one agitating to go riding.

I have bad days too, and they come more often. I don't remember much about them. I think it's supposed to be that way. I occasionally feel guilty that I'm "retired," especially on the good days. I'll work through it. I didn't choose this life. But, every day I have a thousand choices I can make. I'll choose to live well.

Corey D. King

8

Self-Evident

A patriot must always be ready to defend his country against his government.
— Edward Abbey

The patriot volunteer, fighting for country and his rights, makes the most reliable soldier on earth.
— Stonewall Jackson

Patriot: the person who can holler the loudest without knowing what he is hollering about.
— Mark Twain

I have a life beyond Parkinson's. To be blunt, the important parts of my life are not about Parkinson's disease. Parkinson's is an intruder, and does not deserve my regard or my exclusive attention. My intention to live "in defiance of Parkinson's" sometimes means that I ignore it. I can never forget about it (even now, I'm typing at a blazing ten words per minute, and the key I use most is the "delete" key), but I can sometimes choose to think about something else.

I'm not overly concerned about many things these days; having an incurable disease, being completely dependent on medication that I can't make myself, and having an electronic system embedded in my brain and chest with a battery that runs down about every two years gives a person perspective. I try to focus on the big things - contrary to the old saying, it's not all small stuff.

I am a U.S. Air Force veteran. My military service is the reason I have Parkinson's. No one forced me to serve, and it was one of the most meaningful and formative periods of my life. I have to admit though, if my commissioning oath had included the phrase, "...and after you are finished supporting and defending, you will spend the rest of your life freezing, falling, and shaking..." perhaps I would have had second thoughts.

I did things in the service of my country that I believe mattered. I think all of us who serve make a difference. I was not in combat, but I am slowly dying because of the service I performed. I'm not looking for sympathy - there are many who sacrificed much more. I'm simply pointing out that I am entitled to an opinion, and it's this: when I see what our country is becoming, it not only makes me sad, it makes me angry.

Two hundred and forty-one years ago, a group of independent-minded, outspoken misfits chose to risk ruin and death to raise their voices in defiance of tyranny. They took that risk to live in freedom, rather than to live a single additional moment under the yoke of oppression. They chose to live in defiance at the cost of constant vigilance.

Thomas Jefferson said, "...even under the best forms of government those entrusted with power have, in time, and by slow operations, perverted it into tyranny." I believe our form of government is among the best ever conceived by Mankind. It's not perfect, but nothing can claim perfection on the muddy side of Eternity. I also believe that governments cannot be trusted because power corrupts, and because people, even with the best of intentions, sometimes lose their way. Without good intentions, it's almost guaranteed.

Our government was designed with this truth in mind. The three co-equal branches, the checks and balances, the intentional procedural roadblocks that prevent rapid, unilateral changes in the basic structure of governance, were designed to prevent consolidation of power in the hands of a tyrant. However, this elegant machine needs an operator. It needs all of us. "We the people" are required to pay attention and do our job, though, if this inspired structure is to function properly.

Our job is to think; to discern, to separate fact from fiction, and to make judgments based on rational assessment of both individual and common good.

Our job is to act; to make choices based on reason, to be active protectors of our natural and civil rights, and to behave as if we actually believe that all people, and not just ourselves, are endowed with certain unalienable rights.

Our job is to resist; to identify injustice, to speak truth, to insist that our freedoms are respected and all our voices are heard, and to remember that government is our servant, not our master.

Our nation was founded in defiance of tyranny. We must remain vigilant; let us never forget that tyranny grows in darkness, wherever it is allowed to, whenever we see it and do not raise the alarm. We the people have our own destiny in our hands.

I'm relying on you to do the right things. Don't let me down.

Corey D. King

9
Mind Over Circumstance

There are risks and costs to action. But they are far less than the long range risks of comfortable inaction.
— John F. Kennedy

Vision without action is merely a dream. Action without vision just passes the time. Vision with action can change the world.
— Joel A. Barker

Do you want to know who you are? Don't ask. Act! Action will delineate and define you.
—Thomas Jefferson

April of every year is Parkinson's Disease Awareness Month. I have now experienced eight of them as a person with Parkinson's disease. However, every month is Parkinson's Awareness Month for those of us battling the disease, and for our friends and loved ones. We don't need a special month or day to be aware of the disease - we have no choice.

I prefer to think of April as Parkinson's Action Month. I mean no disrespect to the founders of Parkinson's Awareness Month, but my opinion is that simple awareness is just an opportunity for a false sense of accomplishment. Awareness by itself has limited value, except possibly as a salve to the conscience of the person being aware, unless it's followed by action. There are many worthy causes that demand attention, though, and only so much capacity, money, and expertise to go around.

Parkinson's is not a fatal disease. It is progressive, degenerative, and incurable, however, and the degeneration it causes generally means our end of days comes earlier than usual, from a related cause. Sometimes it's pneumonia, brought about by aspiration of food due to swallowing difficulties; sometimes it's malnutrition and general systemic failure brought about by the same swallowing problems. Sometimes it's head injury or complications from broken bones caused by falls. Sometimes it's the complications of slow gastric motility or digestive problems. Sometimes it's brought about by the cognitive and emotional degeneration the disease causes. Those who deal with the disease every day know these things, but we don't dwell on them. Life itself is invariably fatal, and everyone on earth has an invisible alarm clock hanging around their neck. No one knows when their alarm will ring. It is simply the human condition. How's that for awareness? Uncomfortable yet?

Simple awareness is not only valueless, it can be actively harmful if it results in complacency. For example, I am aware of my own mortality. If I thought that the measure of my life was based only on longevity and the avoidance of discomfort, I think I'd be a little concerned. Parkinson's is ugly - it causes discomfort, distress, and both physical and emotional suffering. I am aware, and I choose not to stop with awareness. For my own survival, I choose to move past awareness to action.

Parkinson's is insidious because it tries to steal our will to act, and replace it with despair, depression, immobility and inaction. We fight it every day, and most days we win. On the days we don't, we have to resolve to win the next day. So how do we win when every day is a new fight?

People with Parkinson's are the bravest people I know. Waking up every day to join in battle with the same adversary that put you to bed exhausted the night before is not only brave, it's damned near heroic. But, everyone fights something. It's helpful for me to remember that my struggle is no more imposing than anyone else's just because it's mine. The world is full of heroes. A combat-wounded veteran who has to put on his legs before he can get out of bed is heroic. A single mother working two jobs, spending almost everything on child care, rent, and food, and still managing to put three kids through college is heroic. A teenager living in poverty who manages to avoid gangs, drugs, and violence and make it through medical school is heroic. Anyone who faces fear and does the right things anyway shows heroism and courage.

A colleague of mine used to joke, "I'd love to do the right thing, if I could just figure out what it is." It's a problem. Life is complex, and most situations are painted in shades of gray.

What are the right things? Here is my short list. I think they apply to both living with Parkinson's and everything else; I never claimed to be humble.

— Acknowledge that you're not in control of everything. There's ample evidence it's true - you might as well bow to it. It's a bit liberating to realize that you don't get to call all the shots. I do this by believing that God exists and that the world we live in ultimately makes sense, even if I can't see it and don't understand it. Something else may work for you; find it.

— Acknowledge that, even without control, you have the power to choose. You can't always choose your circumstances, but you can choose your responses and your attitude. Don't squander your ability to choose, but don't wring your hands about the outcome of your choices if you choose badly - just choose again.

— Be guided by the highest principles you can find when you make your choices. This is where beliefs are the most important. For me: God again, and the Golden Rule. Hate, selfishness, and fear are bad foundations for principle. I'd suggest avoiding them.

— Overcome your fears and act. Everyone is afraid. The ones that pretend they're not are usually the most petrified. Act anyway. Nothing good ever happens without action.

Get off your butt and act. Take control when you can, and relax when you can't. Exercise. Learn something new. Water the plants naked at 3 AM. Join Toastmasters and overcome your fear of public speaking. Write a book. Paint a picture. Walk the cat (and let me know how you managed it, if it works out). Learn to play the kazoo. Teach calculus to teenagers. Sing in the grocery store. Call someone you hurt and and say you're sorry. If you love your friends, tell them. If you don't love your friends, find new friends.

Life is precious, with or without Parkinson's. Don't just be aware - act, with a full heart and the expectation of success. And if you don't like what happens, choose again. And act.

10
Watching The Light Fade

It is not death that a man should fear, but he should fear never beginning to live.
— Marcus Aurelius

Death is nothing, but to live defeated and inglorious is to die daily.
— Napoleon Bonaparte

Dilbert: When I die, I want my ashes scattered in outer space.
Dogbert: Cool. I'll bribe an Elbonian general to strap you to their intercontinental missile when they launch it next week.
Dilbert: It's better if the dying and the ash-scattering are separate events.
Dogbert: Don't be a burden on the living.
— Scott Adams

As I was driving to my Rock Steady Boxing class recently, I came upon a terrible traffic accident. The accident had just occurred, and the first responders were not on scene yet. I called 911, and learned that I was one of about twenty people who had done so.
  As I passed the scene of the accident, I saw a man trying to open

the door of one of the vehicles. Through the broken windshield, I saw the unconscious and apparently deceased driver of the vehicle. In the past, I would have stopped to help, but these days I'm more of a hindrance.

Throughout the rest of the afternoon, a thought kept recurring to me, and it's not one I usually have.

I'm going to die.

Everyone dies. For some, it comes during peaceful sleep after a long, productive life. For others, it comes suddenly and without warning, and there's no chance to say goodbye. It's not much of a revelation that I'm going to die. This was not the first time I realized that I was mortal like everyone else, but I couldn't shake the thought that afternoon.

I am not afraid of death. I am neither eager nor ready for it, but I no longer see it as an ending; only a transition. I have no objective evidence to support my belief that we go on after death, but I believe it nonetheless.

That afternoon, it was not the fact of my inevitable demise that occupied me. It was the manner. I could not stop thinking about how I would die. The possibilities spun in my head like a gerbil on an exercise wheel, and distracted me for the remainder of the day.

The subject came up again the following day, as I was chatting with a group of other PWPs (people with Parkinson's). Some wanted to go in their sleep, some preferred a sudden stroke or heart attack. One witty guy wanted to go during sex. No one, however, said they preferred a long, slow decline ending in death by malnutrition, pneumonia, or general systemic failure. That is, unfortunately, how most PWPs meet their end.

We don't often get together to be morbid and discuss death - this conversation was unusual. The subject was on everyone's mind that day, however, and we went with it. I realized something during the discussion. Although I am not afraid of death, I am afraid of the manner of my death. I fear the long slide, the gradual loss of everything I am. I don't want to just fade away.

Of course, it's not inevitable. I am still relatively young, and except for this pesky incurable degenerative disease, in relatively good health. Riding a bicycle is risky (especially in San Antonio, where there seems to be a city ordinance requiring all drivers to try to kill at least one bike rider per day). Shooting as a hobby is dangerous.

Even walking down the street is not without danger. I could step off the curb one day and get snuffed by the proverbial city bus, or step into a storm drain and meet Pennywise the Clown.

I have noticed evidence of more significant physical issues from progression of Parkinson's. I'm dyskinetic for a good portion of the day, and coupled with my balance problems, I am more at risk for falls. When I am off, I freeze and shuffle more often when I walk. I have more trouble swallowing, and I choke more often. Any of these issues could end up being fatal, but I'm not there yet.

Eating and swallowing are a point of contention between Amy and me. She would like to keep me around for as long as possible (understandable; I'm a great guy), and my tendency to choke is a major concern. My speech therapist advised me to eat in small bites, sipping a drink between bites to clear my mouth, and taught me how to swallow to minimize the likelihood of choking. I don't do it all the time, though, and it drives Amy to distraction.

"That last bite was too big, and where's your drink? You've taken four bites without a drink. Are you trying to kill yourself? Why did you bother going to the speech therapist if you're just going to ignore her?"

Amy is right, of course. Parkinson's is changing me in ways I would not have anticipated. I forget to do things if I'm not completely focused on one task at a time, and it's frustrating for Amy to have to remind me over and over again.

For some reason, I leave the drawers in the kitchen half-open about ninety percent of the time. I don't do it on purpose, but I think Amy is beginning to wonder if I'm not just screwing with her for fun. If I get too hungry, I eat too fast, I don't take sips of water between bites, and like John Belushi in the movie *Animal House*, I will try my best to cram an entire meal into my mouth at one time. Of course, it makes me choke, and that makes Amy angry.

I know she's not really angry; she's scared. She sees me doing things that will only get worse as time goes on, and I'm guessing she feels powerless to do anything about it. She probably thinks I am contributing to my own impending death, and it's terrifying.

It doesn't help matters that I hate feeling managed, and I am more childlike in my responses than I used to be. I sometimes resist good advice just to feel a little more independent. It's futile, but I have to be honest. I miss my independence.

There is more than one way to die. I do not want my spirit to fade before my body is done. I want to go quickly when it's my time, but not so quickly that there is no time for, "So long; see you soon."

Not so long ago, I was convinced that when I died, I would return to the nothingness from which I came. I don't believe that any more. I cannot say what will happen. I don't really believe in a literal "floating in the clouds, pearly gates and halos, wings for everyone" afterlife. I have no idea what the truth is, but I'm willing to wait to find out.

I am not willing to go without having said to my family and friends how I feel about you, though. If I surprise you at some point by telling you in the middle of a conversation about bicycle parts or ammunition that I am grateful for you and I love you, bear with me, but believe me. There is never enough time to get it all said, but I'm going to try.

11

The Sound And The Fury

Every time you find something funny in a challenging situation, you win.
- Charles M Schultz

True love is spending one day getting married and the rest of your life feeling glad you did.
- Unknown

When you see a married couple walking down the street, the one that's a few steps ahead is the one that's mad.
- Helen Rowland

My daughter was married a year ago. The wedding planning was flawless, the bride and the ceremony were beautiful, the reception was the social event of the season, and everyone who attended seemed to enjoy themselves. As an added bonus, it worked. A year later, the happy couple is still a couple, and they are still gloriously happy.

My role in planning the wedding was limited, although I was

allowed to attend and even encouraged to speak aloud during the ceremony. However, unless I was specifically asked and provided with an acceptable response beforehand, I was forbidden from expressing opinions about anything important during the planning process. It simplified things, and honestly, I didn't have opinions about some of the most critical issues. I didn't even know there was a color called "champagne." I know what champagne is, of course - it's a beverage that people who are not planning a wedding can afford to drink.

I accompanied Amy on a day trip to look for wedding items several weeks before the wedding, and she asked me to evaluate a piece of cloth and express an opinion about the color. I foolishly tried to comply instead of asking, "well, honey, what do YOU think?" waiting thirty seconds while I practiced my look of attention, and then saying, "I think so, too."

I fondly remembered the days when people asked my opinion and listened entranced while I provided it (you're free to remember whatever and however you want; I claim the same freedom), so I hitched up my jeans and said, "which piece of cloth?"

"Oh it's over there," she said, gesturing vaguely in the direction of a floor-to-ceiling rack of cylindrical bolts of cloth that were all exactly the same color. "The champagne-colored one."

I had been down this road before and I was in no mood to hear that I was being willfully non-compliant, so my dog Izzy and I shuffled over to the rack and began analyzing. After about 15 minutes, we returned to deliver the verdict.

"It looks nice," I said. Izzy glanced up at me, and I could tell she was thinking, "you don't expect to get away with this, do you?" Sometimes having a dog that is smarter than I am is a good thing; this was not one of those times.

"Nice, huh? What about the texture and weight? Do you think it will work as a pleated altar cloth?" Amy asked, instinctively circling to the side to flank me and look for a vulnerable spot.

"It's soft, and the weight is fine," I said with a touch of panic. "I think it'll be great."

I turned to put Izzy between me and Amy; Izzy turned with me and stayed behind my legs. "You started this, you finish it," Izzy's look said.

"Show me," Amy said, her eyes narrowing, and I buckled like a

Kleenex suspension bridge.

"They're all the same damn color; how do I know which one is champagne?"

"What have you been doing for the last 15 minutes? THIS one is taupe, THIS one is ecru, THIS one is sand...and THIS one is champagne."

"It looks nice," I said again, mostly not to admit defeat.

Amy made a sound that defies description, but that every married man knows. This sound is the reason wives win arguments, the reason men go to war, the reason NASCAR and hunting and golf and beer and Bass Pro Shops exist.

When Izzy speaks, I understand her. The reason she is so clear is that I decide what her nonverbal cues mean, and they mean whatever I want them to. Izzy says whatever I need her to say.

When Amy makes The Sound, I am also free to interpret. The Sound usually contains a combination of "you're an idiot" and "I love you," but the proportions of those two ingredients vary with time, location, and circumstance. The current meaning of The Sound is also impacted by how long it's been since the last time she made The Sound, and how many times that day it's been necessary.

On this day, she was forced to make The Sound repeatedly and almost continuously, and the meaning had shaded into "you're an idiot" and "go wait for me in the parking lot while I start the truck," with only a little bit of "I love you," which may not have actually been present.

I can't be blamed - fabric stores are not my natural habitat. Neither is it my natural role to express an opinion about the qualities of the color champagne, as distinguished from ecru or taupe. The changes in our normal patterns of behavior and interaction demanded by Parkinson's disease aren't natural either, but we still manage.

She didn't run me down with the truck (my truck, which she drives whenever we're out together - if I drive, she makes The Sound), but I didn't wait for her to decide. Iz and I crossed the parking lot and found a barbecue restaurant to wait out the remainder of the fabric shopping in relative safety.

Parkinson's disease causes unavoidable friction in relationships, but it's likely that some that friction would have been there anyway. A realistic approach, a touch of humor, and a dog all make things easier. Barbecue doesn't hurt, either. Most days, The Sound has more love than idiot in it, and even if it doesn't, I have faith that it will again soon. Until then, I can hear what I need to.

I didn't choose Parkinson's disease, but neither did Amy. It's changed our relationship significantly. I can't speak to its impact on Amy but, although I have the disease, we both live with it.

When I'm out in the world, I am almost never ashamed of having Parkinson's. The symptoms are troubling and inconvenient, but I am usually able to attribute adverse reactions by people I meet to lack of understanding (or in rare cases, to lack of compassion). I usually don't take those reactions as an insult.

However, with Amy, I have to remind myself that her normal irritation and frustration are not directed at me. Some of it is married life, and would exist even if I were still working and unaffected by a chronic disease. Some of it is directed at the situation in general. We both had hopes for an early, comfortable retirement, full of travel and enjoyment; the early retirement has come much earlier than either one of us anticipated, under vastly different conditions than we imagined. And I think that some of it is directed at the frustration of living with the symptoms of my disease; the forgetfulness, the unpredictability, the advancing cognitive problems, the narrowing and shrinking of my world, the shuffling, freezing and stumbling, the fatigue. I sometimes feel like Amy blames me personally for these things, but I suspect the truth is simpler. I feel guilty I have brought this beast into our lives, and I imagine she must blame me, too.

I sometimes wonder if my choices during my military career ultimately caused the disease, and if, in the final analysis, I actually am to blame. I pursued every duty assignment I received. I accepted risks without discussing them with Amy, partially because I was constrained from talking to her about my work, but also because I had the "old school" idea that it was my job, my duty, my decision. I made the decisions, but we are both living with the consequences. If our situations were reversed, I think I would be fighting back feelings of anger and betrayal. And so, I imagine she must be, also.

We were reminiscing about past vacations recently. After I left the Air Force we were less financially constrained, and we were able to take some memorable family trips. One of our favorite vacation destinations was Park City and Deer Valley in Utah - we loved the skiing there, and spent the Christmas holiday in Park City several years in a row.

We were remembering when our Swiss exchange student Andres set himself on fire with a candle during a Christmas Eve church service. Andres, like our son Andrew, was a competitive swimmer, and his hair was dry, devastated, and nearly explosive from the effects of chlorine. He came too close to his blonde mop with the candle during "Silent Night," and with an audible "whoosh" and a merry crackle, he burned half his hair off. We memorialized that Christmas by pounding out the flames on Andres' head, with Amy being the primary pounder. She predicted the event, and even went so far as to tell Andres to be careful with the candle, but I don't think that had anything to do with the enthusiasm with which she slapped Andres in the head. She was just closest to the flames.

As usual, we were both nearly in tears from laughing, but her tears went on longer than usual. Ever perceptive, I sensed that something was wrong.

"Honey, what's wrong?"

"I was just remembering what a good skier you used to be. You would come swooping down the mountain making it look so easy, and now you can't even walk across the room!" she sobbed. "Dammit, it's just not fair!"

I was taken aback. It was agonizing to see her grieve for the things I had lost, and not just the things we had lost together. She was angry and sad, but not at me. She was angry for me.

I am still sensitive to Amy's anger. Most negative emotions like fear, sadness, irritation, and frustration manifest in Amy as anger, and I mistake the target of her anger sometimes (sometimes not, though - Parkinson's is not insulation from occasional husbandly dumb-shit behavior). Most of the time, she's not angry at me; she's angry at Parkinson's on my behalf, or angry at something that has absolutely nothing to do with me. And when she makes The Sound (or even more devastating, gives me The Look), I'm reminded of something she once told me that I find comforting.

"The opposite of love is not hate, it's indifference."

I know Amy loves me. She's under no obligation to love Parkinson's, though, or to keep all her frustration with our lives together under lock and key. She is honest, and part of her honesty is to admit that it ain't all roses. I have faith in her truthfulness, and if there's something I need to know, she'll tell me.

And that champagne-colored altar cloth was perfect at the wedding.

12

Let It Ride

All the evidence indicates that exercise is one of the best therapies for Parkinson's disease. It's good for anyone, of course, but particularly good for those of us who must consciously decide to make every movement.

At the end of a long day, my eyes are often burning and red. It's not because I've been weeping with joy over my latest Amazon royalty check (last month's was for $3.13), but because I have forgotten to blink my eyes. I have to remember to blink, and if I don't, the trickle of tears down my cheeks reminds me. When I walk, I have to remember to consciously place my feet slowly and carefully, so I don't shuffle and lean forward. On a long walk I don't talk much, and I never chew gum.

Walking with me can be distracting. I don't answer questions, and I occasionally whisper to myself. I haven't snapped my cap (not yet, at any rate). I'm thinking "heel toe, heel toe," consciously concentrating on placing my feet carefully so I don't festinate.

Festination is a mid-to-late stage characteristic of the gait of some PWPs. In a festinating gait, the steps become shorter and quicker, often culminating in a fall or a freezing episode. One of the ways to avoid festination is to consciously lengthen your stride, and to exaggerate the placement of your feet, heel first and then rolling to your toe. It takes concentration, especially when I'm off or headed that way, so I don't shuffle down the street on my toes and eventually land on my hands and knees.

In my pre-PWP past, I was physically active as a scuba diver, skier, runner, tennis player, and occasional bicyclist, and I was willing to try almost anything. I took my physical facility for granted. Unlike my brother Ken, there were sports that I didn't excel in (I was never an accomplished basketball player, for instance), but I was naturally coordinated and highly competitive.

Now, to move I have to concentrate. The natural flow of physical activity and the joy of being "in the zone" are gone, and I miss them. I have not given up, though. I'm still active, but not at everything. Rock Steady Boxing, shooting, walking, and bicycling are my primary physical activities.

I just bought my first bicycle in almost twenty-five years. My son Andrew and my son-in-law Chris both were subject matter experts on the purchase, and both have had a hand in making sure I am equipped to hit the road (and ensuring that I'm ready if I actually do hit the road). Between the two of them, they provided a helmet, a toolkit, a flat repair kit, a water bottle holder, extra tire tubes, and dire warnings not to fall off the bike. Amy, because she knows me, added a first aid kit.

Andrew came from his home in Hawaii to spend a few days with us, and took me out to buy the bike one Saturday. He and Chris had collaborated on a plan. They are both mechanical engineers and excellent riders, and are also veterans of long-distance biking adventures; Chris toured the US by bicycle for almost a year, and Andrew completed the Texas 4000, a fundraising ride from Austin, Texas to Anchorage, Alaska, during his senior year in college. Needless to say, I was in good hands.

Andrew knew exactly what I needed, and knew where to go. He nonetheless took me to two bike shops to ensure I was getting a good price, and tutored me on the wisdom of supporting my local bike shop. I've spent years and thousands of dollars supporting local dive shops and local gun shops, so I took his advice. Andrew is full of knowledge and good opinions. He probably gets that from his mother.

Of course, I couldn't buy a bike without riding it first. I taught Andrew to ride a bicycle twenty-five years ago, but that fact was lost on both of us as I swung my leg over my new bike, settled in, and took off. I made several wobbly laps around the parking lot, and was amused and deeply touched to see Andrew standing by the store entrance, watching me like a hawk, wringing his hands and shifting from foot to foot like I had done for him two and a half decades ago. He displayed extreme self-control by not running along with me, holding the back of the seat so I wouldn't fall, and contented himself by shouting helpful suggestions, like "watch out for the car" and "be careful!" He'll be a great dad.

He even installed hooks in the garage ceiling so I could hang my new bike. I wanted to help, and he allowed me to.

"Dad, I don't think you should get up on a ladder, but you can hand me things. No, not that - I need the drill with a 1/4" bit and a measuring tape. Back up a little so you don't get hurt. And please don't try to hang both wheels at once; it's easier to do one at a time. Hang the back wheel first; that way you can control the front fork and not drop the whole thing on your head."

One sure-fire way to push my buttons is to tell me, "you sound/look/act just like your father." I fervently hope Andrew doesn't feel the same way. Temperamentally, he's more like his mom than me, and when I look at him I see the same strength of character and compassion I see in her. Sometimes he sounds like me, though. I think he did this time, and I hope that's good. I hope I'm right, too, because I'm very proud of him, and I am blessed to be his father.

Andrew went home to Hawaii to work (if you can call that "work"), but he'll be back. I can't wait to ride with him. Until then, maybe Chris will ride with me. I'm not able to keep up, but they're both kind souls and I'm willing to buy lunch.

I ride several times a week now. Just as with shooting, some days are not good riding days, but every day on the bike is a victory.

Corey D. King

13

Who Saved Who?

Be of service. Whether you make yourself available to a friend or you make time every month to do volunteer work, there is nothing that harvests more of a feeling of empowerment than being of service to someone in need.
 - Gillian Anderson

The best way to find yourself is to lose yourself in the service of others.
 - Mahatma Gandhi

Never question the value of volunteers. Noah's Ark was built by volunteers; the Titanic was built by professionals.
- Dave Gynn

In the eight years that I have been an official part of the Parkinson's community, I've volunteered in many places. I've enjoyed them all, but I've been better suited for some of my volunteer jobs than others.

Volunteering isn't much different than being employed (except for the "getting paid" issue). The same interpersonal conflicts, disagreements over strategy or management style, or problems between organizations still happen, and stress is still a part of the job. I want to do a good job when I volunteer, but not for all the same reasons as in the past.

I get enormous personal satisfaction from the volunteer work I do, and I like feeling like I'm still relevant. I get the most satisfaction from talking to people, though, both in large groups and one-on-one. There's nothing particularly unique about my background with Parkinson's, but I have years of experience with talking to people about things that are hard to understand, and I think I'm good at it.

My first volunteer job was with the local chapter of a national Parkinson's organization. They were looking for someone to help run the chapter at the same time that I was mostly over my shock and disbelief and was ready to get involved, and it was a marriage of convenience. The organization had been in place for years and I had no experience with non-profit management, so after a relatively short time I wore out my welcome. I was as happy to go as they were to see me out the door, but none of the conflict was about the PWPs we were supposed to serve; the problems were with financial management and business process, with a little personal animosity thrown into the mix. One of the comments I received on the way out was, "I've been volunteering for these organizations for three times as long as you've even had Parkinson's; keep your opinions and ideas to yourself." My response is not printable; it was clearly time for me to go.

Not long after, I started working with the Parkinson's Action Network, a wonderful organization with excellent people who were dedicated to influencing the United States Congress to spend money on research and programs for Parkinson's disease. I traveled to Washington, DC with PAN to visit with the senators and Congressmen from my home state of Texas. Most of the meetings went well, but it was clear that there was no push that year to fund new initiatives for neurological diseases.

One of our meetings was spectacularly bad, though. The Congresswoman was unavailable to meet with us, so she sent a legislative aide to the meeting. The aide listened to our stories for a short time, and then rather bluntly told us there was no funding and no interest at the Federal level, that we should go home to Texas and talk to our local politicians, and that maybe a venture capital firm would listen to us. She then showed us to the elevator.

Our group of six was quiet for a few floors. Someone then asked,

"Did we just get thrown out of a Congresswoman's office?"

Yes; yes, we had. I was incensed. More experienced members of the delegation advised me to just take it in stride. I did, briefly.

I fired off an email to the Congresswoman's office, venting my frustration and anger. I invoked Texas hospitality; I pointed out that she worked for us; I went into some detail about my military record; I hoped fervently that no one she loved would ever be diagnosed with Parkinson's. I wasn't insulting, but I was pointed and direct, and I ended the email demanding action.

After a few days, she responded with an emailed apology, and suggested we get together on the phone with a colleague of hers from the Veterans Administration to discuss next steps. She followed through, and eventually joined the Congressional caucus for Parkinson's education. I also got a personal phone call and a sincere, heartfelt apology from her aide, who was gracious and kind. There really was no money for Parkinson's programs, but after one false start, they listened. It's a shame the Congresswoman decided to retire the next year.

I continue to volunteer, most recently for the Davis Phinney Foundation and the SA Moves Foundation. Both organizations are very effective at what they do, and both are staffed and supported by smart, dedicated people who care deeply about those they serve. I'm fortunate that my remaining talents are useful to them, and doubly fortunate to be able to spend time with such wonderful people.

I recently spoke to a support group about ways to live well with Parkinson's, and I said I thought the plan should include exercise, attitude, a good medical team, and a support ecosystem. I talked at length about the support ecosystem, composed of care partners, family, friends, support groups, and social organizations, and pointed out that everyone has something to give as well as receive.

People with Parkinson's and other chronic conditions can develop the bad habit of thinking that support only flows one way. Volunteering isn't all about selfless giving, even if it would be nice to think so. I receive as much as I give through volunteer work, and perhaps more. We all have different capacities for giving, and some of us necessarily need to focus on receiving support. Why not think about what you can give back, though? Living well is not just about organizing and using your resources to improve your own life.

Who can you help? What can you do? We've all got God-given

gifts and talents. Where can you use yours to ease suffering, reduce fear, or help push back the darkness for someone else?

14
The Long Journey Home

Do the difficult things while they are easy and do the great things while they are small. A journey of a thousand miles must begin with a single step.
  - Lao Tzu

Everyone is handed adversity in life. No one's journey is easy. It's how they handle it that makes people unique.
  - Kevin Conroy

…not all those who wander are lost…
- J.R.R. Tolkien

   A friend of mine died last week. I first met him at a Parkinson's conference in Atlanta almost a decade ago. He was the leader of the organization that hosted the conference, and it was the first time I had been to a Parkinson's conference or spent time around PWPs.
   James was the sort that never met a stranger. He was frazzled from trying to make sure the conference ran smoothly, but he nonetheless talked to me for more than an hour in the "Night Owl

Lounge" at the conference hotel. Every Parkinson's conference has one - none of us sleep worth a damn, and it's much more fun to make new friends than to stare at a hotel room ceiling.

We chatted late into the night, about everything and nothing. Other people joined the conversation, and have also become friends, but James was the first.

I learned a huge amount about the disease that would be my constant companion for the rest of my life at that conference, and very little of it actually came from James. The lesson I learned from him, just by observing his behavior at that conference and in the years that followed, was about how to live with adversity.

He didn't say it out loud, but it radiated from him like heat from a Franklin stove. The best way to help yourself is by helping someone else. It's a simple concept, but he lived it like he thought of it first, and he had enormous positive impact on everyone he touched, including me.

I met other people there who have been inspirations to me, as well. Gretchen and Michael, Lainee, Jackie, Ron and many others; all astounding in their accomplishments and all worthy of respect and admiration, to be sure, but also all kind, welcoming, and genuine in their concern for a guy from Texas they had never met before but that they welcomed with open arms.

It's odd, almost a statistical anomaly, but PWPs tend to be wonderful people. I'm not sure why. Maybe it's the camaraderie of trying to slay the same immortal dragon every day, or maybe it's a beneficial symptom of the disease or a side effect of the medications (now, that would be poetic justice, since PWPs tend to get the short straw on both counts). Whatever it is, I have never met a PWP who was also an asshat. Sorry - it's such a descriptive term, and it applies so well in some cases.

James was special, though. He was the first of many to show compassion for what I was experiencing, and I knew it was sincere because he had been there, too. He was a role model for me, and I wish I had told him.

I learned that he had died through Facebook. We didn't often communicate (just an email every now and then), but every single time I reached out to him, he remembered who I was and asked if I was sleeping any better. For someone with a disease that impacts memory as well as a thousand other things, that's astounding.

He was loved and respected by literally thousands of PWPs all around the world, and you could tell by the outpouring of sorrow and remembrance that followed the news of his passing. I'll miss him, too.

In the last year, there have been several deaths among my circle of friends and acquaintances as a consequence of Parkinson's. Every one is a personal affront, and although it is not unexpected, it is still jarring.

The unavoidable fact of Parkinson's is never far from my thoughts. It's getting late as I write this, and my last dose of medication is wearing off. My hand and arms are stiffening up, and my back is beginning to clench with my normal evening bout of dystonia. I am tremoring (although not badly, yet), and my voice is getting softer, so that neither Siri nor Dragon Dictate understand what I'm saying. I have resorted to using the keyboard, and the "delete" key is getting a workout, as usual.

I'm grateful my mind is still working after a fashion, though. I'm fortunate that I remember my successes (and failures), my children's birthday parties, and all the many wonderful times with Amy (except for that one birthday I forgot; I'm still sorry, honey).

I'm also grateful for the friends I would not have made except for Parkinson's, for the chance to emulate James and others like him, and for the opportunity, even in a small way, to be of service.

I'm grateful for my entire family: existing, new, and future. And I'm grateful for Amy - neither of us is perfect (especially me), but we're perfect for each other, and as much as we've both changed over the last thirty-two years, that is a miracle.

Those are the facts of my life, walking with this interloper named Parkinson; some wonderful, some not so good. They form my reality, though, and it's a place I want to be.

I feel a little like I've been wandering in the wilderness since my diagnosis. I've struggled to understand who I am, and what my life means. I've fought for control, and learned I have none. I've given up, and been found even before I knew I was lost.

I've learned what courage is, because I've seen it in other people. I've seen true misery, and felt ashamed for the times I've complained. I've watched what fear does to good people, and discovered there is nothing to fear that I don't create. And I've decided that, even if there seems to be more evil than good in the world, good is stronger.

I don't know very much. I don't understand how it all works. I believe, though, that we are here for a reason. I believe that we can discover parts of that reason, but that there is no checklist. I believe God exists, now and forever. I believe we get in God's way too often by speaking instead of listening.

I believe my father regrets what he did to me. I believe he knows I forgive him. I believe I will see him again.

I believe I will be the victor in my battle with Parkinson's, not because the disease will disappear but because I will refuse it permission to steal my hope, joy, and faith.

And I believe that I have reached at least the midway point in my journey. I believe, now and finally, that I'm headed home.

Made in the USA
Lexington, KY
09 October 2018